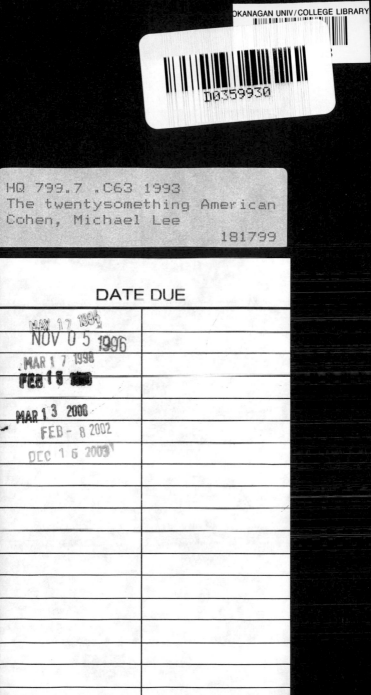

DATE DUE

MAY 17 1994	
NOV 0 5 1996	
MAR 1 7 1998	
FEB 1 8	
MAR 1 3 2000	
FEB - 8 2002	
DEC 1 6 2003	

THE
TWENTY-
SOMETHING
AMERICAN
DREAM

MICHAEL LEE COHEN

THE TWENTY-SOMETHING AMERICAN DREAM

A CROSS-COUNTRY QUEST
FOR A GENERATION

A DUTTON BOOK

DUTTON

Published by the Penguin Group
Penguin Books USA Inc., 375 Hudson Street, New York, New York 10014, U.S.A.
Penguin Books Ltd, 27 Wrights Lane, London W8 5TZ, England
Penguin Books Australia Ltd, Ringwood, Victoria, Australia
Penguin Books Canada Ltd, 10 Alcorn Avenue, Toronto, Ontario, Canada M4V 3B2
Penguin Books (N.Z.) Ltd, 182–190 Wairau Road, Auckland 10, New Zealand

Penguin Books Ltd, Registered Offices:
Harmondsworth, Middlesex, England

First published by Dutton, an imprint of New American Library,
a division of Penguin Books USA Inc.
Distributed in Canada by McClelland & Stewart Inc.

First Printing, August, 1993
1   3   5   7   9   10   8   6   4   2

REGISTERED TRADEMARK—MARCA REGISTRADA

LIBRARY OF CONGRESS CATALOGING IN PUBLICATION DATA:
Cohen, Michael Lee.
The twentysomething American dream: a cross-country quest
for a generation/ Michael Lee Cohen.
p.   cm.
ISBN 0-525-93685-8
1. Young adults—United States—Attitudes.   2. Young adults—
United States—Interviews.   I. Title.   II. Title: Twentysomething
American dream.
HQ799.7.C63   1993
305.23′5′0973—dc20   92–46884
                                                                CIP

Printed in the United States of America
Set in Garamond Light and Gill Sans Light

Designed by Steven N. Stathakis

For my parents, my grandparents, my brother
&
to the memory of Aunt Arlene

ACKNOWLEDGMENTS

My name is the only one on the cover of this book, but there are lots of people who were critical to its completion:

First, thanks to all the people who took the time to speak with me. Without their words and their ideas, this book would not have been possible.

I also want to thank Harvard University and the members of the committee that administers the Sheldon Fellowship Fund. Their confidence that I could actually write the book I had envisioned was at least as valuable as the money they gave me. My agent, Anne Edelstein, had the courage to risk some of her professional time with a previously unpublished author and patiently responded to my innumerable phone calls and questions. Peter Borland, my editor, showed remarkable kindness and tact in dealing with a compulsive and nervous first-time author. His suggestions and his sense of humor were always helpful.

I am indebted also to the many people who allowed me to

sleep on their floors and couches and in their guest rooms during my journey: Jeff Bell, Brent Karren, Michael Rosenblum and Justine Harris in St. Louis; Sondra Hemeryck, Barbara Stoldt, John Sykstus and Jean O'Leary-Sykstus, Ellen Bublick and David Jacobs in Chicago; Raul Yanes in Milwaukee; John Tanner in South Bend; Bill and Susanne Mahoney in Philadelphia; Mat Gimble in New York; George and Nicole Postolos in Connecticut; Adrienne Shishko and Joel Sklar in Boston; Steve Dettelbach and Kristin Bender in Washington, D.C.; Brett Kirstein in Dallas; Jim and Les Kaufmann in Austin; Jeff Levin in Weslaco, Texas; Nancy Talavera in Houston; Josh Force in Lafayette; Barbie Barton in New Orleans; Jeff Seinfeld in Vaiden, Mississippi; Mike Stewart in Knoxville; Charles and Bunny Burson in Nashville; Edward and Gloria Felsenthal in Memphis; Ed and Ann O'Leary in Albuquerque; Linda Osher in Los Angeles; and Gretchen Hug in San Francisco.

I also want to thank the women who transcribed my interviews—Linda Alexander, Amy Anderson, Diana Deal, Nancy Griffin, Johnine Searls, and Mona Shaver. Without them, I never could have finished. Thanks, too, to Judge David Kline, and to Steve Kline for allowing my typists to use their word processing equipment.

A few more thanks: to the attorneys of Susman Godfrey, who allowed me the time to pursue my American Dream; and to Jim Kaufmann, Randi Shade, Martin Siegel, and Miles Tolbert, for their willingness to discuss ideas with me. Finally, I thank my parents for taking the time to read and edit the early drafts of this work, and for resisting—quite successfully—Jewish parents' natural inclination to say that everything their child writes is brilliant. (And no, Mom, you are *nothing* like Mrs. Portnoy.)

CONTENTS

INTRODUCTION

I've had it. For most of my life, my generation has been eclipsed by the 72 million omnipresent baby boomers. Like the pig in the python, because there are so many of them, the baby boomers have defined every era through which they have passed. Even relatively small subspecies of them, such as the roughly 4 million young urban professionals, have made social waves. And now that my peers and I are beginning to receive a bit of attention, we are getting clobbered.

In the last several years journalists, pundits, sociologists, and college counselors have attempted to define the 40 million-plus individuals known collectively as the twentysomething generation. We have become a topic of interest largely because people between the ages of eighteen and twenty-nine are the primary hiring pool and, compared to the generation that preceded us, we are relatively few.

Although the efforts to understand us probably have been well-intentioned, few of these portraits have been sympathetic; even fewer have been fair. One nationally syndicated columnist asserts that we suffer from "herky-jerky brain," that we are "numb" and "dumb" and indifferent to "practically everything on the planet that is interesting, infuriating, maddening, exhilarating, fascinating, amusing and nutty." *The Washington Post* labels us "the Doofus generation" because we are less likely than our elders to follow certain news stories. An editor at one national magazine calls us the "the New Petulants" because we so often sound like whiners. Granted, society's older members have the inalienable right to feel that the succeeding generation is the most barbarous horde of ingrates since the Vandals sacked Rome, but intellectual integrity requires at least an effort to understand the other side of the story.

This running commentary began in 1986 with *The Postponed Generation,* a book by Los Angeles sociologist Susan Littwin. Littwin's thesis, that adolescents today require an extra decade to become adults, is not necessarily controversial and in some instances is correct. However, though Littwin's tone is occasionally evenhanded, just as frequently it ranges from tongue-clucking to castigation. "Having had an expensive education and more advantages than any generation on earth," she writes, "[today's young adults] seem confused, unfocused, and dependent." They have "a high sense of entitlement and a not so high sense of reality" and are on a prolonged search to find themselves, while assiduously avoiding commitment, rejection, the risk of failure, even reality itself. Littwin writes about people in their twenties as Spengler might have written about the decline of Western civilization after a year of est.

Between 1988 and 1990 there were a few articles about today's generation of young adults, but *Time* turned us into a national issue with a cover story in July 1990. In "Proceeding with Caution," two writers in their twenties dub their peers "the twentysomething generation," then sketch an unflattering portrait of their subjects as anxious, indecisive skeptics who desire "to avoid risk, pain and rapid change," and who "feel paralyzed by the social problems they see as their inheritance." The *Time* piece inspired a spate of similar articles in magazines and newspapers across the country, and at least one television news special.

Unfortunately, the *Time* article also catalyzed a sort of bandwagon effect. With a couple of exceptions, everyone seemed to agree that most members of today's twentysomething generation are little more than lazy, self-indulgent moaners. Commentary offered by the young adults themselves only confirmed the point. One twenty-three-year-old wrote, "If you're in one of those 'superior' older groups, go ahead and keep bashing my generation. You can't hurt us any more than you already have." How's that for a good pout?

Fiction writers, including Jay McInerney, Bret Easton Ellis, Tama Janowitz, David Foster Wallace, and Doug Coupland, and filmmakers, including Richard Linklater and Cameron Crowe, have also tried to define what it means to be a young adult in today's United States. If their novels and films accurately depicted the lives and attitudes of the majority of this nation's young adults, the gloomy assessments offered by Littwin, *Time,* and others would be understatements along the order of Custer's horoscope the day before the battle of Little Big Horn—"Avoid South Dakota." But most young adults are not coked-out aspiring authors or rich, spoiled, world-weary preppies. Most of them are not striving to be oh-so-boho in SoHo. Most of them are not hiding from the world by escaping to the California desert, whiling away the days by telling tales and boozing. Most of them are not paralyzed by a crushing sense of "futurelessness," fretting about the likelihood that they will be forgotten by History. Rather, most of them are striving to carve out lives for themselves and, in some cases, their families, even though they face some daunting obstacles—apparently diminishing economic opportunities and increasingly fierce international economic competition, a spiraling national debt, environmental degradation, a faltering public education system, AIDS. Yet if one were to judge today's young adults by the articles, books, and movies about them, one would likely label them the "dis-" generation—disenchanted, dissatisfied, disenfranchised, disgruntled, disillusioned, discomfited, and disconnected.

These efforts to define today's young adults share a common fault. Each attempts to comprehend—or, in the case of the fictional works, has been assumed to comprehend—the experience of an entire generation, yet each focuses almost exclusively on college-educated young adults from prosperous backgrounds. By concentrating on the well-educated offspring of the nation's well-to-do, these works exclude the majority of the nation's twentysomething generation. In 1989 slightly more than 23 percent of people between ages twenty-five and twenty-nine had completed four years of college. What about the other 76 percent? And what about those young adults who did not have the good fortune to be born into affluent families? These people are part of the twentysomething generation, too.

Most of the nonfiction works also share another shortcoming. Reading and listening to them, I began more and more to sense something teleological in their assays, as if they had already reached certain conclusions about what today's young adults are like, then found individuals who could provide sound-bite illustrations of their assertions. The most egregious example of this fill-in-the-blank journalism is Barbara Walters's news special, "Twentysomething: What Happened to the American Dream?," which aired in July 1992. Walters filled one-third of the time with her own words—I counted the lines of dialogue in the transcript, and she spoke in 315 of 944—leaving approximately thirty minutes to be divided among her eight twentysomething interviewees. Moreover, when Walters's guests did respond to her questions, she frequently led them to the answer.

WALTERS: It may make you more afraid [of marriage and commitment] when you grow up in a family where you see divorce.
GUEST: Right.
WALTERS: And either . . . make you say, "Oh well, I can get into this or get out of it," or, "I'll do anything rather than go through what I went through as a kid."
GUEST: Right. Right.

Either because they were awed by Walters's presence or because they were being polite, only twice did any of her guests fail to give Walters the answer she sought. The print journalists had the luxury of including only those remarks that supported their contentions, although Littwin demonstrated her intellectual integrity by including a chapter on young adults who have not "postponed" growing up. The other commentators probably would have done the same if space had allowed, but hey, it's tough to summarize 40 million people in eight pages.

All these efforts to define this nation's generation of young adults left me with one question: *Who are these people talking about?* Having been born and raised in Oklahoma City, I realize I am not the most sophisticated guy around, but I also know there is more to this generation of young adults than the image depicted in the media. So I decided to find out for myself what my peers are thinking.

Financed by a fellowship from Harvard University and what was left of my bar mitzvah money, I drove across the country and spoke with other members of the twentysomething generation. Between October 1991 and June 1992, I interviewed 161 people in fifty-one cities and towns across the country. I spoke with people in their homes and at their jobs, in gyms, in bars, in restaurants, on university campuses, in soup kitchens and recreation centers, in office buildings, and on military bases. I did not focus on individuals from any particular background; rather, I talked with people from as many different circumstances—racial, social, economic, educational, occupational—as I could find.

Looking for people who would speak with me, I learned that Steinbeck was right: "We don't take a trip; a trip takes us." Meeting folks on this journey was mostly a matter of serendipity. With a handful of exceptions, I did not interview anyone I knew. Of the forty-two people whose stories are included in these pages, only Adam, the Wall Street banker, is a previous acquaintance.

I started by asking my friends whom they knew, then I asked those people to suggest names, and so on. By the time my travels were winding down, there often were more than a half dozen people between me and the person who ultimately sat down to talk with me. In addition to these people, I often struck up conversations with folks I met as I was traveling, explained to them what I was doing, and asked whether they could spare a couple of hours to talk with me. About half of them consented.

Because the questions I asked were open-ended and because I was not wedded to a script, each conversation took on a life of its own. Nevertheless, I relied upon a list of questions that I asked everyone. First I learned about their backgrounds—where they were born and raised, what their parents did for a living, what role religion played in their lives, where they went to school, what they do for a living, what choices they made along the way, and why. Then I asked people about the American Dream—how they think others define it, how they define it for themselves or whether that concept is even relevant to their lives.

Why "the American Dream"? Two reasons. First, much of the recent discussion about people in their twenties insists that they will not be able to fulfill "the American Dream," yet none of the commentators bothered to define this phrase. Precisely what will these people be unable to achieve? I wanted to learn what my peers imagine the American Dream to be.

Second, no matter what people think about the concept of the American Dream, it is such a potent and long-standing part of our national mythology that virtually everyone has something to say about it. The American Dream is a Rorschach test for our individual and national psyches, a blank screen onto which we project our personal and collective hopes and aspirations. Not that anyone wakes up and says, "Today I'm going to participate in the American Dream." But as English author Pico Iyer observed, "There still is an American dream in a way that there is not an Italian dream or a Japanese dream. . . . It still speaks very powerfully to the world." And to us. At the very least, that phrase, "the American Dream," is a good conversation starter, and it can tell us something about what people in their twenties want for their private selves.

The last category of questions was about the national situation—what issues concerned these people the most, what solutions they envisioned, whether they voted, and other related issues. I wanted to know to what extent people in their twenties are involved in the public life of the nation, whether they have public selves to complement their private selves.

One person who heard about my project wondered whether what the people had told me about themselves was true. Frankly, I do not know. While I tried to ask probing questions when I felt someone was shading the truth, these folks were the first and last authority on their lives. I did not verify their stories. Why? Because although most of these people did not tell me anything lurid or embarrassing or intensely private, a few did. They were willing to share their stories with me because they did not know me, I was not part of their lives. I was, I think, a combination of confidant, anonymous buddy, and friendly ear. It would have violated the unwritten rules of my relationship with these people if I had tried to check their veracity.

I can say this much: in those few instances when I did have an opportunity to compare the teller's story against reality, the facts always checked out. My intuition also tells me that these people were honest with me. I'd like to think it was because they trusted me, but it probably was because there was no reason to lie, especially since I gave pseudonyms to those few who wished to remain anonymous.

■ ■ ■

Choosing which people to include in the book was more difficult than deciding with whom to talk. I could speak with lots of folks; I could transform only a fraction of those conversations into print.

I deliberately selected those discussions that reflect the broad range of backgrounds and opinions that I encountered during my nine months on the road. Consequently, some readers might feel that some of these individuals express viewpoints that are outside the mainstream. Without examining what precisely *is* mainstream—an issue that I hope you will consider and reconsider as you read this book—I will say that those readers are correct: many of the people in this book are not commonplace. Most twenty-six-year-olds are not their community's elected representative in the state legislature. Most twenty-five-year-olds do not work for a *Fortune* 500 company and own a restaurant, too. Most twenty-three-year-olds are not drug addicts who eat their meals in soup kitchens. Most twenty-five-year-olds do not have the AIDS virus. But I included these "extreme" perspectives so that people will begin to comprehend the vast range of experiences and ideas contained within this twentysomething generation.

A sense of proportionality also influenced my editorial selections. I wanted the book to reflect, at least broadly, the social, economic, racial, sexual, educational, and occupational composition of today's generation of young adults. In this I have been fairly successful, though I must offer two mea culpas. First, roughly half of the people included in these pages have college degrees, which is twice the national average. This is probably because I used my friends and acquaintances as starting points in meeting people, and most of my friends have college degrees and know other people like themselves. Second, not one of the people I interviewed has a physical disability. I believe there are two reasons for this. As a statistical matter, people with disabilities are a relatively small percentage of the twentysomething population. And because our society has only recently begun to make a concerted effort to provide these individuals with access to most buildings and to public transportation, they have tended to live segregated to some degree from the rest of society. Unfortunately, what they say is true—out of sight, out of mind. My book is the poorer for this oversight.

Another factor also came into play in deciding which people to include—quotability. This is a book, after all, and I believed readers would appreciate comments from people who not only said something insightful, but also said it well.

The previous efforts to define the twentysomething generation fall into one of two categories: either a narrative summation of an opinion poll, with statistics and short quotations used to season the results, or one writer presenting his own ideas and asserting that this is what people in their twenties are like. I found both approaches limited.

A remark once made about statistics applies equally well to opinion polls: what they reveal is suggestive, but what they conceal is vital. A survey tells you only that a certain number of respondents preferred one canned answer to another. It does not tell you what an individual thinks and feels, or why—and these are the really interesting questions. Although they are useful, polls are boring because they have no human face.

As for the pundit-as-Everyman approach—well, let's just say I am not as confident as others have been that I can speak for an entire generation. I am Jewish and grew up in an upper-middle-class home in Oklahoma City. I have a liberal arts degree from the University of Texas and a law degree from Harvard. Hard as I try, I do not think I could be my generation's Everyman. But why should I try when people in their twenties can speak for themselves if they are given a chance?

And that's what I have done—provided some of my peers the opportunity to express their views in their own words. In these conversations I listened more than I talked. I strove for the same effect in print. Other than providing a narrative thread, I do very little commenting in these pages. These individuals speak for themselves.

The American Dream is more than a tired shibboleth trotted out by politicians during election-year stump speeches. The concept of the American Dream is part of our nation's secular faith, and chasing the Dream is an act of devotion that all people, regardless of their sectarian beliefs, can perform. That is why I have divided this book into two sections—"Believers" and "Nonbelievers, Skeptics, and Doubters." The believers may define the American Dream in different ways—in material terms, or as freedom and opportunity—but they all agree that there is a dream that is peculiar to this nation. The nonbelievers include people who explicitly reject the notion that there is a uniquely American dream; people who doubt whether it exists anymore, if it ever did; and people who want to participate in a commonly held vision of the good, but who for some reason feel excluded from taking part.

Besides the believers and nonbelievers, there are three pairs of portraits titled "Same City, Different Worlds." These are conversations with individuals who live in the same city, but who, for various reasons, interpret the same facts in drastically different ways. Their lives overlap geographically, they occupy the same physical space, but psychically they might as well be from different planets.

During the course of my travels, I learned many lessons, far more than I probably realize. One of the more irritating ones is that, contrary to my knee-jerk response, the previous efforts to define the twentysomething generation are not completely inaccurate. I did meet people who have postponed growing up. I did talk with individuals who are anxious, indecisive, skeptical, and who are at times overwhelmed by the magnitude of society's problems. But they are only part of the generation.

In a letter I received during my travels, a friend wrote, "I hope you found out what we're all thinking so we can all start thinking it." People who are looking for a pithy generational moniker, a three-word slogan—The (catchy adjective) Generation—might be disappointed by this book. There is no single word or idea that can accurately capture 40 million individuals. A man in Houston said it quite well: "People in their twenties go through college in two years and go make a million dollars on the stock market. People in their twenties do drugs and drop out of college and go live in the streets the rest of their lives. People in their twenties are everything. That's what people in their twenties are." By offering many different perspectives—sometimes complementary, often contradictory—I have attempted to provide a composite portrait of the twentysomething generation, one that approaches the richness and diversity of this generation's world.

As you read this book, you will come across ideas you will find appealing and others you will find appalling, people whose backgrounds are similar to your own and others who will make you wonder, "Did one of us grow up on Mars?" I ask only that you listen to these people with a sympathetic heart, and that you do not allow that sympathy to be bounded by the horizons of your own circumstances.

MICHAEL LEE COHEN
Dallas, Texas

PART ONE

BELIEVERS

THE HOUSE,
THE CAR,
THE KIDS

RENE

"I always had kind of secretly wanted to be a physician," says Rene. "I mean, yeah, my mom and dad knew, but I didn't go around saying, 'I'm going to be a doctor.' " Of course, it would have been unusual for a girl from Bokchito, Oklahoma, population 628, to express such an ambition. "My hometown," says Rene, "I mean, I love it and everything, but, for a female especially, your expectation is to graduate high school and get married. No one ever expects you to go do anything else."

But Rene is very goal-oriented. In a letter she wrote when she was eighteen, she predicted that in ten years she would be finished with medical school and in her residency. She also expressed hope that she would be married by that time. Rene is now twenty-six, and each of those predictions and wishes has come true.

The oldest of three children, Rene was born in Durant, a town in southeastern Oklahoma, just north of the Texas border. She was two when her family made the move fifteen miles east to Bokchito, the area where both of her parents had grown up. Rene's family lived in that little town until she finished fourth grade. Over the next three years, they moved three times to three cities in Texas and Oklahoma as Rene's father, a construction welder, took his family where the jobs were. At the end of the third year, Rene's parents decided it would be better for their children if the family settled in one place. Because all four of Rene's grandparents lived in Bokchito, her parents bought a twenty-acre farm five miles northeast of the town and moved the family back to Bokchito.

The farm where Rene lived was not a commercial operation. "It was more of a fun farm," she says. "Dad bought us each a cow, you know. He was going to teach us responsibility. That was the whole meaning of the farm, we were gonna learn how to work, 'cause we were kinda city kids." Besides the cows, which the children had to milk at 5 a.m. every day before school, they raised sheep and pigs for show, and they also had chickens and cats. "You name it, we had it on that farm. It was like Old MacDonald's. I mean, there was a little bit of everything. We even had peacocks at one time," she says.

She enjoyed growing up on the farm. "It gave us enough room to do what we wanted. Y'know, it had two ponds, it had a pecan grove. It had plenty of runnin', trompin' space that you could ever want, as far as a kid goes."

But as much fun as the farm was for the children, the cost of maintaining it was always a struggle for Rene's parents. "I can always remember," she says, "even from the time I was in junior high, when they moved back to Bokchito and bought the farm and everything, it really became a big burden for them, and it's been a big burden for them ever since—the mortgage and things. And they're stuck there now. With the economy, they've been trying to sell the house for seven years now, and they haven't been able to sell it."

The problem, says Rene, is that her father often goes for months without work. Not because he's lazy; it's just the nature of his trade. Yet even with Rene's mother working as a cook in the Bokchito school cafeteria, they have trouble paying their bills.

"My whole life," says Rene, "I can only remember my parents trying to make ends meet. I mean, not that we were poor or anything like that, but it was always making ends meet. Most people are in that same situation, trying to make ends meet—or, the people I grew up around, they were in that same situation."

Except for the three years when her family was moving from town to town, Rene had always attended the public school in Bokchito, where all the students, from kindergarten through high school, go to classes in the same building. As a senior she was the president of the student council, the 4-H club, and the horticulture club. Unlike most of the nineteen kids who graduated with her, Rene decided to go on to college. Of the six who did continue their educations, Rene was the only girl.

Though she had originally intended to enroll in one of Oklahoma's larger public universities, Rene received a two-year scholarship to attend a smaller public school in nearby Durant. She decided it made good financial sense to get her basic requirements out of the way at the local campus, then transfer to one of the state universities. After two years, however, she liked the smaller school so much, she chose to stay there the entire four years.

She explains: "I liked the class sizes. They were small. The professors knew you by name. They were interested in your plans for the future. And you had a lot of one-on-one teaching, which I knew you couldn't get at a larger school.

"And the biggest thing's that I was comfortable there. My friends, my family were there, within the community. I had a job. I mean, I was just too comfortable to pick up my roots. Plus, just financially, it was a better move as well."

Rene majored in chemistry and biology, a typical path for a student headed to medical school. However, she began to wonder whether she would actually go on to study medicine. "It was something that I just talked about," she says. "It always frightened me. I didn't really think that I could do it or anything like that. What I ended up doing was investigating every other possible health profession besides medicine."

So began Rene's process of elimination. Optometry . . . dentistry . . . nursing. Nursing was not quite right, she says, because "you do your assessments on patients, but you didn't get the true medicine part of it"—which, for Rene, means identifying the problem and figuring out how to fix it.

Rene did not stop there. She also thought of becoming a medical technician, then realized she would be bored running tests. During the summer between her sophomore and junior years, she worked in a lab to see whether she might enjoy being a research scientist. She didn't. But that was the summer she decided she would go ahead and take the entrance exam for medical school, just to see how she would do.

"Did okay on it," she says, "but it really got me excited, thought maybe I could do this after all."

Rene took the exam again in May of her junior year. "It sounds funny," she says, "but there was nothing else that appealed to me. Everything just fell short of going and being a doctor." By January of her senior year, she had been accepted by the medical school at the Oklahoma Health Sciences Center, a branch of the University of Oklahoma, in Oklahoma City.

"Medical school wasn't as scary as what I had anticipated," says Rene. "Once you got over the initial first couple of weeks, you just got into a routine and you did what you had to do." Not that she did not have moments of anguish. "I didn't do too well on my first biochemistry test," she says, "and that was our very first test of our very first set of tests of the first year. And I remember thinking, 'Oh Lord, I'm going to flunk out of medical school. It's going to happen.' But what ended up happening is I did okay on my other tests, and one I did pretty good on, so I was like, 'Okay, I'm gonna make it after all.' " And by June 1992, she had made it; she was officially a doctor.

During the third year of medical school, Rene had to begin figuring out in which area of medicine she wanted to specialize. She arrived at her decision through the same process of elimination that sent her to medical school. "That's how I always do it," she says. "I don't want to limit myself and not look at anything else."

Obstetrics and gynecology? A month during her medical school rotations was enough. Surgery? "It was fun, but the residency is five years long. You're on call every other night, every third night. So it went out the door real early on, just because of the residency and the lifestyle of the residency."

What about pediatrics? "I was going to be a pediatrician when I came to medical school," she says. "But with children, they scare me because they can get so sick so quick. I mean, they can. You see a little child just get close to death so quickly, and I just couldn't handle it."

Rene "was kind of left" with internal medicine. Today she is in the first year of her residency in Oklahoma City. She's working hard, she says, but the internal medicine residency is more humane than most. For instance, she is usually on call every fifth night, and during some rotations she will never be on call.

Rene has spent much of her time working at hospitals that serve poor people. For the most part she likes her job, but she has felt frustrated by some of the patients. She explains: "Outside the medical profession this might sound really bad, but you have this patient that comes in, they've just trounced their body to death. I mean, they've drank two or three cases of beer every other day and dut, dut, dut, dut, dut. They've just really gotten themselves into a pitiful state, and then they come in and they say, '*You're* going to cure me and *you're* going to change everything that I've done. Not only that, I don't have any money to pay for anything and it's your job to find a way around payment.' I mean, the people that use this medical center, they know how to use it. They know what they can get, a lot of 'em do.

"It's not that you don't care about taking care of their physical illness, but they're telling you, 'Yes, you are going to find medications for me to go on. You are going to do this and this and this for me.' And they have that attitude of, like, 'It's the rest of the world's job to take care of me. I don't do anything. I don't work, I don't try to do anything, but it's everyone else's responsibility to take care of me now.' And that's not from a physician's aspect, it's more Rene's aspect of, like, 'That's not fair.' My dad works and works and works, and I know millions of people who go out and work every day just to make ends meet. And yeah, they're not having a good time in life either, but at least they're trying.

"Some of these patients have just had real hard luck at life, and some of them have no means to provide for themselves. It's the younger people who could get out and do something for themselves, and they just refuse to do it because it's their way of life. It irritates me to death—and that's more, not as a physician, but as just a regular old American person. They go out and take advantage of what the system has to offer."

Despite this, Rene is very happy at this point in her life. "I don't think it's so much my career or anything," she says. Rather, it is because of Jimmy, her husband.

Jimmy grew up in Silo, Oklahoma, a small town not far from Bokchito. Jimmy and Rene met at college. They shared the same major, so they had many classes together, and over the course of four years became friends. Their first date was when Rene went home for Thanksgiving during her first year of medical school. The following summer—Rene and Jimmy refer to it as The Summer—

Rene worked at a hospital in Durant, and she and Jimmy went out nearly every night. The next fall, Jimmy began working on his Ph.D. in microbiology at the Health Sciences Center in Oklahoma City, where Rene was a medical student. That September, they were engaged. Six months later they were married.

"Jimmy's a great guy," she says, smiling, "he really is. I don't know who could put up with my being on call and things like that. And he's so laid back that he can blow all the medical school residency stuff off, and when we're together it's just us and not fifteen million other things going on. I think that's the main reason I'm happy, because our marriage is a happy one right now."

Jimmy will have his doctorate within a year or so. Rene is uncertain what will happen after that. "Jimmy has been offered some postdoctoral studies in other places," she says, "and he's going to have to go to a major university outside the Midwest for his postdoctoral studies before he can come back and work in the Midwest and have a decent position somewhere. That's our big question right now, what's going to happen and which way we're going to go. We don't know yet."

Although Rene would prefer to finish her residency in Oklahoma City, it is more important to her that she and Jimmy be in the same city. "We're going together. We're either both staying or we're both going."

When Rene hears the words "American Dream," she envisions a life that she and Jimmy are on their way to building: "The nice house, nice car, Mom and Dad, kids, everything hunky-dory. Everyone's comfortable. There's no illness, there's no bills to pay, y'know, anything like that.

"The other part of my dream is to make sure that my parents or Jimmy's parents, that no one in my family, has to worry about paying a bill again. That would be my dream, for my parents and for Jimmy's parents to be comfortable and not have to say, 'Oh gee, we have the insurance bill this month,' and have to sit around in their latter years worrying about paying a bill. I feel really strongly about that. Jimmy and I would rather do without some things in order to make sure our parents are comfortable. That's my biggest dream."

Although Rene uses the word "dream," she does not necessarily think of her dream as *the*, or even *an*, American Dream. It is simply *her* dream. Yet she does not reject the idea that there is such a thing as the American Dream. "Everyone needs something to focus on, as far as what they want in life," she says, "and if that's what they want and what they think will make them happy, then who can argue with them. I can't argue with anyone who has that dream. It's a pretty good dream, you know.

"I think the worst thing about it is that it's an expectation that everyone has, and it's so hard these days for anyone to make that dream come true. There's so many people that are living in such disappointment because their lives aren't this picture-perfect little setting that everyone is supposed to have. It's getting harder and harder for people to do it, for someone to own a house. It's not so bad here in Oklahoma. You can pretty much buy a house as a young person. But in other parts of the country, it's a lot harder to purchase a home. It's almost impossible for many people."

Rene says, "I just want to take good care of my patients and take good care of my family. That's about it."

Medicine, she explains, "is not my entire life. I feel that if work is interfering with my family, with what life's supposed to be about—you know, having time just to sit down, eat dinner, *talk,* things like that—it's too much.

"The biggest thing is that I'm not going to be able to stay home like my mother was, and I loved having my mother at home. It was great to have Mom there when you came home from school. So sometimes I wonder, 'Well, what have I gotten myself into now?' I want to be a good mother and a good wife, and then I'll do my job."

Rene tells me about remarks made by some of her medical school classmates whose parents were physicians. These people said that they never saw their parents, that their parents were never part of their lives. These stories had a profound impact on Rene. "I don't want to hear my kids, twenty years from now, going, 'God, I never saw my mom. She was never there for me.' I want to be there for my children, even if I might be at the office. I want them to know that, yeah, Mom is there for them."

How does Rene plan to balance her family and her practice? "My dream is to work in a group practice with maybe three to four other physicians and rotate call with them. That way, at least there will be part of my time that is sacred, that is, you know, *our* time. There will be no phone calls, there will be no interruptions. We can just do our thing.

"I've made the best plans I can. Hopefully, once problems arise, we'll be able to work them out."

Because Rene and Jimmy do not know where they will be after Jimmy finishes his Ph.D. next year, and because they have not figured out how they will juggle two careers *and* children, they have postponed having kids for another two or three years. "Oh my gosh," she says, "there's so much responsibility with a child. And once you have a child, it's yours for life. You can't give 'em back. And even when they're twentysomethin' years old, they're still your child. They're there forever, and you better be ready for it. So we're not going to have children for a while. We just got a puppy, and we thought that was a big step."

Although Rene is optimistic about her future—"maybe too much so"—she is less sanguine about the nation's collective future. One of the issues that most concerns her is how health care in America is going to work out. "It scares me," she says. "Is it going to become socialized medicine? Is government therefore going to be telling me what to do and how to do it? Am I going to be working for the government? Which I really, really don't want to do.

"My biggest argument against socialized medicine is, I don't know how they would organize it or who they would get to organize it. And that person could not be changing every four years, or the system would be in constant flux with new rules, regulations, how we're going to do things, how we're not going to do things.

"And plus, I don't want to be told what to do. That's another reason I went into medicine. I want to be a little bit more in control of my life and not have a boss, so to speak. And if government was running it, I would have a boss. I would be told when I was going to work, how much I was going to work, what I was going to be doing and how I was going to be doing it. Which tests I should get, which tests I could not get, which medications I could give my patients, which I couldn't, how often the patient could come to see you. You know, things like that.

"But access to health care is also a concern because, I mean, my parents don't have health-care insurance. My dad doesn't work with one company, so therefore he can't get it through a company. If you go out and try to get this health insurance on your own, it's too expensive. If you're not making any money you can go get Medicaid. But if you're *trying* to make ends meet and *trying* to take care of yourself but you just can't get the health insurance and make that bill as well, then you're kind of stuck out in the cold.

"It's really the biggest question for everyone, because obviously the system we have right now is not working. What we're going to do and how it's going to be done, I don't know. And I think that's what bothers me the most, is that I can't even come up with an answer for the problems that we have right now."

The crisis in the nation's health-care system is not the only problem that worries Rene. "You name it—education, health care, just people having a job. I mean, things are continuing to worsen, and I've seen that just in my own family. My dad just went six months without a job. I mean, that's the worst it's been—ever—for him. Ever. Since he's been working all of his life, that's the worst it's been.

"And I don't see things getting better right now. I think they definitely can get better. But I don't see anyone doing anything, as of yet, other than just solving problems here and there as quickly as they can, which usually turns into ten other problems later on. I think we have lost sight of any goals. Rather than a plan to solve things, we're putting out fires.

"This might sound really strange, but within like the next twenty years, I think the United States could have another civil revolution, the people of the United States going against the government. I could see it happening because so many people are getting ignored within the system. Of course, with our military system I don't see it happening, but it could happen. I mean, if everyone did what they did out in L.A.,* we could have one bad situation on our hands.

"If we continue to have people frustrated to the point that they see no hope at all of things ever getting better and they see no changes, just generation after generation of people who see no hope of things getting better, no hope of getting a new job, no hope of having the American Dream, I think it could happen. You don't think of that happening in the United States.

"But it could."

---

*Rene is referring to the riot of April 29–30, 1992.

SERGEANT SHANE AND CINDY

With his broad forehead, square jaw, and barrel chest, Shane looks like a Marine sergeant straight from central casting. If a pit bull could walk erect, grow a dark wisp of a mustache, and speak English with a slight Floridian drawl, he would be Sergeant Shane. When I met Shane, he was wearing red gym trunks and a white T-shirt depicting a bird that looks like the Warner Brothers' roadrunner marching through the middle of a truck tire, a boxing glove on its left wing and a socket wrench in its right. Printed on the tire's sidewall are the words "Road Runners**MVU-56 USMC." Tattooed on Shane's left biceps is a red rose the size of my fist; the name "Cindy" is emblazoned beneath it. Cindy is Shane's wife, a woman with azure eyes and a sweet smile.

Cindy, twenty-seven, and Shane, twenty-eight, live on a naval base in a two-story house that could have been designed by the same architect who devised the houses for the Monopoly board. Though trained as a heavy-equipment mechanic, Shane is currently an inspector and instructor for the reserve unit assigned to the base. Cindy is a secretary in the legal services office on the base.

Shane and Cindy met when they were students at the same high school in West Palm Beach, Florida, where both of them were raised. Shane was a construction worker, and construction was slow at the time, so he enlisted in the Marines during his senior year of high school. After graduation, he went to boot camp, and he married Cindy when he returned. They have two kids—Shane Jr., four, and Shanna, one—and Cindy is pregnant with their third when I visit. Rudy, an amiable nine-year-old brindle pit bull, completes the cast.

Shane did not intend to become a career soldier. When he enlisted, he thought he'd serve his four years and get out. But in those four years he had gotten married and had a son. "Time was goin' fast," Shane tells me. "I wasn't preparin' myself financially to get out. And then my son came along. Instead of pulling out to the private sector, strugglin' to get a job, maybe not havin' somewhere to stay, not havin' the money to keep me goin' for three or four months while I was out there job-huntin', and havin' to suffer, I decided it was smarter to stay in." Shane has already served ten years and recently reenlisted for another four. He hopes that he will be assigned to Okinawa.

Two words explain why Shane remains in the military—job security. He reasons, "The economy is really bad right now. Jobs are slow. There's no money out there. There's no jobs out there. This is security. I have my family with me. I can take care of my kids, make ends meet. The money's not good, but I can make it."

Shane says that he and Cindy do not have the same financial trouble that plagues so many military couples, that is, spending more than they make. He explains, "We can fluctuate with our budget. We don't accumulate a lot of bills. We have a lot of plastic, but we don't use it that much. And if we do use it, we pay it off right away."

Cindy adds, "We don't overextend ourselves." They don't live extravagantly, either. For instance, they have seen only one movie since Shane Jr. was born four years ago. They took their son to see *Teenage Mutant Ninja Turtles*.

"Are you happy now?" I ask.

Cindy: "Yah."

Shane asks, only half sarcastically, "Are we?"

Cindy again says, "Yah," though I sense some reservation in her voice.

Shane's conception of the American Dream is straightforward: "More kids, nice home—with a swimmin' pool—couple of nice cars, and watchin' the kids get through a nice education."

Cindy chimes in: "Now *he* says 'nice cars'—he's talkin' BMW or somethin' sittin' in the driveway, a five-acre lot, big wooden house, pool, Jacuzzi. That's his idea of the American Dream."

"Is that yours?"

"That *would* be mine. But that's not gonna happen for us. If I have a nice house, it doesn't have to be a fancy one. I don't have to have a Mercedes sittin' outside on my yard. I'd have a decent car. And if we can pay our bills, I'd be happy."

Cindy thinks the American Dream has become too expensive. "No one can afford it anymore. Back in the fifties and sixties things were a lot cheaper. Things just aren't working anymore. Most people can't even afford to eat, let alone buy a house. You can't even buy a house anymore for under a hundred thousand dollars. Who has that kind of money anymore?" She and Shane felt the same frustration when they tried to buy a car. "We went out to look for a new car. We couldn't *find* a new car under twenty-five thousand dollars—I mean, not a family car. We need a nice, dependable car with four doors. I want air-conditioning. I want heat. I want a stereo. But we can't find a nice car that's something we can afford."

Cindy says, "Unless we win the lottery, I don't see us ever having that much money." Until Shane gets out of the military, "there's not an opportunity to make a lot of money. Maybe when he gets out, things will change."

Cindy and Shane also have somewhat different definitions of success. Shane's is simple: "Success for me is having money in the bank to cushion you if you need it. Kids' education paid for. Being able to get up and go and having the money to afford to do that."

Cindy's perspective is a bit more complex. "It'd be nice to have some money," she says. "Then again, I can only have so much money earning what I do. If I wanted to, I could go back to school. But I don't feel it's good on the children, having to work all day and then go to school at night. I feel successful. I'm good at what I do. I'm happy without the money."

I ask what's important to them and, without hesitation, Cindy answers: "My family's important to me, and that's all. As long as we stay together, that's all that's important to me." She points out that Shane has been twice stationed in Okinawa, and that both times the tours were "unaccompanied," a military euphemism that means Shane had to pay to bring his family to Japan—no small feat on a soldier's salary. What's more, although they could buy supplies at the base PX and eat in the commissary, they could not live in military housing, nor could Cindy work on base to supplement Shane's income. "We lived from paycheck to paycheck," says Shane.

When I ask Shane what's important to him, he replies, "Their education is gonna be real important. Their health, their education, their well-being."

I note that he has mentioned his children's education several times during our conversation, so I wonder whether he regrets not going to college. "Very much so," he says. He explains that his father had offered to pay for a college education, but "I was young and I had enough of school. I joined the military thinkin' I would join for four years and get out. But within that four years I had gotten married and had a son."

He continues: "I started savin' for college—you know, they have that G.I. Bill, two for one. I'm savin' all that right now. I'm goin' back to school. I've taken some courses. I've taken an architectural drafting course, and I've taken some math courses, and I just took an accounting course. Been a long time since I've been in school. Years. It's pretty hard to get back into it 'cause I have to work, take care of the family. But once we get settled—like when we get to Japan and I know I'm gonna have three years—then I'm gonna start back to school two nights a week. Whatever it takes to get some kinda education, so I can get out of the military when I'm thirty-eight years old and fall right into society."

Although Shane has for the most part enjoyed his time in the Marines, he also feels frustrated because he does not have the opportunity to use all his talents. He says, "The military promotes you according to what they need, not what you're capable of doing. If it wasn't for the security and the kids, I would get out of the military—and start makin' some money." He insists that he will not allow his son to repeat his mistakes. He will even work a second job if that's what it takes to send Shane Jr. to a private school. With complete conviction, Shane says, "He's gonna be somebody. He's goin' to college. He's not goin' in the military. He's not gonna spin his wheels like I do."

Cindy does not echo her husband's regrets about having skipped college, though she wonders whether it might have been a good idea for her children's sake. She explains, "When they go to school, I'm gonna have a hard time helping them. I see myself taking college courses at night, trying to keep up with my kids, so that when they come home saying, 'Mom, how do I do this?' I can help them." She admits, perhaps a bit wistfully, "I think college would've been fun. It would have been neat. But even when I was growing up, I wanted to go out, get married, and have kids." College simply was not an option in Cindy's mind.

When I ask Shane and Cindy about the national situation, Shane expresses bitterness about the disparity in the nation's distribution of wealth. "The rich get richer and the poor are gettin' poorer," he says. "If you have a lot of money, you can make a lot of money. If you have *no* money, it's really hard to start makin' money. I'm workin' on my second million dollars right now—I gave up on my first."

Shane and Cindy are also angry about the unwillingness of our national representatives to raise soldiers' salaries, while they raise their own without compunction. Shane becomes angry as he explains: "They can sit down and vote and tell the military—that has to go out and maybe not come home to their families again and die for their country—that they can have a four percent pay raise. But they close their doors at the end of the night and vote themselves into a twenty-five percent pay raise. Now who's gonna be foolish enough to vote against that? If I could sit down and write my paycheck out to be twice of what it is right now, you don't think I would do that? And that's exactly what they're doin'. They wanted a fifty percent pay raise. Their justification was they have to own more than one home because they're in Washington, D.C., so long, so they have to maintain two different homes. Well, I'm sorry. I don't make *any* money and I don't even *own* a home. And they're gonna tell me I get a four percent pay raise? It's a screwed-up system.

"They should not be able to vote themselves into a pay raise. We should vote on whether they're doing their job to get the pay raise. And the American public should vote whether we should get a pay raise. I'm sure right after this little conflict we had, this [Persian Gulf] war, they would've voted us much more than a four percent pay raise." An ironic suggestion from a man who has never even registered to vote.

"A lot of people misunderstand the military. They *think* that the military has a lot of money. The reason they *think* that is 'cause a lot of soldiers drive nice cars. But they can't afford to own homes, some of 'em don't have kids, so the only thing they have to spend that money on is a car. But that's all they own. Soldiers don't make any money. I probably make fifteen thousand dollars a year. That's nothin'. A kid comin' outta high school probably makes that."

When I suggest that they might be receiving benefits that make up for the relatively low pay, Shane retorts, "They're cuttin' those benefits."

Cindy explains, "We have CHAMPUS medical insurance. It used to be our deductible was a hundred dollars. They raised it to three hundred dollars. Within a normal year, your children don't go to the doctor that much to where you can meet a deductible like that."

And remember, Shane adds, "we're paying three hundred dollars on fifteen thousand dollars income. But the senators have a physician right there, and they have free medicals, free prescriptions. Everything is free. They pay nothin'. But they're makin' a hundred and twenty-five thousand dollars a year."

Cindy tells me about an instance when she tried to get a prescription filled for Shanna. The base pharmacy was out of what Cindy needed, so she had to go to a pharmacy in the city. When she went to the base pharmacy to have the prescription refilled, the pharmacist refused because the prescription originally had been filled in town, even though Cindy explained why she had to go off base. "But," she says, exasperated, our national representatives "can walk across the street and get free medicine and free medical care. We don't get anything."*

When Shane retires from the military—at the ripe old age of thirty-eight—he thinks he might "open up a business, workin' on heavy equipment." Or he might "get a nice civil service job—I could always work in the post office and collect another pension, let the government continue to pay me—buy a home down in Florida, retire down there, live out the rest of my life there, and enjoy watchin' my kids and my grandkids."

Cindy is not as sanguine about their prospects. "That sounds like a pretty picture," she says, "but we'll see what happens. When he gets out in ten years, if we can afford to buy a house, we will. Like I said, maybe things will change.

"We started planning after we had both kids. Now we plan things. We have a savings account. We put money away so that, should anything happen, we have some money. So hopefully in ten years we're gonna have some money. Shane's got some money goin' to a fund so the children have college money. So hopefully our plan will work out, and in ten years he *can* retire and we *can* go home and buy a house and watch our kids go through high school—'cause that's where they'll be when he retires, they'll be just starting high school. And then once they finish high school, we can send them to a college if they want to. And then I can go sit on a beach, lie in the sun, and do absolutely nothing, like you're supposed to do when you're retired."

*Until 1992 the Navy maintained a medical clinic that offered free medical care and free prescription drugs to members of Congress. However, in the wake of the check-bouncing scandal at the House of Representatives bank in 1992, Congress changed the rules. Now members of Congress must pay for their medicine and a $520 annual fee for routine medical care.

Note: Since our conversation, Cindy gave birth to their third child, a girl.

ROD

Rod, twenty-three, just wants to be middle-class. But it's not so easy to be middle-class anymore, even for a painting contractor who works sixty-five hours a week. "To be middle-class you need to be what used to be considered real wealthy," he says. "Any new people that move in here in this neighborhood are driving Mercedeses, I mean brand-new ones. And you would never see that in this neighborhood ten years ago, because people that drove Mercedeses wouldn't think about moving into this neighborhood. They had more money than that. People that were moving into this neighborhood had VWs and *maybe* a Cadillac, an older one. It's like, that's just the way it is now. And maybe I'm wrong, but that's the way I see it."

Growing up, Rod was solidly middle-class. He has lived most of his life in his parents' home in Woodland Hills, a suburb of Los Angeles. "It's one of the better areas in the Valley, I think for sure," he says. Rod's father used to work as a contract negotiator for an aerospace manufacturer. (A "very high-stress job," notes Rod's mother, who has just brought us something to drink.) A series of strokes forced Rod's father to retire early. Rod's mother was, for most of Rod's life, a housewife who devoted herself to raising Rod and his older sister. These days, Rod's mother designs jewelry and teaches oil painting classes once a week.

When Rod was in junior high, his father had his first stroke. Rod says, "I couldn't deal with that, the feelings and what have you." That, says Rod, is when he turned to drugs.

"It wasn't a daily habit, but a definite habit started, smoking half a pack a day. Smoking was just for fun, then, y'know. But of course a year later I was a pack a day. Y'know, fourteen years old, smokin' a pack a day, drinkin' every day by the time I was fourteen. I always thought I was havin' a good time, but I was to the point of even bringin' it to school and gettin' high before school and having thermoses of liquor in my lockers, y'know. The kind of stuff that, just, a fourteen-year-old kid can't handle, man. Even an adult can't handle.

"I cleaned up the first time when I was fifteen. My mother just gave me an ultimatum—'I'm shipping you away to a boys' camp, or you can seek some help for your problem.' I thought I was so brave, but I took the easy way out, y'know. Of course I'm not gonna be shipped away. And I got some help that way."

After Rod graduated from high school, he became a painter. "I was definitely lost," he says. "I didn't know what I wanted. I just took what was available. I thought I wanted to be in construction, y'know, and this was a quick in for me 'cause I knew a guy that was a painting contractor. And I like to work with my hands. I always have been the kid on the block that fixed everybody's bicycle, I was building treehouses. It's just always been the way I've been.

"And y'know, I caught on really quick, and I started makin' money really quickly. I mean, I started out making fifty bucks a day. Two hundred fifty bucks a week is more than a lot of people make now, y'know, lower-class people. Walkin' down the street in my painting clothes, I would pick up a job." Rod snaps his fingers, as if to say, "Like that."

"Construction was *booming* then, and people were paying high wages," he says. "I mean, by the time I was nineteen, I was running a crew of five guys and I was makin' about five hundred a week plus bonuses, y'know. When I was twenty years old, I made sixty grand that year. And I was partyin' it up big-time—goin' away every weekend, just doin' whatever I wanted to do, buyin' whatever I wanted to buy. Nothing outrageous, of course—suits and stereos and trucks. You know what I mean.

"At that time my bills were about twenty-eight hundred dollars a month, and the minimum I was makin' was four grand a month. I mean, I had money in my jackets that I forgot, hundreds of dollars that I forgot that I left in a coat pocket. Y'know what I mean, just stupid stuff like that."

Weekend trips and shopping sprees were not the only way Rod spent his money. His "main gig was drinkin' and smokin' pot." That his business partner was also an alcoholic did not help. "The old man that I was workin' with, he started drinkin' again. We were knockin' off work at noon, drinkin' till ten o'clock at night, y'know. Makin' money hand over fist, though, 'cause he had all of these old-timer contacts. They all drank too, and it was, y'know—

"I couldn't see past my shadow, y'know. So I thought I was just gonna be ridin' the fast lane like that." And after two and a half years of sobriety, says Rod, "I went right back to where I was, man.

"I ran a red light in the middle of the night. A cop followed me. I actually ran from him, realized that I wasn't gonna get away. Slowed back down, got out of my car. They arrested me, took me to jail. The policeman walked me through the jail and told me, he said, 'You're a young kid. I just wanna show you what your future's gonna be like if you continue doin' what you are doin'.' And he walked me through the facilities there.

"They have maybe ten cells down at West Valley, and a big drunk tank. He's like, 'This guy has been in and out for the last three years and this . . .' He just gave the whole rundown, and he says, 'I'm gonna release you on your own recognizance this time. But I don't ever wanna see you down here again.'

"And I don't know. Just clicked, y'know. I walked home from there to here. It was about ten miles, and it was, y'know, a.m., early a.m. It just gave me a lotta time to think. And I went to an Alcoholics Anonymous meeting that day. And it's been clear as a bell to me since that that's the only way I can be the way I wanna be."

As symbolic proof of his commitment, Rod shows me the gold AA pendant—a triangle circumscribed by a circle—that he is wearing on a gold chain around his neck. The sides of the triangle stand for "service," "unity," and "recovery."

Rod made approximately $90,000 in the year and a half when he was partners with the old man. Great money for a painter. But once Rod became sober again, he could no longer work with the old man. Rod explains, "Jobs that he was trying to handle were falling apart, and he was losing money all the time—losing it meaning blowing it, y'know, *my* money. When we were drinkin' together, it was different, because he didn't have anything to hide from me. But when he started having things to hide from me, like, it wasn't okay to me anymore for him to be drunk at five o'clock in the morning."

When Rod ended his partnership with the old man and, more importantly, his access to the old man's connections, Rod's annual income dipped, from $60,000 to $50,000. Still a respectable income, even in California. "It was just cool to me," he says. "I was young and very successful. I thought it wasn't gonna end. I thought it was just gonna get better and better and better and better.

"And it didn't." Rod laughs.

His annual income plummeted from $60,000 in 1989—"my great year," he says—to $18,000 in 1991. So far, 1992 has not been any better. "I was slow this year," he says. "I worked maybe three weeks a month, and it was for wages that I worked for when I was seventeen. It's been a real tough year."

He explains: "This is a hard, hard business. I mean, it's hard. Painting contracting, you open up the yellow pages and there's a hundred of them, in the Valley alone. The illegal aliens are working for so cheap. Y'know, they gotta earn their money to live, too, but I can't compete with that.

"I'm just gettin' burnt out, y'know what I mean. It gets old. Really does."

Rod used to employ as many as twelve painters but now uses only two regularly and occasionally a third. He tells me: "I don't think I'll be self-employed ten years from now. Where I'm at right now, the stress isn't worth it to me. And I'm makin' less money than I probably could workin' for somebody.

"I'm giving it my last shot right now. My wife is working with me, and she's very organized, and she's got a good business head on her shoulders."

Rod has known his wife, Marcelle, since they were in junior high, which is when they started what became an on-again-off-again romance that lasted through high school. They were on again as high school seniors and, except for one six-month period, have been on ever since. They have been married for nearly two years. In addition to helping with Rod's business, Marcelle also works full time as a personnel director for a temporary employment service.

Marcelle has not always had to work. "There was actually times where Marcelle didn't work for six months, and I covered everything no problem, still having an easy time," says Rod. "But I mean, my salary got cut in half and then some."

Until a month ago, Rod and Marcelle were renting a two-bedroom house in Woodland Hills. Over the past several months, however, even though as a couple they were making approximately $50,000 a year and even though they had sold one of their cars to reduce their debt, their bills—rent, utilities, car payments, car insurance, medical bills—began to overwhelm them. Besides overextending themselves, they had also had some bad luck. For example, one of their cars was stolen, but because the insurance paid them only one-third of what they owed on the loan, they will be paying on the note for three more years.

Rod did not save much money from his financial heyday, a few thousand dollars at most, and nothing is left of that. Since then, he has not been able to save a dime. So, "just gettin' tired of bein' a slave" to his bills, Rod and Marcelle last month moved in with Rod's parents.

The couple considered renting an apartment instead of moving in with his parents. But it would be tough to find any apartment in this area, let alone a decent one, for the $200 a month they pay Rod's parents. Plus, Rod notes, "I have two dogs, and I have a lot of equipment—work equipment, motocross gear, my wife has a motorcycle. Those two sheds out there are basically full of my stuff.

"And apartments and me don't mix. Around here, you move into an apartment, and everything you own and your car get ripped off. It's inevitable. The last apartment we lived in, a lot of my work equipment got stolen, my stereo got stolen outta my truck, all my tapes and CDs. That crap just gets old."

Rod explains that living with his parents is good for everybody: "My father's employer didn't give him his pension for about a year and a half, so he just got buried. And so they're on major catch-up, y'know what I mean. I mean, they're behind on stuff and they just barely get by. And with all the stuff that needs to be done around here, it just couldn't happen for them. And they can't sell the house in this market right now today and get what they need to get for it. My mom also, during my dad being sick, refinanced the house, y'know, so it's a big payment here, like about twelve hundred dollars a month. So with them bein' in their situation and me and Marcelle bein' in our situation, it just kind of worked out. I'm gonna do a lotta work around here. I pitch in on the rent. I'm able to pay my bills on time, and they are too now."

Still, says Rod, "it was very frustrating and demoralizing. Hell, I couldn't do anything. I was out there trying to get work, and when I was gettin' work I was workin' as hard as I could. I mean I was puttin' in ten hours a day and just movin' backwards.

"The major strain that it put on was my relationship with Marcelle. It was the hardest time we've ever had in the last, y'know, eight years, or six years actually. It's easy for me to say I can roll with the punches. I mean, I'm a pretty easygoin' guy, but I'm also talkin' about movin' back into a place I lived in for almost twenty years, actually eighteen years, with *my* parents. So I'm just moving back onto my own turf. And my parents aren't major rule-makers either, y'know. Never were. But for Marcelle, it's like foreign for her. She's not gonna have her own kitchen. And it's a little different for a woman. It was hard on her, big-time, but it's a lot easier than she expected it to be. So it's definitely lightening up around here."

Rod points out that moving in with his parents was difficult for Marcelle not just because she was entering unfamiliar surroundings, but also because Rod's lack of direction distressed her. "I always had a good job, and I worked hard," he says. "And when work started gettin' really bad for me and I was thinkin', 'Y'know, maybe this is a good time for me to get back into school,' all of a sudden here I am, this guy who's really stable as far as she's concerned is now a little bit unsure of himself. So it scared her a lot."

Rod is not sure how long he and Marcelle will be living with his parents. "I would like to say a year, max," he says.

These days, Rod regrets not having gotten more schooling, especially about business and legal principles, such as pricing, cost analysis, and liens. "It's just obvious," he says, "the more I get into the business world, the more I know I need to educate myself more and more. I'm learning lessons, too many of 'em, the hard way.

"I learned how to do my job and the business end of it from the old man, and he had been a painting contractor for like thirty years. And back in his day, a handshake was as good as gold, y'know, and he never changed from that. His biggest contract was the front page of a piece of paper. Basically, that's all he taught me.

"I wasn't armed with the right tools business-wise, y'know. I thought that I knew the trade, the rest is just a piece of cake, when it's actually the other way around.

"Generally, I would say this is probably the most wishy-washy I've ever been. I guess it has a lot to do with the times. Just a little bit of confusion. I'm not going to say a whole lot, because I know what I'm confused about. Just work, and what I really wanna do. I have to make a decision, y'know what I mean." However, except for his plan to enroll in a course on small-business management at a local community college, Rod has not yet decided what he really wants to do.

Rod may be uncertain about how to get there, but he knows what he wants from his future. "My American Dream," he says, "would be to own my own house, in a more mountain area that's not full of smog and gangs, and just have a good, peaceful life. Couple of kids and just get along. I don't need to be high on the hog. I just wanna be, y'know, middle-class, happy. Not a lotta stress, which is what I have right now, lot more than I wish to have ten years from now."

A minute later he seems to contradict himself. He says, "Everybody wants to have the white picket fence, the girl and the boy and the dog, the motor home, and I think that that's a bunch of bullshit. The American Dream mainly to me would be to have a great amount of spirituality, y'know what I mean, just to be okay with whatever situation is goin' on. Of course you're gonna have your problems, but I think that too many people get into having so much and getting stressed out.

"I have a great friend—I *had* great friends that either got into contracting or into business for themselves that I can't even talk to 'em anymore. They're just assholes. It's not their fault, I mean, they got caught into the stress of not having any time for themselves."

Rod tells me a story illustrating this point, about a general contractor with whom Rod had worked many times. "I didn't even give him bids on the jobs that I did for him," says Rod. "I just did 'em and billed him for it. He knew how much I was gonna charge, that's how many jobs I did for him." And they were not just professional acquaintances; they were also friends.

In 1991, Rod's financial nadir, he had the opportunity to act as the general contractor for some people who needed major repairs on their 10,000-square-foot Malibu home. These people offered Rod $500 a week, on top of the painting contract, to hire the other subcontractors—the carpenters, the electricians, the plumbers. But instead of taking the job himself, Rod recommended that they hire Rod's friend, the general contractor. "I gave up five hundred dollars a week because I wanted to do the right thing and have the right guy do the right job," he says. The homeowners hired Rod's friend. But instead of hiring Rod and his partner to do the painting, Rod's friend hired "dirt-cheap labor" and undercut Rod's bid.

Rod explains: "See, this is the American Dream for him. He bought a house, he had a motor home, a wife and a kid, another one on the way. He had two new cars, which he couldn't afford. He even had to borrow money to look like he could borrow money. So he got himself so deep in a jam, you know what I'm sayin', he got himself so deep in a jam that he had to screw over one of his best friends—and try to pretend like it didn't happen and tell me that they decided not to use me.

"That guy took a lotta money out of my pocket on that. He screwed me out of one of the bigger contracts of the year for me.

"Sure, money's important. Money's not gonna make you happy, but it's gonna make you a lot more relaxed. If you're chasin' money all the time, it's hard to be happy, y'know what I mean. But you can have a lot of money and be an asshole." Rod laughs.

Rod also believes that the house-in-the-'burbs American Dream has been priced out of reach. "In California today, to buy this house that we're in right now, you're lookin' at almost four hundred thousand dollars.

"I have friends of mine that live in Florida. She is a hairdresser and he is an accountant, and they just bought a house that they can walk to the beach from, for like seventy grand. It's as big as this house, in a better location. Y'know what I mean. In California, I don't know. It's just wacked out here.

"It's changing a lot around here. I don't know if I'm just more in tune with it now because I'm older and I have a wife living with me and I'm concerned about her well-being, too. It's already bad. It's already bad crime-wise. My wife got her car stolen at gunpoint at a mall down the street from here. Her father almost had his car stolen at an intersection. They tried to come and grab his keys and beat him up. Luckily he's a strong man and he was able to defend himself. Just that kinda crap, y'know. Down the street at another mall a couple of months ago, there was a night stalker. He was just picking women off every night. Same mall, they couldn't even stop the guy. He was getting into their car with them and makin' them drive him to a place, raping 'em and killin' 'em. And that's not like 'Wow.' You just get hardened by it. And I don't even live really deep into it."

Rod tells me that his punishment for drunk driving was eighty hours of cleaning litter along the highways. "You won't believe how many people live in the bushes along the freeway. It would blow your mind to get down in those weeds and you find all these little huts built. There's little camps in there. I mean, there's full-on fireplaces built out of brick and mud, with barbecues on the top of 'em, fireplace at the bottom, and couches and—it's just a mind-blower, man.

"Every once in a while they go through and—" Rod smacks his

fist into his other palm, symbolizing destruction. "That was unbe-lievable. I wouldn't do it. I mean, I needed a gas mask to do it. People were puking in this crap.

"We're just tired of this rat race out here. People don't even wave around here anymore. I mean, very few. I used to think I wanted to be in the raciness. But as time goes on and on and it just gets more and more and more crowded here, it just gets old."

Rod wants to move to a smaller city. "Not a two-horse town or anything like that, but a little more smaller of a town. People in smaller towns aren't greedy. They even have time to say, 'Hey, buddy, how ya doin'.' They're not blowin' their horn all the time, and when they go into the market they're not, like, frustrated be-cause there's ten people in line and they need to get goin', man. That's a shitty way to live. And I think the majority of people live that way, y'know.

"It's terrible. But I'm kinda trapped here right now." He chuckles.

Rod believes that, ultimately, the two things that are most im-portant are "just bein' happy and havin' a good relationship with my wife. I think they kinda go hand in hand."

Rod tells me that he is optimistic about his future. "Things'll be good," he says, "I'm sure of that. I mean—it has to be." He laughs.

LESLIE

Leslie, twenty-eight, is an Army brat, the only child of a career sol-dier from the back hills of Kentucky and a Korean woman. Her par-ents met and married while Leslie's father was stationed in Korea. Born in San Pedro, California, Leslie lived in Washington, D.C., Ja-pan, Hawaii, Louisville, Heidelberg, and Waco, Texas, before her parents finally settled in Killeen, Texas, where her father completed his twenty years by working as a computer programmer and oper-ator at Fort Hood. He is now retired from the Army and works for a defense contractor in Killeen. Leslie's mother is a homemaker.

After graduating from Killeen High School, Leslie attended Texas A&M. She initially majored in chemical engineering, then switched to biomedical engineering. She says some of the experiments conducted in her physiology labs, particularly those performed on live animals, made her squeamish. Consequently, unlike so many of her fellow biomedical engineers, who went on to become doctors, dentists, veterinarians, or research scientists, Leslie stopped with her bachelor's degree. She also met her future husband, Clay, at Texas A&M.

After college Leslie and Clay, who already had been dating awhile, went to work for the same large defense contractor in Fort Worth. Leslie worked in the systems engineering group, which she describes as "totally theoretical, nothing hands-on." She helped to design computer systems for futuristic aerospace vehicles, such as the Orient Express, a hypervelocity vehicle that may someday fly as fast as twenty-five times the speed of sound, traveling the distance from Texas to Japan in three hours.

Leslie and Clay decided it would be foolish if they both worked for a defense contractor, so Clay accepted a job offer from a major electronics firm in Houston. The defense contractor created a job for Leslie so that she could continue working for the company in Houston. She became the liaison between the company and NASA's Johnson Space Center. Before they started working in Houston, Leslie and Clay eloped and were married in Hawaii. After a year in Houston, the electronics firm assigned Clay to Richardson, a suburb of Dallas. Leslie, who'd "had enough of defense," quit her job with the defense contractor and went to work for a large consulting firm in Dallas.

Unfortunately, consulting required Leslie to be away from her husband far too much. "I got assigned to a nuclear power plant out of town, and I was only seeing my husband on the weekends. And it doesn't get any better. The higher up in the company you go, it's still consulting. You still have to go where the clients are, and they're out of town."

So Leslie left the consulting firm and took a job in the Dallas office of one of the nation's largest public accounting firms. "I basically made the change for personal reasons, to try to get something a little more stable, where I'm in Dallas a little bit more," she says. "It's a lot different than consulting was because, typically, you do go out to the clients and they are out of town, but it's more like day business trips. You go out for a couple of days or maybe several weeks of a couple days a week. But you're basically in town, and that's a big distinction."

Leslie feels as if, in almost every way, she has lived the middle-class American Dream: "Went to public schools. Middle-class. Went to a public university, had a few scholarships. Got a job in engineering, got a job now consulting. Got married, bought the house, had the dog, the whole bit." But the dream ended with her divorce.

"Twenty-four when I got married, twenty-seven when I got divorced. It was a very, very big shock. There were a lot of signs along the way that I should have paid attention to, and I just didn't. His parents were married, then they divorced. They remarried each other a year later, and they redivorced each other. And then they each went on and married someone else. And at the time when we separated, his brother was in the process of a divorce, and his father was in the process of a divorce, so all the men in that family were in the middle of a divorce. I just think there were a lot of outside circumstances that played into it.

"We bought a house. To him it wasn't a home. Which is kind of strange. It's going against everything you hear, that most people are nest-building. 'Cause that's what I wanted to do—buy a house, kind of make it a refuge from work, someplace you could go home to. It's home, it's not just a house. And to him it's *just* a house. It's brick, it's glass, it's wood. It's a place you drop your stuff off, go out and have fun and come back. You sleep there and it stores your toys. So we had some basic philosophical differences."

Leslie concedes that Clay is not solely responsible for their marital problems. She may have been uncompromising ("I'm hard-headed. I admit it. But everyone says that about him, too"), and she may not have been as supportive as Clay needed her to be. Leslie also believes she had an "unhealthy dependence" on their marriage, that she put too much pressure on the relationship because she expected too much from it. "I used to say, 'My family comes first.' 'I put you first, before my job.' 'I get my happiness from our relationship.' 'When we're doing fine, I'm happy.' I think that was probably a little unhealthy on my part. Of course, it's easier to say that looking back at it than when I was doing it. It took the divorce for me to realize that what you need to have are two people who are basically happy with themselves first, and then you can *share* your life together. But if you're not happy yourself, you're not gonna be happy in the marriage, and it's gonna have problems. That's part of what happened in my case.

"The divorce hasn't left me bitter or cynical or anything like that. The way I try to look at it is in a positive light. I learned a lot from it. And one of the things that I've learned is that you really need to be able to take care of yourself on your own, that you should not depend on another person. And it may not be divorce. It may be death. You might be totally happy and you get this knock on your door and your spouse or whatever has been in a car accident and is dead. And there you are. I think I was a little too dependent before, emotionally.

"And I think that financially it taught me a lesson, too. It's a good thing that I had a job where I could take care of myself because I wasn't able to depend on this other person to provide for me. So this whole thing of divorce has kind of tainted my outlook. It's kind of sad because I look at it as having been very trusting and wanting to stay home, if I were to have children, for the first three, four, five years, whatever, to give them a good start. Then when they went to school, go back to work myself. That was what I always had intended. But now with what's happened, the way I look at staying home with the children, it almost puts the woman in a vulnerable kind of a position because you're totally dependent on this person for the money. And *you're* losing *your* skills and marketability. If something were to happen, you would basically be left without means for yourself.

"I'm not sure how I want to handle it now. I still think it's important to stay home with the child. What I would try to do now is try to work part-time, whereas before I would have wanted to stay home full-time to raise it. But now I could probably compromise and do both, and that way still give attention to the children and still maintain some means of being able to look out for myself."

Despite the divorce, Leslie would like to be married again someday. She says, "It's a lot more fun to share things with somebody and to have a family, that whole bit. I just think I have to be really careful about who that person is. So, I'm hopeful, hopeful that the next time will be the right one. But I'm not pursuing it. If they want to, they can call me and we'll go out.

"If you're gonna get serious about it, I would probably go to a counselor before you got married. I think there would be less divorces if people went to a counselor before they got married. They have all these little tests and questions and things to bring up that really ought to be discussed beforehand. I think that would be the thing. The next person I'm involved with, if I get serious, we're off. He'll have to put up with me and go."

Leslie tells me about her vision of the American Dream: "I think most people, for the American Dream, think of the material side of it. You want to have enough obviously to be comfortable. But I think most people—or, at least, I do—should get a lot of their well-being from their relationships with people. I don't think when people die, on their deathbed, they ever say, 'I wish I had worked more,' 'I wish I had just written one more paper.' It's always 'I wish I had spent more time with my son,' 'I wish I had spent more time with my wife.' It's always personal.

"I see a house. I see having a job where I'm making enough money where I can take care of myself. Doing something which I enjoy, which maybe is a little fulfilling. I don't expect the world. I don't expect to be able to afford to do all these things if I'm saving whales. I see a husband and I see children. I see just being able to do things with them—travel, show them new things, and teach them things. A dog and a cat. Pretty standard stuff, really. I don't really feel this burning drive to be extremely successful in the business world. I don't feel this burning drive to leave something behind when I'm gone. I don't really feel the need for that type of glory. I just wanna be happy. I just wanna live my life and be happy and have good friends and family around and be healthy and travel."

Because Leslie emphasizes her personal life in her vision of the American Dream, she will likely quit her job with the accounting firm. Although she has enjoyed the travel and working with a cadre of intelligent, well-educated young adults, she says, "This company is very difficult as far as maintaining a personal life, a family. I don't know what the divorce statistics are for the partners and managers here compared to the population as a whole, but it's a very stressful job. It demands a lot of your time and you're away a lot of times. A lot of people who do put family first tend to leave because it's very difficult to have that here."

I ask whether it has been difficult working in professions largely dominated by men. She tells me a story from her days with the defense contractor in Fort Worth:

"I had just started and so had this guy. We sat next to each other. Well, this one particular manager would keep dropping off these little menial things on my desk for me to do, which I didn't mind doing because I'm new. I figured, I'm the low man on the to-tem pole. I'm staff, I need to do this type of work. But he never dropped any of this type of work off on the guy that sat right next to me who was also new. Never did. It was always brought to me. And I did it and I did it and after a few weeks, I said, 'This is ridic-ulous. He's not giving you any of this—typing or copying or what-ever it was—to do. He always brings it to me.' So finally I went up to him and said something about it. I said I don't mind doing my share of the work, but I don't understand why.

"He just kind of looked at me and he was like, 'You mean you're not a secretary.'

" 'No.'

" 'You're an engineer?'

" 'Yes.' I'm getting mad now. He thought that I was a secretary down there and had been giving me all this stuff and he just *as-sumed*. Oh, I was infuriated. I was just infuriated by that. He never dropped anything else off again."

Leslie adds that she does not feel she has been the victim of sexism at the accounting firm. "For the most part I'm demanding enough where, if I see something happen, most of the time I'll ad-dress it. I'll just say, 'Why is this happening?' Having an engineering background, I think they look at me a little bit differently. I don't let myself get pushed around or taken advantage of. I think they kind of see me as more serious type of person."

A lot of national and global issues worry Leslie, but one of her principal concerns is "the destruction of the American family." One of the problems, she says, is Americans' breezy attitude toward di-vorce. "With all the divorces and how quick people are to do it, it really does impact the children, how they look at families and the security and stability. Looking out for 'me' versus 'us' type of thing. That's really troublesome."

Leslie sees self-absorption as the other problem. She says her ex-husband would make remarks such as, "It's hard for me to be selfish, but you only live once and you shouldn't have to compro-mise what it takes to make you happy." Leslie says, "If he has that attitude, and a lot of other people have that same type of attitude, the American family structure is just going away. It just can't last with attitudes like that."

■ ■ ■

Note: After I spoke with Leslie, she left the accounting firm and accepted a job as a sales rep for a medical equipment company in North Carolina.

ANN

Two years ago Ann had a "revelation." She was the assistant manager of a Friendly's, one of those "family restaurants" where everything, from the tabletops to the scrambled eggs, tastes as if it has been fashioned from injection-molded plastic. Ann was twenty-five and had been working at one or another Friendly's in suburban Cleveland for almost ten years, five of them as an assistant manager. One day she asked herself, "Is this what I'm gonna do, flip burgers all my life?"

Ann, twenty-seven, was born and raised in the Cleveland suburbs. Her father was a blue-collar worker at a steel mill; her mother was a housewife. When Ann was twelve, her mother, a borderline diabetic, died of a vascular problem associated with her condition. Ann's father was working the swing shift and it eventually became clear that, without his wife, he could not earn a living and still have time to take care of his children. So Ann's father and her two younger sisters moved in with Ann's paternal grandmother, while Ann and her older brother went to live with their father's brother and his family.

A couple of years later, the steel mill where Ann's father worked was taken over by a large conglomerate. Ann's father, who had been laid off periodically over the preceding several years, was laid off permanently. He and his brother decided to head to Houston, Ann says, " 'cause it was booming there and they were able to find a job." At this point, Ann's older brother moved out on his own, and Ann moved in with her two younger sisters at her grandmother's.

Ann's grandmother did not need any financial help to take care of Ann and her siblings because Ann's grandfather, a former executive who had died a few years earlier, left his wife "pretty well set." But Ann has "always been kinda on the responsible side"; she didn't want to depend on anybody. Once she turned sixteen, she started working after school behind the fountain at Friendly's.

She still relied upon her grandmother for food and a roof over her head but took care of everything else herself.

Ann graduated a semester early from public high school, but she did not go to college, a decision she regrets. (Both of her younger sisters went from high school directly to college. "Because I told 'em," says Ann, "an' they seen how I struggled.") Instead, Ann moved out of her grandmother's house and began working full-time at Friendly's.

"I was Friendly's gung-ho," she says in her Midwestern twang. "I wanted to be a manager at Friendly's. That's all I wanted to do."

Only seventeen, Ann was promoted to assistant manager. Then the company decided that an assistant manager had to be eighteen, so they reassigned Ann to work behind the fountain. When she was twenty, Friendly's again made her an assistant manager. A few years later, she began the company's five-part management training program. But she had a personality conflict with one of her managers, who, she says, was very egotistical and sexist. The company tried to help Ann by moving her to another Friendly's. By that point, however, Ann had grown so frustrated and discouraged with the company and with her own life that she decided not to reenter the training program and began examining her alternatives. She remained an assistant manager—until two years ago, when she had her revelation.

Actually, it was less a revelation than a realization that finally dawned on her after a couple of years of steadily creeping unhappiness and boredom. According to her nutshell version of the story, she had been at Friendly's for ten years, and "it was time to change." The unabridged story is a bit more complex.

"When I 'uz in my early twenties," Ann tells me, "I worried about, you know, havin' the nicest car, wanting to have this and that, worried about it if I didn't." Then she turned twenty-five and said to herself, "Gosh, where am I goin'? I'm still here at Friendly's. I'm paying an arm and a leg for a nice car just to keep up with everybody.' And I just started thinking about it. Took a long look and decided that that really wasn't important, that my happiness was more important. And material things wasn't going to give me happiness.

"Think that when you reach a certain age, an' everybody's different, you kinda look at yourself, an' you look back on what you've done. An' you change. 'N' I kinda looked and said, 'I don't wanna go this route.' 'N' I changed."

That's when Ann decided to become what she had always wanted to be—a nurse.

She explains: "I felt like I was being taken advantage of at Friendly's. There was no advancement. I wasn't gonna go anywheres. And I wanted a job that I could be able to support myself, and then when I was older there'd be other avenues that I could spread out to. In nursing there are all kinds of different ways that you can go with that. You can be fifty years old and still be a nurse. But you can work in a doctor's office. You don't have to be on your feet all day, and it pays well."

She continues: "I like working with people. And when someone's sick and you go in and do anything for 'em, they really appreciate it. That makes you feel good. I mean, they can't pay you enough money to have that feeling. There's no money value on that."

After two years of school, Ann is just one year away from becoming a registered nurse. She plans to work for two years as a sort of generalist before she begins specializing in obstetric care.

Before graduation, however, Ann will be married to her fiancé, Bobby. They met while they were working at Friendly's. Bobby, a systems analyst for a division of a large automotive parts manufacturer, was moonlighting to make some extra money for a down payment on a house. They've been engaged for a year and have even bought a home in North Ridgeville, a middle-class suburb of Cleveland. The new house is just four minutes down the road from another Friendly's, so after the wedding Ann is going to transfer there. And they're planning to start a family in two years, so Ann will have at least one year to work full-time as a nurse.

If all of these things turn out as Ann and Bobby have planned, Ann will have achieved much of her American Dream. She'll be a nurse. She'll have a home, her own family, a car for each of them. Materially, the only difference between Ann's American Dream and what she perceives as the textbook definition will be the absence of state-of-the-art appliances in Ann and Bobby's home. "I don't necessarily have to have all the luxuries," she says.

Yet Ann wants more than the material components of a comfortable life. She also wants something that few others I talked to mentioned explicitly—"free time."

She frets, "Everybody's wrapped up in having to go here and there. I don't think that people have enough time just t'go out and enjoy outside or stop and do things."

Ann herself is a perfect example. For the past two years she has worked nearly full-time as a waitress at Friendly's. That's in addition to thirty hours per week devoted to her professional studies. She also spends one day each week taking care of two "little ladies" at a local retirement community, helping them with their shopping and their housework. There's church every Sunday, too.

Her voice tinged with genuine longing, Ann tells me, "I'd love to have a day where I didn't have to look at my watch. I could just, you know what I mean, take my time 'n' do whatever I wanted. My goal's that one day I don't even have to bother lookin' at my watch. I'm always on such a timetable. What would I do?" As Ann ponders this question, her voice trails off, as if she is nearly overwhelmed by the incomprehensibility of the concept of spare time. Unfortunately, when Ann has children, she will not have any more free time than she has now. She plans to work part-time, on weekend nights, so that she can maintain her professional skills.

And there's one more thing Ann will have to take care of before she feels completely successful—her debt. Most of her credit card debt is from school—tuition, books, supplies. She also has car payments. She has only one more year of school, so she thinks she'll have her credit cards paid off by next year, and she has only another eighteen months of car payments. She hopes for the day when she won't owe any money and will have enough so that, if she wants to go shopping, she won't have to say, "Aww, I can't buy that" and will feel sufficiently comfortable to "at least check the price tag. That would be nice."

Right now, Ann's only worry is the state of the U.S. economy. According to one of the elderly women whom she tends to, "We're headin' right for a depression. She sees the signs. She's lived through World War One and Two and gone through the Depression. She says things are really gonna change.

"I don't per se have to worry about having a job, 'cause nursing, that'll be there. But you get worried about what'll happen to the economy. Will people be working? Is everything gonna shut down? I hear stories about the Depression, you know, where people didn't have enough food or housing. I just wonder where it's gonna all go." Ann's worries are well founded. Her father has been laid off twice, first by the steel mill, then by the large national homebuilder for whom he worked in Houston. Now he's back in the Cleveland area doing odd jobs to earn money.

"I'm a little bit concerned, especially just starting out. We just bought a house. Hope that we can keep it." A nervous little laugh sneaks out.

Still, Ann feels good about her life. She says, "I am approaching twenty-eight soon, and I'm not feeling depressed by thirty coming up. At least I'll have somethin' I can say I've achieved in my life. I'll go to my ten-year reunion next year and be able to say I'm somethin'."

BILLY

Billy, twenty-five, was born in a small town in southern Oklahoma. His father was an Air Force pilot, so he and his family moved every couple of years until Billy was seven. That's when his parents divorced and his mother moved with Billy and his sisters back to that same small town in southern Oklahoma, where his mother's family still lives. Since then, Billy has seen his father a few times—"in between, here and there," says Billy, "but nothing really stable. I wouldn't *care* to see him for that matter."

Financially, Billy's mother had a difficult time when she first divorced her husband and moved back to Oklahoma. "I think we were probably upper-lower-class," says Billy, not meaning to be cute or ironic. "It went up and down, depending on financial help from my father, work on my mother's part. We lived in the housing projects, then just kinda moved up from there."

Not long after Billy's mother had moved back to Oklahoma, she married a man who is now a plant manager at a facility that makes and tests various kinds of machinery. Along with their marriage came better financial times for Billy's family. "When my mother met my stepfather, they moved into a three-bedroom home, and they've just kind of moved up ever since. They've done real well together."

While Billy was growing up, his mother worked on the assembly line at a now-defunct defense plant in Gene Autry, Oklahoma. Consequently, says Billy, he and his older sisters "kind of helped raise ourselves while she was at work, and my grandmother played a big part in raising us." Billy tells me, "There was just a bond there, somethin' that wasn't there in the family."

Billy attended the local public schools all the way through high school. In the summer before his senior year, he married Karen. Billy was eighteen, Karen seventeen. Billy says, "Both of my older sisters got married at the age of eighteen. At that point, I think I was kinda goin' on my sisters' dreams. Neither one of them were goin' to college. They just dreamt of getting married, having a family, settling down 'n' having, you know, a dream, a white picket fence or whatever. And I just kinda wanted the same thing. And, I don't know. We thought we loved each other. It was just one of those things. We should've waited, an' now I know."

At that time, however, Billy and Karen were not in the mood to wait. Neither Billy's nor Karen's parents wanted their children to get married, so Billy and Karen issued an ultimatum: either they received permission to be married or Karen "was gonna get pregnant." Their parents acquiesced.

In his Oklahoma accent, in which "you" becomes "ya" and "for" becomes "fer," Billy tells me: "Karen's parents were not *poor,* but they didn't have a lot of money, and my family either. And so we paid for the wedding ourself. We saved the money, paid for everything ourself, and that was one issue with her mother. Her mother signed, we got married, and that was that. We continued to go to school, though."

Billy and Karen saved enough money to pay for the wedding but little else. So they lived at first with one set of parents, then with the other, before they finally could afford to rent a house for themselves.

After Billy graduated from high school, he went to work as a pharmacist's assistant. Karen was finishing high school and working at a fast-food restaurant.

Billy and Karen's marriage lasted only two years. Says Billy, "During the course of that year after I had finished high school, I figured out that I could do more, I could be more, and that living in a small town, doing little odd jobs, just wasn't what I wanted." But he insists that his changed ambitions did not cause their divorce. "Oh, no," he says. "We just felt like it would be better if we just went our own ways, y'know, grew up on our own."

While he was finishing high school and was married to Karen,

Billy, who had been at best an "okay" student, was not sure he even wanted to go to college. "I had different dreams, y'know, different aspirations in life. They changed after I got divorced. I'm *glad* they changed," he says. "Actually, my mom was a big part in getting me to go to school, also. She talked me into going."

Once Billy decided that he wanted to go to college, he still had to find a way to pay for it because his family did not have the money. That's when he enlisted in the National Guard.

Billy had friends who were already serving in the military. He says, "It was kind of a quick thing. I knew it was there. I went out there and talked with 'em, signed the line, and left. There was really no thinking in between, because if there had been I probably would not have done it.

"Actually, they promised me some things that never held up. Like basic training, they told me that it was gonna be a little more than what it was. I don't know that it's a fact that they *lied* to me, it's just they didn't tell me the whole truth, y'know. They just left a few things out, just the way I would be treated, the schedule that they put you on as far as getting up, going to bed, eating, things such as that." A bureaucratic oversight later provided Billy with an opportunity to leave the military at the end of his basic training. Yet despite being misled about the realities of basic training, he opted to stay.

After basic training and advanced individual training as a heavy-equipment operator, Billy enrolled at an Oklahoma state university. He was initially a psychology major, but after working with children in conjunction with one of his classes, he changed his major to special education. Four and a half years later, in December of his final semester, Billy was called up for Operation Desert Storm, the war against Iraq.

Billy recalls: "I think everything was happening too quick to be scared. I was nervous, probably. And we weren't real sure where we were going when they called us up. You go through a lot of stations. They brought in people and they took over a coliseum there in southern Oklahoma. You go through 'n' you get your shots 'n' you get weighed 'n' you make your will out 'n' you just do all these different things. No one never told us where we were really going, so we didn't really know. But we all had a good idea. They said, 'Oh, probably stateside, probably stateside,' but we all figured Saudi Arabia.

"I don't think any of us were really down about going until the morning that we loaded the bus t'go to Fort Sill, in southwest Oklahoma. The families were out there and we were leaving. That night, before we left, they had a little program at the coliseum for us where all the families could come and listen. They had singers 'n' the mayor was there. That's when it kinda hit us. We went back and slept at the armory. They locked us in so everybody would be there and no one would run off.

"The next morning we got up, we loaded the buses, the families were there. They lined the road, y'know, to watch us leave town. That's when it really hits you, y'know, 'Well, maybe we're not comin' back, or maybe it's gonna be a long time.' "

"We got over to Fort Sill and we stayed there for a few days. I remember calling home on Christmas Eve. My whole family was at the house, y'know, they were opening presents. My grandmother was there. The first Christmas that I'd ever been away from my grandmother an' my family, as far as that goes. I don't think it was a real Christmas for any of us because, I mean, I didn't have any presents t'open or have any family around. They were all sad because I wasn't there. The nieces and nephews knew that something was wrong, y'know. They didn't know what it was, but it just wasn't Christmas." Billy and the other soldiers flew out on Christmas Day.

"The flight over was very crowded," he says. "We were side by side. If I was facing east, then there was someone facing west with their knees right up against mine, someone on the north and south of me, y'know, just pressing up against me. It was cold in the airplane. It wasn't a commercial flight, it was a military flight. And we just tried to get comfortable and sleep sitting up as much as we could. We kinda told jokes. We tried to keep each other calm. It's not that anybody was freaking out or overly nervous or anything, it's just, we weren't sure what we were getting into and we tried not to think about it.

"When we landed, we didn't know what to expect, they hadn't told us anything. We landed at the airport there, in Saudi Arabia, we got off the plane—and there was nothin'. You could see these old houses that were thrown together, tin pieces up. At the time we thought they were houses. Later, I don't know what they were. You could see sand everywhere and sand was blowing. You couldn't hardly keep your eyes open because of all the sand.

"There were people rushing everywhere. At that point we were just kinda stunned, y'know. And they kept moving us over here, move us over here, move us over here. We found our gear and we stayed there until someone came and picked us up. They took us to housing quarters. We stayed there the whole time as far as a central place to leave our gear and t'sleep when we were back in Saudi Arabia. I guess it was an apartment-type building, and we lived on the fifth floor. It had been empty for eight years. It was built for the people over there. They didn't want to move in. They like roaming with their camels and stuff, so we were told.

"When we got over there, it was just a state of limbo, really. We didn't know what to expect—if we liked it, if we didn't, if we were scared, if we weren't. After a while, when we got settled in, it was just rush, rush, rush, hurry up and wait, y'know, that type thing. And it was disgust with just the military in general, pulling you away from your home and taking you over there and having you *sit* there. For a while, when we weren't doing anything, we felt abused, y'know, used, taken from home too early. Maybe we could've spent Christmas day with our family, we thought. So, bad attitudes started to filter in.

"Later on, when we started to work, you kinda forget. When we were at Fort Sill, I had a sergeant there that told me not to feel bad, that whenever we got there that our family and everything that meant a lot to us and that mattered over here would go to the back of our head, and we really wouldn't think about it, and not to feel bad about it because it was a survival technique, really. And we didn't really believe what he had said about putting everything to the back of our minds. And after we got over there, it *did* kind of go to the back. I mean, we had to deal with the issues at hand and, after a while, you almost really forget about home, except at certain times. So he was right."

As a heavy-equipment operator, Billy mostly hauled tanks, bull-dozers, and armored personnel carriers from one place to another. "I never fought," he says, "I never fired my M-16."

"What was it like?" I ask.

"It depended on where we were at," he tells me. "If we were in our truck making a haul and we weren't close to a base or somethin', we wouldn't hear the sirens go off. What would give you the warning was when bombs started going off, then you would know somethin's starting. And if you were back at the barracks, then they had alarms that would sound, and you would know that something was getting ready to happen. Bombs would explode, the building would shake, windows would rattle. You could hear it, you could see it, you could feel it. You don't know what to think, y'know. And you're driving down the road, and you see one go over your head and go out in the distance and blow up or you see fires. It's like somethin' you see on television, y'know, that you don't really think about. And at that point you just do what you have to do and then think about it later. You get back with all the guys and then maybe sit down and talk about it, y'know, and try to joke about it or find somethin' funny in it, just to lighten the conversation some.

"But I was around a lot of exploding and things that had exploded. The building that blew up that killed the American soldiers was probably a mile or two away from where we were at. We felt that impact."*

Among Billy's strongest memories from the war are images of people dying, in wrecks and in explosions, and their corpses. He shows me snapshots that the military censors did not bother to look for. Most of them are from the four-lane highway that runs between Kuwait and Iraq. The soldiers called it "Death Valley." There are pictures of distorted bodies, disembodied arms, legs, and heads. Most of the corpses were charred beyond recognition by the explosions that killed them, though some had been desiccated from days of exposure to the desert sun. In one of the pictures, the corpse's flesh had been seared off, though eerily, surreally, the man's clothes remained mostly intact, leaving a denuded skull atop a dressed body. Another man's body remained upright in the passenger seat of a Mercedes truck, a charred memorial to his own death. A third body lay on the ground, arms outstretched, as if the man had been crucified there on the sand.

"I wasn't used to all the dying and dead bodies," says Billy. "It was hard for a while, but you get used to it."

After the Iraqis had fled Kuwait and this brief, shining war was over, Billy and thousands of other U.S. soldiers were dispatched to Kuwait to help the Kuwaitis "pull things together up there." Billy tells me, "I remember driving down the road and kids on the side of the road, hungry, begging for food, you know. I'd throw out the MREs [meals ready to eat] that I had. They would give us a case

---

*Billy is referring to the Iraqi missile that demolished a barracks housing some of the U.S. troops. Twenty-seven soldiers were killed; another 98 were wounded.

when we left, in case our truck broke down or whatever, we'd have somethin' to eat. And candy, I'd throw out a Starburst, you know, one here, one there. I've got a picture of a little girl on the side of the road shooting the peace sign at us, y'know, just standing there. I don't know. It's something you see on television that you don't think should ever happen, but it does. I'm not glad I went through it, but it was an experience that I wouldn't trade for anything.

"But I don't feel like we accomplished what we should have. I think we shoulda moved in and corrected the situation and then come home. I feel like we went over there and slapped the Iraqis' hand and they backed off and we left, and now they're gonna try it again. Being over there, seeing all the destruction and what happened to the people over there, and going through Kuwait and seeing the roads all with big holes in 'em from the bombs and—dead people—'n' women 'n' children scared to death, 'n' buildings broke in 'n' houses blown up 'n' cars burnt 'n' just—I don't know. I didn't feel like the right people, or the people that needed to give us the go-ahead t'correct the situation, was seeing it firsthand and didn't really realize what was going on. I don't think that Hussein was hidden that well, y'know. I think we should've gone in, we shoulda done something with 'im, killed 'im, and got 'im out of there. It would've been the best for all sides involved. I just don't think it was handled properly."

Four months after the war was over, Billy was told he would be shipping out, but he was ambivalent about returning home. "Well, I thought I would be real happy," he says. "I wanted to come home, but then again, I wanted to stay." What Billy did not want to face was a second marriage that was falling apart.

Billy married his second wife, Janet, the month before he was called up for active duty. They had been friends for a long time before they ever considered marriage. Janet and her family lived near the same small town where Billy had grown up, and their parents knew each other. Billy and Janet dated on and off for less than a year and had been considering getting married about the time Saddam Hussein's tanks rolled into Kuwait. Janet was also a member of the National Guard, and, thinking that they might be activated for service, the couple decided to go ahead and get married.

Billy says, "We had planned t'wait t'get married and then we just kind of thought it would be better that—since we were going to get married when we got back, and we had a date set 'n' everything—that we would just move it up, kind of up the benefits that we would receive while we were gone. So we got married."

But Janet was not called up. Her daughter from a previous relationship, Jessica, contracted a severe ear infection that required hospitalization. Janet was discharged from duty so that she could remain stateside with her daughter.

When Billy went to Saudi Arabia, Janet moved in with a woman who lived in Billy's hometown. This woman was married to a man who was serving with Billy in Saudi Arabia. While Billy was in the desert, he learned from Janet's roommate that another man had become part of Janet's life. (Turns out that Billy, who had been faithful to Janet, was not alone in his misery. He says, "There were a lot of the wives that didn't hold true while we were gone. There were a lot of 'Dear John' letters while we were over there.")

Billy returned to the United States at the end of June 1991, but did not arrive in his hometown until the beginning of July. "When we got back, I didn't see either one of 'em, really. I just kinda kept my distance. We had a few discussions when I got back and decided that it wasn't gonna work out.

"I think that one of the reasons that I did get married was because of Jessica, more so the baby instead of the mother, really. Not that I didn't love Janet, because I did. But kids—I just have a thing for kids. I really like kids and I've always wanted kids. I think that's what kinda drew me—drew us—together."

Later he adds: "Janet and I had somethin' between us, somethin' that I thought was real special. And I *wanted* it to work. I wanted t'be married and I thought it *would* work. But, it just didn't. And I don't believe in staying married just t'please someone else, y'know. I mean, if it's not gonna work, it's not gonna work." In August 1991, less than a year after they were married, Billy and Janet were divorced.

Billy officially graduated from college while he was in Saudi Arabia. When he returned to the States, he immediately began submitting applications to school districts throughout Oklahoma. Within a few weeks the suburban junior high school where Billy had done his student teaching contacted him and offered him a job. Eager to get away from his hometown, Billy accepted and began teaching that fall.

"I like kids. I've always liked kids. And then I like trying to teach them something. I know that things were taught to me—or people tried to teach me things—when I was younger, and I didn't listen, and I went ahead 'n' did it my way. I know that's probably what will happen with other kids, but, I don't know, I think I have something valuable that they can learn and that I can teach them. And not just through academics but through life, y'know. I just think there're so many things out there that they need to be aware of and t'be taught, that somebody needs t'do it, and why not me."

But as much as Billy enjoys his teaching, there are things about his work that frustrate him. For instance, he says, "I feel like teachers are underpaid, period. I just don't feel like the public understands how much teachers really mold kids' lives."

Perhaps even more irksome to Billy is the disrespect with which so many students treat their teachers and the unwillingness of parents to help the teachers deal with this. "Teachers," he says, "are being run over by kids because the kids have so many rights. Y'know, this right's being abused if you do this, if you do that. If they have a weapon, maybe it's because they didn't know any better and they don't have to be kicked outta school.

"I think that if school was run more like basic training, I think it would be better. Not with weapons or anything like that. But the ways they go about teaching you and making you respect life and love and parents and the things in life that are worth respecting.

"Structure—I believe kids need a lot of structure. An analogy I used the other day was, it's like cows in a fence. If you go along the fence all day, just goin' around and around the fence and keeping the cows in, y'know, they're going t'be there. And that's what I think used to happen. Now, we just walk the fence every so often, and when there's a hole, we don't find it 'n' the cows get out.

"A small example is, like, backtalk, or cussing or flipping you off or something like that. I mean, to me, that's total disrespect. T'me, disrespect is disrespect and it oughta be dealt with in a strong manner, and we just don't have the capabilities of doing that. Parents may push their kids around and say, 'Well, they're my kids,' and they don't really have a lot t'do with their kids. But if one thing goes wrong, then they're in there and they're wantin' to sue.

"Personally, I think a lot of it stems from the home—parents not being there, parents not making them show respect, letting them run around and do things because maybe they're scared of 'em, y'know.

"I just think parents need to take control of their kids more.

And it's hard, because both parents are out working or not at home. I know it's hard, but it's gonna have to happen. We're getting away from the family, and it's goin' downhill quick."

I ask, "Are you happy at this point in your life?"

"Yeah," Billy replies, "I'm happy. Maybe a little lonely, but happy."

He tells me, "I have a friend, a real close friend, that I met when I came back from Saudi Arabia. We just kinda run around together sometimes. It's kind of a support system for her and for me both.

"But, right now, I'm looking at trying to make a life for myself, by myself, with myself. Because of the simple fact of, I had quite a bit, twice, and I lost it twice, as far as material things go, when I got divorced. And now I'm back, I've got a few things. Not a lot by any means, but I'm happy right now. I don't know, I just felt like I've been cheated in life. I know it happens t'everybody, but I just don't think it will happen to me again, as far as getting involved and then getting ripped apart. I think there's a lot more searching that needs to be done as far as getting involved with somebody than what I've done in the past, a lot more understanding between the two people, maybe.

"I wanna have kids, I know that. And I don't have to be married to have kids, and I know that—and I may not be. But I know that I will have kids one day.

"Going through what I've gone through, I know that I could bring up a child and instill in them the respect and the judgment that I think should come about. You don't have to be a family unit as far as husband-wife-kids 'n' all that to instill in your kids what you believe and what you think would be best for them."

Given that Billy does not see the traditional nuclear family as the only kind of family, it is ironic that this is precisely what he imagines when he hears the phrase "American Dream." "The first thing that pops into my mind," he says, "is a little house 'n' a little white fence 'n' kids 'n' a husband 'n' wife 'n' a pie on the windowsill, y'know, the old American Dream that I think has been from way back. But that's not what happens. I guess it could, but goin' through life, you just see it a lot more so not happening than happening.

"I don't know that I've ever been in that dream, or that I've ever had that dream for any length of time. Maybe I had thought I found that dream, but I haven't yet. I would like to.

"Problem is, the family is breaking up. Mothers and fathers getting divorced and the kids living with the mother or the father. I think that back in my grandmother and grandfather's time, the family held together, a lot more so. I just think there was more structure for the kids, and discipline, and we didn't have the riots 'n' the gangs 'n', you know, the drugs 'n' stuff.

"I don't think we're being strict enough all the way around as far as punishment goes—with kids, with criminals, with anybody that's breaking the law. I know there are individual cases, but I don't think you're going to stop it by slapping 'em on the hand and sending 'em on their way and letting 'em do it again.

"As far as *my* American Dream, I would like t'be financially stable. I would like to have the house and the car and the kids. And a wife, or a family unit. Like adoption. If I never got married again and just adopted kids, I still think that's a family. I think that I could fulfill my American Dream without a significant other.

"As far as being happy and having things out of life, it doesn't have to be extravagant. Just being comfortable in my life. And nowadays, there's so many different things as far as people and relationships go, that I think it's whatever makes you happy is what you should pursue."

Billy continues: "I think the freedom of choice means a lot. And I don't think that a lot of people realize how much that does mean until they're put in a position where they don't have that freedom of choice."

"Can you be more specific?" I ask.

"I know gay people have a lot to deal with. A lot of people don't understand the lifestyle, and they think if they don't understand it, then it's not right. Or they think that if you've been brought up a certain way, that's the way you should live.

"I think you should have the freedom that everybody else has as far as having friends and being able to go places and do things with whoever you want it to be with, whether it be male or female, as long as you are living within the realm of society, not breaking the laws. I don't think that society should depict who you can and can't be with."

I ask Billy whether he is gay. He says yes, but that it has only been in the past year, since his return from Saudi Arabia, that he has had the courage to admit this to himself. He then says: "There are just a lot of people that don't accept homosexuals in this world, and if you choose to live that lifestyle and be in a profession which chooses not to recognize that, then you have to hide it. And I don't think it's right t'have t'hide yourself."

Fewer than a dozen people know Billy is gay. He has told a few friends and, although he has never openly admitted this to his mother, he is certain she knows. Other than these people, no one knows—not his friends or commanders in the National Guard, not his teaching colleagues, not even the other members of his family or his other friends. When Billy enlisted eight years ago, he was asked whether he was homosexual. At that time he had an inkling that he might be gay, but he had never had a physically intimate relationship with a man, so he said no. (In retrospect, Billy thinks this may have been denial.) The school administrators have never asked the question.

Billy says, "I don't change any at all. I don't change the way I talk, the way I dress, the way I act. I *do* leave a few things out. If they did ask, I would tell 'em the truth."

I say, "But as long as they don't ask, you don't tell them."

"Exactly."

While Billy says he would tell the truth about his sexual orientation if he were asked a direct question, he hopes he never has to face that situation. "I would hate to lose my career in the military," he says. The military would discharge him if he revealed his homosexuality.* And though Billy believes that there is a state law that would prevent the school from firing him just because he is gay, he understands that "there are ways that people get around that."†

At first Billy found it difficult to have to hide his sexual orientation from people. "But," he says, "I guess you just learn how to get around things."

I ask Billy whether he feels excluded from participating in the American Dream because he is gay. He replies: "I still think that the

---

*The Clinton Administration is seeking to end the military's prohibition of gays in the military. However, the administration has met stiff resistance in Congress. It is uncertain whether the legislature will allow Clinton to fulfill this particular campaign promise.

†Billy is mistaken. In Oklahoma, a teacher may be dismissed if he engages in "criminal sexual activity," and sodomy, even between consenting adults, is classified as a criminial sexual activity. However, according to local attorneys who deal with legal issues in education, no teacher in Oklahoma recently has been fired solely for being homosexual.

American Dream is there for me. It may be changed, y'know, a little bit. But yeah, I still see the dream there for me. I see it there for everybody. I don't think there should be any limitations on why you can't have or can have the American Dream—the family life, the home, the car, the stability.

"I think I may have it. I may never reach that point, but I don't feel that it's closed off to me. I just think we all need to get together as a world and become educated and realize that not everybody's the same and that it's okay."

The world, however, has not reached the understanding that Billy hopes for. "The fact that people are being so judgmental," he says, "that worries me a lot. People are being killed because they're black or white. People are being killed because they're gay. If you don't fit someone's image of what they think that you should be, then they just kill you.

"I think we need to make the people more aware of things that they don't wanna become aware of. As far as dealing with the race issue, that's come a long way. As far as out in the open, the homosexual issue is coming out in the open. But you can't push things that people don't like too fast or else you see just mass confusion and killing. I think we're headed in the right direction, but there are just a lot of things that can be done to prolong life for people that don't fit the public's image of what a person should be.

"I think that people are willing to change, willing at least t'try t'change."

At the end of our conversation, Billy says, "There are so many people that are gay that can't express it or that never express it because of the way people think or what may happen to them. I just think it's sad. I see my gay friends being more stable, more structured, dealing with the community more, trying to help out society more. I just think that going through what they go through, as far as being treated, that they see the world differently. They're trying to make it a better place and they try harder. They see that there needs to be a change and they try harder. Their heads may be getting beat up against the wall, but they still push for change because they live in America and they want to be able to live in America, and that means living the way you want to live."

Billy offers a final suggestion: "Just fight to be what you want to be. Because unless you do, nobody's going to fight for you, and then you're gonna die not being what you want to be. That's sad that people have to die and they haven't experienced what they want to experience or they're not who they wanted to be or that they lived a lie. That they had to live a lie."

BRIT AND KELLY

"It was fate," says Kelly.

Kelly, twenty-six, makes it seem as if she and Brit, twenty-seven, were destined for each other. Perhaps their meeting was purely coincidental. Granted, both moved with their families to Houston when they were five—Kelly from San Antonio, Brit from Freeport, a small town on the Texas gulf coast—but thousands of people moved to Houston in the late sixties and early seventies. And sure, each of them is the youngest child of devoutly Christian middle-class parents. But that's like saying you're the youngest child of a middle-class Jewish family from Long Island; you're one of millions. What's the big deal if Brit and Kelly ended up at the same small university in Nacogdoches, Texas? Others made the same choice. And so what if Brit and Kelly shared the same last name even before they were married? There are lots of Chapmans.

Actually, that's how they met, because of their last names. It was Kelly's first class on her first day as a student at Stephen F. Austin University. She sat in front of Brit, and when the teacher called the roll and said, "Chapman," Brit and Kelly both said, "Here." They laughed and introduced themselves to one another. They soon became friends.

Later that year Brit transferred to Texas A&M to study landscape horticulture. He wrote a few letters to Kelly, who was still in Nacogdoches, but other than that they did not keep in touch. The following year, Kelly transferred to A&M, though not for Brit. One day they ran into each other at the library. (It must have been fate, says Kelly, because she "didn't attend the library very, very much.") Although each was involved in a serious relationship with someone else, they renewed their friendship. After their other relationships ended, they started dating each other. Four years later, they were married.

"It's just kinda strange," says Brit, speaking softly and deliberately in a pleasant Texas drawl. "Y'know, a lot of times you hear, 'You'll really know when you find the person that you're meant to spend the rest of your life with.' Lotta times that's hard to believe for people that haven't experienced it. But I couldn't imagine growing old and spending the rest of my life without her. 'N' she had the same feelings."

Maybe it *was* fate.

And talk about made for each other. Kelly's outgoing; Brit's more introverted. Kelly's a little high-strung, but Brit's laid-back. They even hold hands as they sit on their loveseat and tell me about themselves.

Most important for them, Brit and Kelly agree that God should be at the center of their marriage. They go to Sunday school together. They say grace before meals. They attend marriage seminars sponsored by the Christian Crusade. They read the Bible and devotionals together. Brit plays softball and flag football with a few fellow church members, and Kelly attends aerobics classes at the church.

Our religion "is the core of our marriage," says Kelly. "We can just feel God working in our lives when we pray." Kelly's proof? Her seven-year struggle with bulimia ended not when she turned to her parents or to group therapy, but when she turned to the Lord. As soon as she started praying, she says, "the desires went away. That's how I know Jesus is alive and walking. That's my proof."

However, even though they believe God is working in their lives, Brit and Kelly must still render unto Caesar. With his brother and father as partners, Brit runs a landscaping business that his father started while Brit was in high school. Shortly after graduating from college, Brit took over the business from his father, who had accepted a job as a sales rep for a company that sells chemical analyzers to oil refineries. Most of Brit's work is landscape maintenance for office buildings and for condominium and apartment complexes. Brit's older brother oversees the labor of their eleven employees, while Brit handles the business end of things.

When Brit first took over his father's business two years ago, it was struggling with debts to a variety of creditors, including the IRS. Today the business is financially stable. The bank holds a couple of notes on some of the company's equipment, vehicles, and other property—typical business debt, but that's it.

In fact, the business is actually doing a little too well. Brit tells me, "We have canceled a few contracts because we were just really gettin' too much work. A lotta headaches were coming along with the work. There's a little more income with it, but it wasn't worth the sacrifices we were having to make as far as our personal time together."

Why, in a sluggish economy, is the family business doing so well? "We try to do the right things to earn our customers' and our friends' respect," says Brit. "I think that that's a key to success."

After graduating from A&M, Kelly initially accepted a job as a public relations director for an advertising firm in Houston. But a few months after their wedding, she went to work for Brit's company. Now she keeps the books and the payroll and handles customer relations. Her office is one of the rooms in the tastefully decorated (Sante Fe style) condo in southwest Houston that she and Brit call home. Kelly says that working with Brit and working out of her home is "perfect" for her.

Happily married for two and a half years, a prospering business, a "perfect" job. Sounds like an American Dream coming true. And for Brit and Kelly, it is.

Brit, who every month reads a book "concerning business-type principles," says that financial independence is certainly part of his and Kelly's vision of the American Dream. "Money plays a part of it," he explains, " 'cause we definitely have things that we want out of life. We would like a nice house. We would like t'get t' th' point where we're not worried about if money's gonna always be available to us."

Still, although he and Kelly want things to be even better, they realize how good their situation already is. Brit acknowledges that, for many people, the American Dream "is havin' your own business, and we already have that in our twenties. We know we are very fortunate t'have that. We don't have people hangin' over our heads tellin' us what to do and worryin' about losin' our job. We know as long as we work hard and make the proper decisions that we're always gonna have a good job available to us."

But as far as Brit and Kelly are concerned, more important than a thriving business is "just bein' able to have peace about what we do for a living." For instance, Brit declined a lucrative landscape installation job offered to them by one of the most successful topless bars in Houston. Although they passed up good money, Brit says, "we decided that it's better for us to turn that down and be able to come home at night, go to sleep without knowin' that somehow we helped out a less-than-good cause."

Kelly joins in: "I think maybe the American Dream would be to have your own business 'n' to be able to work out of your home. An' to have a family and not to have to send them to day care or do whatever, to raise 'em here. So I think we're on the right track of what our dream is, which is to have a house and two cars, your basic 2.5 kids and a dog and a yard." But, she adds, "we're not lookin' to have the BMW, the Mercedes, things like that. That's not important to us. The happiness comes first."

Brit elaborates: "We just wanna make a good living and have enough money to get a few things, have enough money left over to save for a rainy day. But beyond that we are not driven, driven, driven to work seven days a week."

For Brit and Kelly, time is ultimately more important than money to their happiness. That's one of the reasons they've canceled or declined a few contract offers—to have time to be with each other, time to be with their families, and "time to go to church and be with our Christian friends and draw off of their strength and their relationship with Christ."

But just as finance plays a part in their American Dream, it is also one important element in Brit and Kelly's happiness. Kelly says she's "just uncomfortable" when she is worrying about being in debt. Consequently, she and Brit are adamant about living within their means. They have almost completely paid for their condo, which they bought just before they got married. And unlike many of their friends who have the same disposable income, Brit and Kelly don't take fancy vacations to Jamaica. For them, short weekend trips, nothing more.

"It's more important for us to just save the extra amount of money that we have," says Brit.

Brit and Kelly are committed to putting money away because they want to be "financially stable" before they begin having children. And for them, financial stability includes a nice house "in the environment where they'll be more comfortable living in" and the wherewithal to send their children to a parochial school.

Money, however, is not the only reason Brit and Kelly have been, as Brit says, "a little bit hesitant" about having kids. "We're a little concerned with the way society in general is getting."

One of their principal concerns is crime, particularly violent crime. Fortunately, neither Brit nor Kelly has been the victim of such violence, but both have had some property stolen. Now Kelly rarely goes out by herself after dark, unless it's driving home from aerobics. Brit accompanies Kelly to the grocery store as often as he can because they've heard so many stories about people being abducted in grocery store parking lots. They also keep a couple of cans of Mace in the house in case someone breaks in while they are at home.

Brit frets, "It seems like every year that goes by, there're just more and more things that surprise us, as far as crime-wise. Just seems to be more and more of it."

According to Brit, the other issue that most worries him and his wife is "how the government is taking more and more of the religion and God away from the public schools."

For example, Kelly describes "these meditation things" that she says are being introduced in the public schools. "It's more of a New Age-type cult thing. It's kind of a hidden thing," she tells me. "It's where the kids maybe get around in a circle and they have to visualize, say for instance, a dolphin. Maybe it's their friend and they can tell the dolphin their problems. They should be real quiet, the lights are low. They say, 'This is how I feel. This is my problem.' When actually that is a New Age type of thing that they're doing. They're not trying to communicate with God."

Brit declares: "Seems like the country was built on Christian principles. And America was such a great country for so long. Still is. It seems like every year that goes by, an' state an' church are separated more and more, seems like the country just falls off more and more. Seems to be a parallel with the amount of government takin' religion out and also America's debt getting worse, crime getting greater. Just seems like those two things are related."

According to Brit and Kelly, the only solution to America's moral dissolution lies in the ballot box. Kelly says, "I think that Christians need to take more responsibility in who they vote for. Because who you're putting into office, these are the people who're making the decisions for us and the community."

Brit continues, "That's one of the only things I think we *can* do. The people that run the government, they're up for election every so often. Really research and see the way that they've voted on certain things."

"Such as abortion," adds Kelly. She and Brit, both Republicans, vote in nearly all the major state and national elections and are unwaveringly opposed to abortion, even in cases of rape or incest. Kelly insists that ultrasound "can prove that there's a living person, a baby, inside your body that you don't have the right to get rid of."

Still, despite the growing specter of violent crime and the apparently widening chasm between the sacred and the secular, Brit and Kelly will probably start having children in the next year or two.

"Think it's a little scary," confesses Brit, "the thought of raisin' kids in today's world. But that's none of that we can't handle."

THE HOUSE,
THE CAR,
THE KIDS...
AND A WHOLE
LOT MORE

DOMENIC

It's only midafternoon, but for Domenic it is nearly the end of a long working day. He has been up since a quarter to one in the morning, which is when he must get out of bed to be at the market by 1:30. He works for his two older brothers, who own a successful wholesale produce company in South San Francisco. They sell fruits and vegetables to grocery stores throughout north central California.

The youngest of four children, Domenic, twenty-four, was born and raised in the suburbs south of San Francisco. Although he owns a house into which he will soon be moving, he still lives with his parents in Millbrae, twenty miles south of San Francisco on Highway 101. His father is a first-generation Italian-American who has worked in the produce business for more than thirty-three years. Today his father works for Domenic's two brothers. Domenic's sister also works at the brothers' business one day a week. Domenic's mother, who is from Italy, is the only member of the immediate family not directly involved in the produce business. She has been a mother and housewife all her adult life.

Domenic attended the local public schools and graduated from the public high school, where he was a standout in football and baseball. During an all-star football game, he took a painful hit from a fellow who went on to play major college football. Despite the injury to his shoulder, Domenic played one more year of football for a junior college in nearby San Mateo. He had intended to earn his associate's degree there and then transfer to a four-year college. But during his freshman year, his older brothers started their produce business and asked Domenic to help them. "It was," says Domenic, "a offer I couldn't refuse."

Occasionally jamming his words together because he is speaking so rapidly, Domenic explains, "When I got out of high school, my dad really wanted me to go to college, so I went to college. I wanted to go. I wanted to play football. I had no intentions of working at the market the rest of my life.

"As it turned out, I went to junior college for a year. My brothers offered me this job, without pay. I just did it pretty much to help them get off the ground. I knew if I went to work for these guys and the thing went belly up, I could buy an education. I could go out and I could go to school and I could pay for my own. That's why I did it. I did it because I thought it was a good opportunity, I could make a lotta money. I mean, I've seen a lotta people go to college, you know, four, six, eight years, get their master's, come out and make thirty-five, forty thousand dollars a year. That's not what I wanted t'do. I mean, to me, the thing was, work now, do the best I can now, make as much money as I can while I'm young and retire by the time I am forty-five.

"What happened was, I went to work for them, things took off, we did absolutely fantastic. After six months' time they paid me— good amount—and said, 'Look, you gonna go back to school or are you going to work for us?' So we sat down, the three of us, and we discussed it and hammered somethin' out. And it was pretty much that I would work labor another couple of years, and then they would expand the company by getting my dad, which we did, and then I would take over the original part, which is citrus, which is what I sell.

"Young blood in that market is good. People selling against us are getting old. Not that they don't care about it anymore, but they

made their money. So I mean, it was a good opportunity—for everyone.

"I work between ten and twelve hours every day, five days a
week, minimum. That's minimum. When we first opened, it was between sixty and ninety a week. Granted, I make good money and all
that, but, at the same time, I don't think there's too many guys that
are my age that would devote their life to do what I do. I mean, a
lot of guys would see the money that I make and say, 'Hey, I would
do it for that kinda money.'

"Yeah, but when you get right down into it and you see what
it's all about, you have to know what you're doin', first off. Secondly, you make a mistake, that's your reputation, you're not gonna
make any more money. I was trained by my brothers and my father,
y'know, three of the best guys in the business probably. Without
those guys I wouldn't know what I know today. And you never
know it all. You learn until the day you die in this business. Y'know,
that's what I like about it, because every day it's changing. You see
it when you go to the store, there's a different item here, or this is
new and that's new. Things are high-breed [hybrid] and things are
different every day. So, I mean, you can never stop learning in this
business."

Continuous learning is not the only thing Domenic enjoys
about his work. He says, "I wanted to do something where I could
make money. In other words, I could be in charge of my destiny. If
I sold good, I would make money. If I didn't, I would be responsible for myself. Which is where I am now, but I'm in the produce
business."

I ask Domenic whether he has any regrets about not finishing
college. He tells me: "If I get an education, if I get four years of college in, and I end up doing what I'm doing *now,* which is selling
produce, it's not so much as a waste of time, but I could've been
making money for four years, cutting my work span down four
more years. Now I grant, after I quit and during the course of my life
while I'm working, the investments that I make, having the education would help me greatly. In other words, if I had the education
of an investment broker and I got back in the produce business,
sure, if I become wealthy and I'm makin' a lot of money in the produce business, I can make twice as much investing it properly with
my own mind than paying someone else to do it. So that part of it
I miss.

"Where I'm standing right now, and I'm twenty-four years old, I have a home, I own my own home. It's my third home. I bought my first home when I was twenty. I bought it, rented it out, sold it. Bought another one, rented it out, sold it, bought this one. And not too many people can do that out here in California, I don't think.

"It's a good time in my life. Things are goin' good, our company's goin' good. And I don't think I would be in this position right now if it wasn't for the decision that I made in 1986."

The commercial success of the produce business is only one aspect of Domenic's current happiness. There's also Sherry, his fiancée. Sherry is a grade-school teacher. She lives with her family in a house just around the corner from Domenic and his parents. Sherry and Domenic grew up together and attended the same schools from kindergarten through their first year of junior college. They began dating during their senior year of high school. Domenic can even remember the precise day of their first date—November 3, 1984. When I ask him how he can remember, he admits, "I guess 'cause she just basically told me."

After more than six years of dating and a one-year engagement, Domenic and Sherry will be getting married next week. Domenic has been working with his future father-in-law to remodel the house Domenic recently bought, and Domenic and Sherry will move in after the wedding. Domenic tells me that he and Sherry will not begin having children immediately. They'll wait a year or so, then they'll have three, maybe four. And as long as Domenic can afford it, Sherry will stay home to raise their children. It is, he says, a mutual decision.

"I don't think I could be any happier," says Domenic. "From a financial standpoint, I do fine. From a personal standpoint, my family's healthy. I have *my* health right now. And that's the bottom line to me, the most important thing. I know the owner of a chain store out here, and when he was twenty-nine years old, diagnosed with leukemia. The guy was a multimillionaire at twenty-nine. And I'll never forget, he told me, he said, 'What did I do, who did I screw, to deserve this disease?' And he died two years later, he was thirty-one. I'll never forget, he always told me, he goes, 'It ain't worth any amount of money, what you do or the money you make, if you aren't healthy, you have shit. Look, I would give everything away, everything away, to be livin'.' That's the bottom line, I think."

How does Domenic, a young man whose life is going so well,

define the American Dream? "Gettin' t'my age, gettin' a job—gettin' a good job—getting married, having kids, starting a family, taking vacations once a year or twice a year, enjoying your life, work hard, buy a home, make investments, and work as hard as you can as long as you can until you can retire. If you can retire when you're forty, do it. If you can retire when you're thirty-five, do it. And just be as healthy as you can."

He continues: "When I was growin' up—I'm obviously still growing up, but younger, y'know, sixteen, seventeen, in high school—and this American Dream came up. You know, it's stamped on you, *this* is the American Dream, so that's what I perceive as the American Dream. But y'know, I'm sure it's different to everyone. I like the idea of the American Dream, that everyone can grow up, afford a house, raise a family, y'know, never get divorced. But that doesn't happen, y'know, the odds are against you.

"Like, lot of my friends. They live at home, they pay rent, they don't have jobs but they have a college education. They see what I have and, not that they're envious or anything, but they hate us. They say, 'Hey, I wish I had that, that would be great.' Whenever I start complaining about anything, they go, 'Hey, don't *you* complain, look at what you've got.' And then I get defensive, like, 'Hey, I work hard for what I have, I'm not handed anything.'

"But the American Dream has meaning for me because I've grown up hearing this is what the American Dream is, and now I'm achieving it. And once I have a child, that will be more of an American Dream—having a kid, having a wife, having a house and being happy and everyone healthy. That to me will be more like an American Dream. I don't think you have to be a millionaire to have the American Dream. I don't think it is important.

"My father, he grew up in a family of seven, one of seven boys. His paycheck when he was a kid went to the family, to help support the family, food, clothing, everything. And his oldest brother came down to San Francisco and got a job and started with nothing. And then my father got married and came down, started with nothing. He went through it and built himself up. Now he's well-off today, and all of his brothers are. They did it, why can't we do it?

"In other words, I've been lucky enough to grow up in a family that, like I said, is middle-class and upper-middle-class. So I got a head start. Being that I grew up in a successful family, I shouldn't be a bum and sit back and leech off my father and wait for him t'die so I can have his money. I mean, I should learn t'make my own money. I should be that much more of a person. I shouldn't take what I have and sit on it. I should take what I have and make more out of it.

"I think that right now, if I put my mind to it and work hard, I can pretty much have what I want. I'm not saying I can own the New York Yankees. I'm not talking about that 'cause I don't want that. But I could do what I want, make the money I want to be comfortable. So I'm optimistic, yeah. It doesn't worry me 'cause, right now, what I do and the people that I'm doing it with, which is my family, everyone works hard for one common goal. It's a good thing. I mean, we argue 'n' we fight. It's not *The Brady Bunch,* y'know, it's far from it. But I've got a good chance. I've got a chance that not too many people have, 'n' I don't want to screw it up."

Though Domenic acknowledges how fortunate he has been, he does not think the American Dream is beyond the reach of others who were not born with his advantages. "If you have nothing," he says, "make more out of yourself. If you grew up in poverty, you have nothing, you don't need money to go to school. If you go to a public school and you study, they'll give you a scholarship. You'll get money from the state, you won't owe anyone a penny. You can become that doctor or that lawyer. But the person that grows up in the ghetto or grows up very poor can make it, can be successful. Mean, you don't have to have a lot of money to get an education. If you're poor, you can get grants and funds and make it through college and make something of yourself."

Still, Domenic realizes that it may be hard for someone today to duplicate his father's achievements. "I think the United States used to stand for the Dream—you can come here and, if you work hard enough, you can get what you want and you can be successful. I know a lot of people like that. What it stands for now, I'm not so sure. I think you can still come here and be successful, but I don't think that it's now like it used to be forty years ago, fifty years ago. I think a lot of the avenues for success have been exhausted by bigger businesses that monopolize them."

Fortunately for Domenic, he is already on one of those roads to success, and he plans to travel even further along that path. "I want to start investing my money," he says, "just always want to keep movin' up. From the house I'm in now, I eventually want to sell it and buy a bigger house. I'll sell it and buy property, invest in the stock market and lotta other stuff. That's what I wanna do, just become more successful financially. On a personal standpoint I want to have a healthy family, I want to have kids that I can raise with respect and be proud of."

Referring to his financial ambitions, I ask Domenic, "Sounds like a treadmill. When does it stop? When do you say, 'Enough!'?"

"It's sad," he replies. "It's pretty sick, actually. I don't know, it's hard to say. When you're happy, you stop. I mean, I like the house I'm in, I'm happy where I'm at. If I were t'stop making money tomorrow, I could be very happy where I'm at. But if I'm not gonna stop making money tomorrow, then I want more. I want that bigger home or I want a nicer car, this, that, and the other thing, and I won't stop until I stop makin' money."

"Does that worry you, that that could be kind of consuming?"

"Yeah, I don't think that's a good thing. But I mean, if you're makin' that kinda money, you have t'do something with it. In other words, you have to invest it. You get a house, you get a bigger payment, you get the write-off. You can't make that kinda money and live in a house that costs you a hundred thousand dollars and bank it, 'cause you'll get murdered by taxes.

"If you're gonna make it, you might as well make it work *for* you. That's what I mean by going up and advancing. If you can make it, you have to make it work for you. I don't mean, you know, I have to have a bigger and better thing. I'm content where I am. I like where I'm at.

"I would just like to have a home out in a suburb, more in the country type of setting. I would be a little more happy there, let's put it that way. But at this point, it's not realistic 'cause I don't have millions of dollars."

Even if Domenic never can afford to buy that house in that sylvan suburb, he still will consider himself successful. The only element missing is children. And when he and Sherry have children, he wants them to be educated. "I'm not," he says, "but I want them to be.

"This goes back to another question you asked me, when you said do I regret not having finished college. I guess in a way, if you get right down to it, I would have to regret it a bit. You can't throw away an education, you can't put a value on it. In other words, once you have it, you can't throw it away, no one can take it away from you. And I'd like to see that if I have kids.

"My father wanted to see that of us, but all of us saw the money in the business and wanted to go after it. With an education, you could probably solve more of the problems in the world than I could without one. I have my ideas, but the way things are goin' now, what I see on the news, and with the ecology of the planet and with all the other things, to me, you get scared to even have 'em, even have kids. 'Cause what's gonna happen in fifty years?

"As far as the ecology of the planet goes, it scares the hell out of me. You got a lotta people that are uneducated in other parts of the world *and* here. I think more so in other parts of the world, though, Mexico, all over Europe, where they have no plans, no plans of ever recycling, no plans of ever stopping the pollution that they're emitting. And that scares me because, I mean, you only have so much to work with here. You can't move t'Mars. So that's what scares me. I think that's a real serious problem, and the ozone and all that.

"I think the world—I think in the United States anyway—we're starting on the right foot. Because I know, like, my fiancée's a schoolteacher, and they're doing a whole unit on pollution and on the environment. When I was in school, I never did it. They have to do a unit on the environment, and that makes you aware as a young kid. My nephew comes over t'the house, and I'm eating ice cream and I throw the wrapper away. He goes, 'Don't throw that away. You can recycle that.' That's good, that's a start. You have to start from the ground floor up. You can't tell people that have been throwin' away beer bottles for twenty years to recycle. They're gonna tell you, 'Sorry. *You* recycle.' Those people are finished, they're done. You have t'start with the young people and educate 'em and say, 'Hey look, if you don't stop polluting, you're not gonna have a world.' That's not a solution, but I think it will help. But I don't have the answer for that."

Domenic is equally concerned about the national debt. "You can't spend what you don't have, and that's what our country's doing. That drives me crazy. I understand that money has to be spent. Certain programs, in depressed areas people don't have money to support these programs that they need, such as, y'know, health care, activities for kids to keep 'em off the streets and out of trouble and off of drugs. But spending money for other things—limousines, presidential limousines, lunches for Congress, phone bills, elaborate vacation homes—to me, that's a bunch of junk.

"The only answer that I could have would be, stop spending the money that you don't have. And once you stop spending money you don't have, then there's gonna be monies that you're gonna find you have to spend. Once you find those monies you have to spend, you have to evaluate those and put priorities on those. Once they're prioritized, then you cut back on those, which is being done now. I mean, I'm sure they are not spending money on things we don't need, at least I hope they're not.

"You know, it's funny. I don't have the answer. I don't think anyone has the answer, and I think that's why the problem gets worse."

A few minutes later, Domenic adds, "I think at *this* point, when you're so far in the hole, you have to start running the government like a business. I don't think that twenty-five years ago, when we weren't at this point, that it needed to be run as a business. But if you take a company and you buy it and it's bankrupt, what do you do? You restructure it. You have to restructure the United States, and by doing that you have to run it like a business.

"I think the problems can be solved. I think that there *are* people out there that can help solve these problems. I don't think it's one person, though. I think it's gonna take, y'know, Congress, the President, the people of the United States, everyone pulling together to solve this debt, to turn the country around. Everyone has to change a little bit. Everyone has to help. It's too big of a problem.

"I'm pretty old-fashioned—I mean, I think that I am anyway, pretty old-fashioned. I just think you need to work hard to be successful. And I think our problems can be solved in this country and, y'know, throughout the world, but people have to work together. It'll never happen unless people work together."

Note: Domenic and Sherry are now married. They have moved into the house that Domenic bought and remodeled before their wedding.

VALERIE

Valerie, twenty-six, a black woman who lives in Chicago, is a model of the well-rounded individual. While she's at the office, everything about her is consummately professional, from her midnight-blue suit to her affable but direct manner. But she's also an avid football fan, and she'd be going to this weekend's football game between Notre Dame and Tennessee if she were not recovering from a horrible cold. She regularly reads *The Wall Street Journal, Business Week,* and *Black Enterprise,* as well as "trash" like *Cosmo* and *Glamour.* During the workday Valerie focuses on efficient solutions, bottom lines. In her off hours, she loves traveling, skiing, horseback riding, and cooking, and her favorite pastime is that quintessentially American hobby—shopping.

The elder of two daughters born to "old" parents—both were in their late thirties when they had their first child—Valerie was born and raised in southeast Chicago, not far from Soldiers Field. Her father is a political science professor at a Chicago university; at age sixty-five he is still actively teaching, writing, and serving on committees. And for most of Valerie's life, her mother served as the vice president of a community college. She died a few years ago, during Valerie's senior year of college.

For the first four years of her life, Valerie and her family lived in an apartment complex that was filled with the families of interns and residents who worked at Michael Reese Hospital. Then her parents bought a house just a few blocks away. In contrast to the ethnically mixed group at the apartment complex, Valerie's new neighborhood was populated almost exclusively by middle-class black professionals.

As befits the child of two educators, Valerie has had one of the finest educations this country can offer. First she attended an unusual grade school. "It was the pet school of Michael Reese Hospital," says Valerie. "It got computers, microscopes, and all kinds of cool stuff." She then attended a Catholic high school, which she describes as "one of the outstanding schools in the city." Next came a bachelor's degree in finance from Notre Dame and, finally, an

M.B.A. from the University of Michigan, one of the country's premier business schools.

Two summer internships—first with General Electric, then with the Chicago branch of the Federal Reserve—convinced Valerie that finance was not her calling. "I liked the theory," she tells me, "but in terms of a day-to-day existence, I was bored out of my mind." So she looked for something more "people-oriented," and after sitting through "hundreds" of corporate presentations during her first year of business school, she decided to try advertising.

A summer job at a big agency in Chicago convinced Valerie that she'd enjoy the work. She didn't enjoy the firm as much; its style was "not as professional" as she would have liked. She later accepted a permanent job from another very large Chicago agency, the advertising equivalent of IBM or General Motors. She has been there for more than two years and is now an account executive for one of the country's largest airlines. She and her assistants oversee "strategic direction and creative development, media planning, and research activities" for the airline's local markets nationwide. "It's definitely a challenge," Valerie says cheerfully.

Valerie's version of the American Dream is almost identical to the election-year archetype conjured up by politicians. Valerie defines her American Dream as "a spouse, a couple of kids, and being able to give my kids everything that I'd like them to have— education, opportunities, knowledge, that kind of thing—without spoiling them. Being able to have enough money for my children to be able to live a comfortable life and have the type of education that they would like. As you look at statistics, you see things that say in the year 2010 it will cost two hundred thousand dollars for a four-year public institution to send your kids to college. My sister and I kind of think, 'What are we gonna do? What are we gonna do?' We'll have to marry professors at good schools where our kids can go for free. Just being able to give your kids everything that you've had, all the opportunities that you had.

"It's not just having the money to do it. It's being the kind of person and having the kind of spouse that has that same kind of dream for their kids." Though she'd like to be married as soon as possible—"yesterday" would not be too soon—Valerie is single and is not seriously dating anyone. But she's not worried. "Whatever happens will happen," she says.

Having a house is also important to Valerie's American Dream.

"Growing up in an apartment is something that I would never want my kids to have to do," she says. "For four years of my life, which I probably can't remember, it was no big deal. But I was glad my parents bought a house as an investment. And we had a backyard and had bikes. All the kinds of things that I think help you to develop into the kind of person that you are. So I'd love to have a nice big house, love each of my kids to have their own room. For personal development and privacy and all those other kinds of things, I think it's important." Valerie recently bought a town house in Hyde Park, a comfortably integrated neighborhood near the University of Chicago. She likes the feel of the neighborhood. And Hyde Park is less congested, not to mention far less expensive, than the more popular Lincoln Park area north of downtown.

Valerie adds: "When people ask me what I want in life, I always tell them, 'I wanna be happy.' And that seems like such a broad thing to people. To me, being happy is enjoying my life, enjoying what I do for work, enjoying what I do outside of work, having friends that are true friends, special and important people who would give me the shirt off their back as I would do for them. Being a good person, being good to other people, giving in instances where I can give to people who are less fortunate than I am. Those kinds of things are all very important to me."

If her "dream of dreams" comes true—that is, if she wins the lottery and decides to use the money for something other than travel—Valerie will go back to school and become an interior designer. She then will open an interior design firm "specifically for middle-class, middle-income people, who don't have the kind of money that a Michael Jordan has to decorate a house. People who have a reasonable income and just don't have the ability or the talent to go out and pick out stuff to decorate a house." Opening her own business would give Valerie the opportunity to apply everything she learned in business school and everything she has learned so far in her career. Besides, she asks, why should she work for someone else doing something she merely likes, when she could work for herself and do something she truly loves?

As a member of the Black MBA Association, Valerie has on occasion spoken to high school students about staying in school. "It's a real challenge," she says, "to see kids who have not had the same opportunities that I've had, with two parents who were educators, who understood the value of what you were doing in your life and how education is gonna be a key to success in your life. Kids who come from single-parent families, or parents who are both on drugs and could care less, or people who are fourteen years old and pregnant. It's just such a devastating situation out there.

"Those are the kinds of programs I really try to get involved in and say, 'Hey guys, if you put your mind to it and you work hard, these are the things that you can have.' It's not so much saying material things, because they can go out and sell drugs and buy things that I can't afford today. But it's long-term benefit. Are you gonna be around in ten years to enjoy that big house that you have bought? Or will you be laying dead in the street because of a drug deal gone bad?"

Though she remains optimistic, Valerie is nevertheless realistic about the effect her words will have on many of the kids in the audience. Valerie says these kids see "Johnny over here deals drugs. And he's got a Mercedes and he's got a big house and he's got a lot of gold chains and he's got five girlfriends. So that looks like the great life. That's all they see around them. That's all they have to look at as role models. They can't even comprehend what I do. They can't even comprehend that there's another way of life."

Drugs and the violence associated with drug dealing are not the only issues that concern Valerie. "There's no end in sight to the kinds of problems that we're facing at home. You see people wandering the street, homeless, and you look at the unemployment rate, and you look at all the things. And you think, I understand the global importance of being involved in international agendas and making sure that the situations in Germany and a variety of places are resolved. But I wonder if the sacrifice that we're making to focus our energies there versus here is gonna have a long-term impact on what happens in this country. And is anybody going to come to *our* rescue when we as a country are in trouble domestically? There needs to be some more focus on a quote-unquote 'domestic agenda.' "

I ask Valerie why she did not mention racism as one of her greatest concerns. She says, "I think it's a big problem, but I think that the things I mentioned are bigger. They go across all races."

Valerie believes her contemporaries "really are involved and wonder and think about the future, think about the life that their kids are gonna have, think about how we're gonna afford to send our kids to college. And how are we gonna have a house. And how are we gonna keep drugs out of our kids' hands. And how are we gonna protect our kids from the environment falling apart and AIDS and all these other things that are going on around us.

"Looking back at the kind of life you grew up with and the kind of life your children will probably face is a scary, scary prospect."

LLOYD

Though you can't be certain from his accent—Lloyd pronounces it "New Orlins," not "N'awlins," as most natives do—Lloyd's family has lived in southern Louisiana for generations. His father's ancestors arrived here in 1719, settling in an area known as the German Coast, up the Mississippi River from New Orleans on the way to Baton Rouge. His mother's grandparents came to the Crescent City from Italy early in this century. Both of Lloyd's parents were born and raised in New Orleans, and Lloyd's father went to college at Loyola University in the city. Lloyd's father has declined promotions that would have required him to leave New Orleans because he wanted his sons to grow up here, near their grandparents and the rest of their family. Because Lloyd's family has such a long history in this area, "a sense of place, tradition, a sense of history" are important to him and to his family; hence the Roman numeral III at the end of Lloyd's name.

Like his parents, Lloyd, twenty-eight, and his younger brother were born in New Orleans and spent much of his childhood there, in an area known as Lakeview. When Lloyd was nine, his family moved to Metairie, the suburb where his parents still live.

Lloyd's father is a sales representative for a company that manufactures thread and sewing accessories. His mother works at a market research firm. Their income provided Lloyd and his younger brother with a middle- to upper-middle-class existence. In his subtle Louisiana drawl (a long "i" becomes "ah," "there" becomes "they-uh") Lloyd says, "There was never anything that I needed that I didn't have or, in most cases, that I wanted."

From kindergarten through high school, Lloyd always attended private schools; from fourth grade on, private Catholic schools. Just like his father before him and his younger brother after, Lloyd went to Jesuit High School. He was in the accelerated program and missed graduating magna cum laude by a hundredth of a point.

Given his rigorous academic training under Jesuit tutelage, his very good GPA, his high SAT and ACT scores, one might predict that Lloyd breezed through Louisiana State University. But he didn't. It took him seven years to graduate with a final GPA of 2.5.

"I have a theory about that," says Lloyd, explaining the difference in his academic performance between high school and college. Jesuit, he reasons, was so disciplined and so rigorous—boys only, khaki uniforms, military shoes polished to a mirror shine, name tags, clean-cut and clean-shaven—that he didn't respond well to the "very loose atmosphere" at LSU, where "no one's telling you you have to go to class and you're in classes with *girls* for the first time.

"I'm not trying to make excuses," he adds. "I mean, everyone has to find their own self-discipline."

What did Lloyd do while he was finding *his* self-discipline? "I'd go out a lot," he says. He grins jovially as he recites his former social calendar: "Tuesday night was 'quarter beer' at Murphy's. Wednesday night was five dollars 'all you could drink' at Murphy's. Thursday, it was one dollar fresh-squeezed screwdrivers at Fred's." And, "of course," he went to all of LSU's games, football, basketball, and baseball. He also spent much of his time at fraternity-sponsored events. In fact, Lloyd, a member of Delta Tau Delta, refers to himself as "the Delt for the Eighties" because he attended LSU from 1982 to 1989.

Part of the reason Lloyd took seven years to graduate is that he took a relatively light schedule, anywhere from nine to fifteen hours a semester. He missed one semester altogether because he came down with mononucleosis and hepatitis. He also changed his major four times—from accounting to political science to psychology and, finally, in his last semester of psychology, to advertising. His parents "weren't too happy about it," he admits, "but my parents have always supported me in whatever I've done." And, he adds, without a trace of irony, "the last couple of years I paid for it myself."

"Why all the changes?" I ask.

"Didn't know what I wanted t'do," he explains, "and I enjoyed college and college life. And I put off responsibility as long as I could. Things were just too much fun."

However, things turned "from being fun to kinda lonely" once

Lloyd's really close friends had graduated. That's when he said to himself, "Well, I better start working and get out in the work force." He accepted a position as a field supervisor for a market research firm in Baton Rouge. A year and a half later, the mother of one of Lloyd's high school friends heard about a job opening at the Louisiana Restaurant Association, a trade group that represents restaurant owners and suppliers. The woman contacted Lloyd, who applied and was selected to become the association's director of communication.

Two and a half years later, Lloyd is still the association's director of communication. He edits and writes the association's monthly newsletter and a bimonthly magazine. He handles media relations, public relations, and various "special projects." He is also a one-man research department and an occasional lobbyist at New Orleans City Hall and at the state capitol.

Lloyd finds his job both challenging and satisfying. He is never at risk of being in a rut, he says, because the content of the magazine and the newsletter change every month, and the special projects and lobbying are never the same. Lloyd's work also provides him with an outlet for his creativity, as well as an opportunity to brag about New Orleans, the city he loves so much. The people he works with are "fun." And Lloyd enjoys it when one of his friends calls to ask Lloyd to help set up a dinner for an important client at a famous restaurant, and Lloyd knows the owner. "I guess I feel important that way," he says.

Although he would like to earn more money—"Who wouldn't?" he says—Lloyd is not looking for a better-paying job someplace else. He explains, "I like what I'm doin'. I really do. I mean, I'm sure I could make more money if I wore a beeper and sold fax machines. But I don't wanna do that. I kinda like my position here, an' I like my title, too—'director of communication.' It's a good title to have." He asks, "If I'm content here, why should I look elsewhere?"

Lloyd imagines himself remaining with the association for at least ten years, maybe longer. When I ask him why he is so devoted, he answers, "Loyalty means a great deal. 'N' I think loyalty's rewarded." As he says this, he adjusts his emerald-and-navy-striped rep tie, which is held in place by a tie clip shaped like a fork and knife.

Lloyd's definition of the American Dream is simple: "Get married, have a couple o' kids, be in a steady job, live in a nice house in a nice subdivision" in a suburb of New Orleans or somewhere in southern Louisiana. "I want to spend all my days here," he says. "I just have a real love for this area."

As for fulfilling that dream, Lloyd is making progress. He has a steady job. He is not dating anyone seriously, but, though he describes this as a "missing point" in his current happiness, he's "not really looking for that" right now. As for the kids, he thinks he'll get married first.

That leaves only the house. Lloyd is saving his money for a "considerable" down payment. To help reduce his expenses and enable him to sock away the cash more quickly, he lives with his parents in their house in Metairie. He has lived there, free of charge, since returning from Baton Rouge two and a half years ago. He anticipates that he'll stay another year and a half before he'll have saved enough money.

I ask whether, as an adult with a well-paying job, it is difficult living at home with his parents. Lloyd tells me that his parents respect his privacy, so there is no problem. He also adds that, although he initially worried about what others might think of him, he dismissed those thoughts as "foolish," because what others think is irrelevant. Besides, he remarks, a couple of his friends have similar living arrangements. As far as Lloyd is concerned, living with his folks is strictly a financial decision. Why, he asks, should he pay $500 a month rent when instead he could put that money toward a down payment? He concludes, "It's a way of helping myself, and I don't see anything wrong with it."

When Lloyd shifts his attention from his own life to the national situation, his concerns seem to be governed by his political affiliation.

"Well, I'm a staunch Republican," he says. (A bumper sticker declaring "Rush is Right"—a reference to archconservative talk-radio personality Rush Limbaugh—confirms the point.) "I worry about the national deficit. I worry about government interference, government regulations. I really think that our economy, if we don't do something to reduce our national debt, we're gonna be in a lotta trouble, if we're not already there. It's just amazing that in our lifetime, we went from being an economic—*the* economic—superpower, we were the biggest creditor, and now we're the biggest borrower. We're really second fiddle to Japan, Germany, and who knows who else. And there's no reason, for the resources that we have in this country, to be that way.

"I think it's because of Congress. An' I see this from the regulations that they try an' impose on small businesses. Eighty-five percent of all businesses in the country are small businesses, and they just try to tack things on to them, on to them. And they don't realize that by overregulating these businesses, you're either gonna put some of 'em out of business, or you're gonna decrease employment, because they're not gonna be able t'employ as many people as they would. I think that's a big problem. I think we need to encourage small business an' small-business development.

"I just want us to be a number-one power again, that we once were. 'Cause I just think it's tragic that we were once up here and now we're down here, economically." Illustrating his point, Lloyd raises one hand above his head and lowers the other nearly to the floor.

"You look at how much I'm making now and when my parents were my age. They didn't make that much, yet I think they probably lived a lot better than me. Money just doesn't go as far as it once did. In the past, people would get houses that are much bigger than the houses there are now, for considerably less. Seems that money was more real, I mean, even ten years ago. Now it's nothin' to go through, if you're out, fifty or sixty dollars. Ten years ago, it was a big deal if you went through twenty dollars. I know, I was eighteen at the time and I'm twenty-eight now, but just seems money's not worth as much as it once was."

Lloyd concludes: "Things aren't *all* bad. We still live in America. It's a free country. You can do or become whatever you wanna become. No one's gonna tell you you can't do that. If you wanna become an astronaut, you can become an astronaut. If you wanna write a book, you can write a book. The only thing that limits you is your own personal limitations."

DEXTER

A born politician, Dexter loves meeting people. He always tells his friends, "First impression is always the last impression. When you meet somebody, you never turn your back to 'em, always show 'em a good face. You never know what might happen one day."

Dexter, twenty-five, is black. He is the youngest of his parents' five children. He was born and raised in the self-proclaimed "Frog Capital of the World," Rayne, Louisiana, a town of 9,000 people—or, in the eyes of a pol like Dexter, 7,200 registered voters—in the southwest ankle of this boot-shaped state.

"All my life I've been here in Rayne," says Dexter, his voice a smooth, Paul Robeson-esque baritone. "Attended school here, I've been livin' here ever since. Don't plan on staying here too long though."

Dexter lives part of the time with his parents, who are still married after thirty-one years. Dexter's father drives a truck for a sanitation company. His mother, who has "always been in the cooking business," works in the cafeteria at the local high school. "We always had somethin' t'eat, so I'd say we were middle-class," says Dexter, adding, "It's not that expensive in this town to live, so, you know, you could go along and get on without a lot of money."

After graduating from Rayne High, Dexter went to work as the assistant banquet manager at a hotel in Lafayette, fifteen miles east of Rayne. Describing that hotel, Dexter effuses, "Man, it's totally awesome. You see so many people walk through the doors, y'know, everybody from presidential contenders t'music stars. Everybody comes through hotel doors, y'know, an' I like being around people like that. It motivates me."

Dexter worked at that hotel for four years, and during his last year there, he began a second job, as a manager of a nightclub in a little town north of Rayne. He would spend his days at the hotel in Lafayette, then drive to the club. On Mother's Day, as he was driving home after a night at the club and a full day at the hotel, Dexter fell asleep and rear-ended another car. He decided he could not keep both jobs, so he kept the nightclub position because it was closer to home and gave up the job at the hotel.

A year and a half later, Dexter still manages that nightclub, though that's not the only thing this enterprising Louisianan does to earn a living. Dexter organizes promotions and sells air time for a radio station. He also runs a car detailing business, Cars by Dexter (one free wash with five paid), which employs a couple of guys part-time, and along with one of his friends he maintains some of the nicer lawns in Rayne. Working upwards of seventy hours a week—he claims he needs only forty-five minutes of sleep to be ready for the day—Dexter says he earns more in a day than many people in Rayne earn in a week, and he says he tries to save as much as sixty cents of every dollar he earns.

"The most important thing is t'make money and save it," he says. "Because I see people standin' on corners, older men in their sixties and seventies, an' I always say to myself I don't wanna be like that when I get old. So that's why I work so hard now and try to save, because I don't wanna be like that. And it's more easy to fall into that trap than to keep goin' the right way."

Dexter tells me that many of the people he knows in Rayne fall into that trap. "It's really from laziness, though. People just don't wanna work. There's nothing *but* work in Louisiana. But you can't be choicy when you don't have the education or you don't have the transportation t'go someplace else."

Why, I ask, don't people take the jobs that do exist?

"Shame," he says. "For instance, here in Rayne there's a fast-food restaurant. They hire people daily, but most people that I know, they party so much and drink the best of liquor and the best beer, eat the best foods, that it would be shameful for them to go work in a fast-food restaurant. That's what it boils down to, being shamed. But a hundred and eighty dollars a week comin' in is better than nothin' comin' in, y'know what I'm sayin'."

Of course, Dexter does not save all his money. Some of it goes to support his three-year-old, Tyrone.

Tyrone lives with his mother, Melinda, in a town about twenty miles north of Lafayette. Dexter rents an apartment there, because the radio station for which he works is in the same town, and he has to check in daily. This arrangement allows Dexter to see his son every day. Dexter stays in Opelousas during the first part of the week.

Later in the week and on weekends, he sleeps at his parents' house in Rayne because it is closer to the club.

Dexter has been dating Tyrone's mother for about three years and, though he thinks he loves his son more than her, he says he does love Melinda. Yet his feelings for her do not prevent him from playing around with other women. "Oh yeah, daily," he says. "Even with my barmaids. That's the way I bring 'em in. You see, like I say, I'm in the nightclub business. It's out there. And I've always said if it's out there, I'll take it, 'cause you only live once. Until I get married, then I'll stop."

How would you feel, I ask, if Melinda were seeing another man?

"I wouldn't say anything," he tells me, " 'cause I know what I've been doin'. I mean, when we first got together it would have bothered me, y'know. But after you been with someone so long, it's like gettin' a new car—at first you don't want nobody to drive it, then you say, 'Aw, well, material thing.' That's the way I look at it."

I ask Dexter to explain why he and Melinda are not married, and he says: "Well, at the time, it just wasn't there, y'know. It wasn't in the bag, in other words. Street talk, y'know. I guess there's a timing for everything, and the time just wasn't right. I always said I'd never get married until I'm thirty. 'Cause at that time, with the money put aside, I would be ready. 'Cause I see people get married daily, and they fight and scrumble t'pay bills and stuff like that. It's not worth it."

Nevertheless, Dexter insists he will marry Melinda, probably before thirty. "I will. I promise you. I'll send you an invitation," he says with a laugh.

Besides his work and his son, Dexter's other major commitment is to politics. When cable television arrived in Rayne, Dexter always would watch the news. He says "I fell in love with politics, met a lot of people, and they put me on the right track."

He tells me, "There are some lawyers I know right now, doctors and businesspeople, that can't walk in the district judge's or the district attorney's office and see The Man, y'know what I'm sayin'. And I can just walk in there without knocking on the door."

"Because . . . ?"

"Because I've been affiliated with politics all m'life. And I have a large gathering of people that follows me when I go out to vote, either helpin' myself or helpin' other candidates." In fact, I was introduced to Dexter by the son of a Louisiana state senator for whom Dexter had campaigned in the previous election.

Dexter explains how he gained his following: "I use to deejay when I was comin' up, and I had a large gathering. I use t'put on talent shows every Sunday. I done it all. I use t'be a lifeguard at the swimming pool, so I always was in the eye of the people. Still in the eye of the people—black and white—in this town. I go to the mall and my girlfriend will say, 'We'll never finish shoppin' wit' you,' 'cause if they have two thousand people in the mall, at least nine hundred people come up to me an' shake my hand, 'What's goin' on, Dexter? How you been, man?' That's the way it is." (After our conversation, Dexter, a gifted and tireless self-promoter, insists that we have our picture taken by the staff photographer at the Rayne *Acadian-Tribune* so that everyone in town will know that I interviewed him.)

Although Dexter says that when it comes to local politics he is "on the outside lookin' in," he tried in 1990 to become part of the system. Crossing over from the Republican party to the Democrats—"A man has to do what a man has to do," he says— Dexter, then only twenty-three, made a bid to be Rayne's city marshal.

"I ran weak all over town except for south side," he says. "The major white polling place, I finished third there out of four candidates. The rural area's what killed me, like the country area." Still, he feels he did pretty well, coming in third out of four candidates with 1,000 of the 4,700 votes cast.

Dexter is not disappointed with the results because that election told him what he needed to know. He wants someday to be elected to the Rayne city council, and his unsuccessful campaign for city marshal enabled him to see how he would do in the black neighborhoods, where he would be running. Dexter tells me that in that area, he received 95 percent of the vote.

When I ask Dexter to tell me why politics is so important to him, he says, "It's a marvelous arena where people can come together. Sometimes that's the only way you can get t'people, is with politics, y'know where I'm comin' from." Although his answer is not wholly disingenuous, it is certainly incomplete. Politics, as he points out, is a way to get not only to the public, but also to the public's purse. With remarkable candor, he tells me, "It's a lotta money t'be made in politics."

"How so?"

"Well, you gotta get the right man in the top office. Start with the governor if you are doin' on like the state level. And then when I'll become councilman, my man,* he'll be governor then, so everything will be working out just fine." After that, says Dexter, the key is to be awarded contracts to work for the state. "Washing the state cars, stuff like that. Right here at Crowley they have state trucks, I'll get the contract for that. That's what I'm really after."

"Does that bother you at all, that wheeling and dealing?"

"No, it doesn't. It doesn't really bother me because maybe I was born for that, I think. Some people say I'm crooked, and I always would tell 'em to show me one person that I ever crooked, an' they can't name anyone. I've always helped people. Always. People's homes that burnt down, I'll take 'em out to the millionaires in town and make 'em give 'em a donation."

"How do you do that?"

"Well, they know me. I have a big mouth in town. I'm really out there, with everybody. So they—" Dexter stops in midsentence and, as if he is realizing it for the first time, says, "I have a strange life."

Continued involvement in politics is certainly an important part of Dexter's American Dream, though he does not immediately say so. When I first ask him about this concept, he casually tosses out the first thing that comes to mind, saying, "Everyone wants to own their own home, drive a nice, fancy car, have a good job. That's the American Dream. Mine is to own my own home, fancy car, and I want to own and operate a hotel," preferably in New Orleans.

But a few minutes later, he lays out The Plan. "Everything I do, I do with a plan," he says confidently. "I'll be elected in ninety-four, September of ninety-four, I'll be elected t'post of city councilman in Ward One. I'll be out of the nightclub business and be back in the hotel business, where I really wanna be. For those four years I'll be here in Rayne. I'll be reaching almost thirty at the time. I'll get married, then I'll be out in New Orleans." By the time he's forty-five, Dexter intends to retire and become a "public servant," perhaps a preacher. "The plan is already drawn," he says.

Recalling his remark about procuring state contracts, I challenge him. "Doesn't sound like much public serving," I say. "Sounds like serving yourself in a public capacity."

*Dexter identified this individual. However, I thought it impolitic to repeat this information.

"That's individual accomplishments, alone, until I get about forty-five. Then I'll change."

"Think you'll change?"

"I *will*, because I am scared right now. Sometimes I ask myself, from all of this dirt that I do, I think The Man upstairs want me to be a preacher. That's what I really think."

When I point out to Dexter that "dirt" implies something crooked, he says, somewhat defensively, "Well, yeah, I mean, nothing's ever right in the public's eye. When you have a large bank account at a young age, and the first thing they say, especially in the black community, 'He's either dealin' drugs or he's doin' somethin', y'know, illegal.' Y'see what I'm sayin'.

"Let me give it to you like this. I run a nightclub. You come in the club, you lookin' for a hooker, I can tell you where to go get a hooker at. If you're lookin' for some dope, I can tell you who to see for dope. That's what people don't understand, I'm in the place where everything happens, y'know, and they take it in a wrong way. You see where I'm comin' from now.

"I've never done anything illegal," Dexter insists. "One of the guys I clean yards for is the assistant district attorney, and the man would pull my coat quick, y'know what I'm sayin'. It's jealous people, y'know. They put rumors out about me, that I'm a crook. So I'll say, 'Well, you gonna make me a crook, I'll be a crook.' But I can go to the bank and laugh."

For Dexter, merely getting by is insufficient. But he believes that, as a black man in the United States, particularly a black man in Rayne, he faces greater challenges to success.

"From what I see, as a whole, the United States has always been against the black man. The U.S. is always be a who-you-know place to live in. I've never traveled, y'know, and I haven't vacationed in L.A. for a month or New York for a month, but I know right here at home, if you don't know any white man that has clout in the neighborhood, it's rough for you to live. I mean, you can go out and work and make a living to pay your bills, but if you want to get beyond that, y'know—"

Although it is difficult for people who lack connections to succeed, Dexter feels as if he is "pretty well set up. Lotta my friends, sometimes they say, 'There you go again, talkin' about them ol' politics.' It pays off in the long run. Trust me. For instance, because o' the people I know, I could walk in the bank tomorrow and get a loan, an' the man would say, 'No problem, Dexter, anything you need.' But you take another man, a young black man that's working, with good credit, he can walk in the bank, and they wouldn't even give 'im a loan. You know why? Maybe because one o' his cousins defaulted on a loan, or his mom had defaulted on a loan. That's the way they operate in this area."

Dexter does not believe the situation will improve for the blacks in this area. "Not in my lifetime," he says, "because those that's there now, their kids is in the same business they're in. One bank that the man is president, his son is vice president, and the guy ain't nothin' but about thirty-two. So you see, they're groomin' their families. You know, it might seem strange to you, but this is a rough place to live. This town is not made for the black man."

I ask Dexter why he seems to be succeeding while many other blacks in Rayne do not. He believes it is because he is not afraid to talk with people, not even politically powerful whites. "I can talk with anybody," he says. "I have sat there and talked one-on-one with the governor, and if he say anything that pisses me off, well, I'll just tell him like it is. The big shoe don't scare me."

According to Dexter, the only way things will ever improve for blacks is for them to become directors of banks and corporations. For that to happen, blacks will have to "stop sellin' themselves" and directly challenge the political power of whites.

To illustrate his point, Dexter tells me of a local black incumbent who decided not to run for reelection because he didn't want to run against a white challenger. "That's horrible," says Dexter, "you losin' power right there. And then he, the black man, gets out in the community and say he coulda beat the white man. I say, 'Well, you do me a favor—you beat 'im and retire next day.' That's the way you do it. That's why a lot of blacks don't succeed. We call 'em 'Uncle Toms.' "

Dexter explains why he is unafraid to challenge white political hegemony while, according to him, older blacks are. Earlier in our conversation, Dexter told me about "racial riots" in the early 1980s at his high school. (Judging by his description, these disturbances were interracial brawls, not full-blown riots.) He says that older blacks "grew up with that movement, you know, back in the sixties, when they were fightin' for rights *non*violently. Where the age I grew up, we were fightin' for rights violently. So it doesn't bother me, y'know."

Despite the obstacles that blacks face in Rayne—and in the United States—Dexter thinks of himself as an American. He says, "This may hurt me politically when the book is published, but I don't consider myself as an Afro-American. I consider myself as an *American* American. I was born in America, I was raised in America, and I will die in America. My ancestors came from across the waters, too, but roots die off and stuff like that. I'm an American American."

SUZANNE

"Wonderful. It really was," says Suzanne, twenty-three, describing her childhood in Vaiden, Mississippi. "There's no Front Street left now, but it used to be, like, buildings all the way down. You'd get off the school bus, and my father used to have his own business right down the road. We would just come on an' go up an' down the street. It was just so much fun, just goin' in, visitin' with people. It was like Mayberry."

Tucked in the piney woods of rural Mississippi, just east of Interstate 55 and seventy-five miles north of Jackson, Vaiden does resemble Andy Griffith's hometown. There is only one main road, Highway 51, for the 763 folks who live here. There aren't any stoplights to slow people down—not that anybody drives that fast in Vaiden—and only a dozen or so stop signs. Assuming the headstones in the town's cemetery are an indication, Vaiden has lots of Joes, Jims, and Billys, and more than one Rose and Vera.

The youngest of three children born to dedicated Baptist parents ("Every time the door was opened to the church, we were there"), Suzanne was born in Jackson, the state capital. Soon afterward, her father's parents died and left him their dairy farm, which consisted of eighty cows and a house on 110 acres in Vaiden. Suzanne's family moved to Vaiden and has been living there ever since.

Suzanne's parents never operated the dairy farm as a commercial enterprise. Instead, unlike many of the people in Vaiden who work in factories in Winona, a town about ten miles to the north, Suzanne's father earns his living as an insurance agent. Suzanne's mother is a recently retired maintenance administrator for the local phone company. Their combined income provided Suzanne's family with an upper-middle-class life.

Their income also enabled Suzanne's parents to do what virtually all the white parents in Vaiden did—send their kids to a private school. Although Vaiden's population is almost evenly divided between whites and African-Americans, Suzanne says that, when she was growing up, virtually none of the white children attended the public high school. Instead, their parents sent them to one of the private academies in the area. (This has not changed. According to a teacher at Vaiden High School, only two of the twenty-nine students who graduated in 1992 were white; the other twenty-seven were black.) Suzanne's parents were no different from the others, then, when they decided to send Suzanne to Winona Academy, a Christian day school.

Suzanne believes that one of the reasons her classmates' parents sent their kids to Winona Academy was so that their children would not be in school with black children. She supposes that her parents felt similarly. She says, "How can they say that Vaiden High School is not a good school, because my uncle is principal there, y'know? So what other reason could there be? I really don't know." (She later qualifies her remark by saying that her parents genuinely thought that she would receive a better and more Christian education at a private school.)

She adds, "I can't really say that I *wanted* t'go t' the public school there, y'know. 'Cause you are what you hang around, y'know what I mean. You are what your friends are."

"Meaning?"

"Meaning, like, if I hung around with somebody with low morals, then I would not have high morals. I'm not sayin' that all the people at Vaiden High School are like that. I don't know. I hate t'stereotype. I'm just sayin' that I don't wanna talk like most black people around here talk. I'm glad that I have good English, an' I'm glad that I went to Winona Academy, in a way.

"Now, if everybody had gone there, I'da had no problem with that. I'da enjoyed it. But not bein' the only one, the only white person there. That's bein' a minority. I don't wanna be in a minority." Suzanne thinks that, because of this, she understands a bit better how blacks must feel all the time.

After graduating from Winona Academy, Suzanne transferred back and forth between Mississippi State University and a nearby community college. She finally decided Mississippi State was too big and returned to the community college to complete the requirements for an associate's degree. She then attended Delta State University and graduated with a bachelor's degree in general studies. Together with a summer at Ole Miss and a semester off ("I just played"), she spent five years finishing college.

Suzanne regrets not having taken school more seriously. She says, "Oh my Lord, I've always played. I've never studied. I never studied in high school. Everybody says, 'College—those four years are the best years of your life.' Well, so I took it literally, y' know. So I never studied. I jus' played around, an' my degree is not worth the paper it's written on. I mean, I would have really gotten a better degree or sum'n. Let me just put it this way, I'd've specialized in some kind of field.

"I blame it on this, that nobody just really sits you down and says, 'Look, *this* is the real world an' this is what it's like. You really cannot play around your whole life and jus' luck up an' get a job an' luck up an' have money or whatever."

After college Suzanne looked all over central Mississippi for a job, but she didn't "luck up." She eventually did find work, as the receptionist at the Vaiden Medical Clinic, which had been closed for a decade or more before reopening in July 1991. When she started working at the clinic, it was open only three days a week, so she earned extra money by working at a Stuckey's on I-55. "Man, I hated it," she says, and warns me as she laughs, "Don't ever eat anything at those places." When the clinic began operating four days a week, she quit Stuckey's and started working at the clinic thirty-five hours a week.

She says, "It's just the worst job I've ever had." I ask her to elaborate, and, after noting that it has been "a real bad day," she tells me: "Where do I begin? Let's see. I do not like my immediate boss. She has less experience and less education than I do, an' she acts like I am a total idiot. (That'll be all right. She'll never read the book.) The doctors want ya to lie for 'em an' tell people that they're not here. An' today I was sittin' there just tellin' this lady, 'Okay, she's not here. She's already left for Jackson.' An' out she goes, right in front of her. An' I just, I just wanted to *die*. I mean, I have to live here, you know. She lives in Jackson. No sweat off her back.

"I mean, it's just awful. When you're in school, you can always say, 'Well, this is just, you know, a job right now, and I'm gonna get a better one.' But you know, you're like slapped with reality. I'm out of school and I'm workin' in this crappy place and have no money. It's just awful."

To make matters worse, Suzanne cannot afford to rent an apartment of her own. Consequently, like the 68 percent of this nation's eighteen- to twenty-four-year-olds who live with their parents or some other relative, she has no choice but to live with her parents.

Suzanne has not enjoyed the experience. "I guess 'cause I'm the youngest," she explains, "they just still think that I'm in high school or sum'n. They have to know when I'm leavin', where I'm goin', who I'm goin' with, you know, that kind of thing. Just really drives ya crazy after bein' out five years, then ya come home and they want to know everything and you're just not used to it."

One of the people Suzanne used to go out with was Lee, her on-again-off-again boyfriend of the past three years. Suzanne and Lee are currently off again—for the twenty-fifth time, she estimates.

Although Suzanne loves Lee, she will never marry him. "He's stuck here," she says. "He'll live here forever." Moreover, she says, if she were to marry Lee, who lives in Winona and repairs heaters and air conditioners, "we'd be poor, and I'm not inta that."

"Isn't love enough?" I ask.

"No! It's not enough," she exclaims. "You think about children. You bring children in the world. An' I know my sister thinks that love is enough, you know. She resents my parents for working all the time. When she was sick there was nobody to stay with her, she had to go to school anyway. She resents that. *I* would've resented not havin' the right clothes to wear. I guess I'm materialistic, in a way—I'm not as much as I used to be—but I don't want my children to have to struggle or anything. That's terrible. It must've sounded terrible. But that's just the way I feel."

She adds, "I know bein' poor is not the worst thing in the world, but it's sure not the best thing."

Suzanne explains that it is not just Lee's lack of ambition (though she says he has none) that would leave them in penury. Vaiden itself is also to blame.

"There's no future here, really," she says. "I'm not seeing the town growin'. It's just unreal how things have gone down. The drugstore recently closed, like just last month. I just can't imagine livin' here, 'cause it's just depressing. I don't really see any kind of future for anybody here—any young person—myself.

"I mean, I love it here because I know everybody. It's just not a fun place to live, though. It's my home, it'll always be my home, but I don't want to live here."

Suzanne's next step is to move out of her parents' house, by autumn if possible. To do that, she will have to find a better job or go back to school. If she returns to school, she'll finish her bachelor's degree in history so that she can become a teacher. If she lands another job, she hopes to become a sales rep for a pharmaceutical manufacturer.

"Those are like *the* best jobs in the world," she effuses. "Everybody wants to be a pharmaceutical rep. Because they start you out at thirty plus commission an' give you a car. They sell to doctors, not the general public. It's not a real gross job or anything. You don't really have to come in contact with a lot of . . . *lower*-class people, I guess you'd say. Not that I have a problem with that at all. I'm just saying it's a nice job. It really is. The money's enough for me."

When Suzanne thinks about the American Dream, she asks herself, "Is there anything that you could invent to be rich? Is there anything left to do? Do ya see what I'm sayin', is there anything left to invent? I've sat an' wondered an' wondered, an' I've pretty much gotten away from that because I really don't think that I could come up with it if it was, you know. But I do sit and think about it a lot.

"I used to be real optimistic and everything, y'know. An' now, ya see somebody ridin' down the road and they have a nice car, and you're thinkin', 'They must sell drugs. What *else* can they do? Or who did they know?' It's just mind-boggling to think, *when* do you get financially stable? I don' understand how my parents do it. I used to be real optimistic, but not anymore."

"Optimistic about . . . ?"

"About life. About the American Dream. You think, 'Well, I'm gonna do better than my parents.' You want to. I mean, we weren't just destitute or anything like that. But I mean you just wanna do better. You just wanna have a meaningful job and—this may sound materialistic, but—you wanna have nice things and you wanna be able to go places 'n' see the world, you know. You can't do that if you're poor.

"I just wanna be able to find a job that I like to do. I have no idea what that is, right now. I wanna get married and I wanna have two kids, you know, 'n' that kind of thing. I guess career right now is really the most important thing to get on track first, then comes marriage 'n' I guess family."

I ask, "Isn't it hard to get on track if you don't know what you want to do?"

"Yeah," she says, "ya oughta try it. It's awful hard.

"I jus' don't know about anything," she continues. "I don't know what I wanna do. I was tellin' my boss, I asked her, 'Is it terrible that I do not know about my love life, what I wanna do, or about my life in general? I don't know anything?' She said, 'No. You're young. Don't worry about it.'"

However, though Suzanne might be able to disregard her doubts about fulfilling her American Dream, when she thinks about the state of our nation, worry seems to be the only thing she can do.

"I don't even watch the news. It depresses me. Not to be fanatical about religion, but I really do think the world is going to end. It just seems like that, and I wonder, during World War Two, did they think, 'Well, this is it?' I guess every facet of America scares me.

"Do you read the Bible? Have you ever read it? Revelations, that's just what I think. I think 'tribulation' has come. I really do. It's the time where the Antichrist comes and where Jesus, his second comin'. There'll be a seven-year period in between the Antichrist and Jesus's second coming to this earth. During this seven-year period, you'll have no food 'n' no water. Nothin'. You'll just starve to death. 'N' if you don't have the mark of The Beast, then you will probably die. . . .

"I hadn't seen any signs of the Antichrist. But it's kind of scary 'cause everything that happens in Revelations is happening right now. Like you can't tell the difference in the seasons. In a lot of places, like in Russia, they did not have bread. I don't know if you'd ever heard the song 'bout a piece of bread would buy a bag of gold, but that's about like it was in Russia. An' I just hope we don't come to that. Economically, they say we're recovering from the recession, but I just really don't see any signs of it. And if it is, then it's a very slow recovery.

"Oh, it's inevitable. I mean, you could prob'ly slow down the process. I don't know if we could. I am all for 'Save the Earth,' you know, because I really don't want it to happen in my lifetime. But I really do think it's gonna happen one day, and it's nothin' we can do."

Despite her apocalyptic perspective, Suzanne does not blithely ignore the immediate problems that plague our society. Take segregation, for instance. She says, "There's still this old way of thinkin' that, 'Hey, I'm better than you jus' because my color is different.' "

She tells me several anecdotes to illustrate the racism that still pervades human relationships in Vaiden. One of these is a story from her childhood, sometime in the early seventies. It is about Eddy, a young black man who used to help her mother's parents with chores around their house. It was a holiday, and Suzanne and her family were at her grandparents' house for the holiday meal. Eddy was there, too, working for Suzanne's grandfather.

"They gladly gave 'im somethin' to eat," she says, "but he couldn't come in and sit with us. An' I wanted him to so bad, but they made him eat on the carport, an' I just couldn't understand that."

Suzanne cried during the family dinner. One of the adults said to her, "Aw, Suzanne, be quiet. Eddy's fine where he is."

Race relations in central Mississippi have not improved since then. For example, three years ago Suzanne and some of her college friends were at a bar in a town twenty miles south of Vaiden. A couple of black men walked in and ordered drinks. After they had been there a few minutes, someone said, quite loudly, "What the hell are they doin' here?" A few moments later, that same person walked over to the black men and repeated himself: "What the hell are y'all doin' here?" ("Jus' made 'em feel real unwelcome," says Suzanne, seemingly unaware of the magnitude of her understatement.) The black men took their drinks and left.

"They weren't hurting anybody and they weren't doin' anything. I don't see why they had to leave," says Suzanne, genuinely puzzled. A second later she adds: "They'd be crazy t'stay."

According to Suzanne, blacks and whites in Vaiden still don't mix. She says, "You just don't do that. 'Cause we couldn't go t'the same places. We couldn't do the same things, y'know. An' people would look at you like, 'My gosh, she's white trash. What's she doin' with those niggers?' That's what they'd say."

When it comes to racism, the churches in Vaiden are no better than their parishioners. Suzanne says there are two Baptist churches in Vaiden, one white, one black, and if a black person were to walk into the white church, the people would "freak smooth out."

She continues: "I know that people in my church that're deacons, they would have a heart attack if some black person walked in. I don't know what they'd do. I just don't believe in that, 'n' that's one of the reasons that I don't go to church like I should. They're just hypocritical.

"I'll make sure that my children know that jus' because someone else's skin is not the same color as mine is, that they are not any less a person. I don't want them to think that they're better than anybody."

Suzanne notes that, although she is a Republican and votes conservative, "I am liberal in the way I think." She explains: "When I think of conservative, I guess, I think of somebody who wants to stick to their old ways. What I'm tryin' t'say is that I have nothing against people that are gay. I don't have anything against people that are black. I'm just kind of liberal, really liberal for where I live. 'Cause everybody here is like, 'Gay!? Oh my gosh' or [under her breath] 'They're black.' Are they white or black? What difference does it make, y'know."

Note: In June 1992, Suzanne moved from Vaiden to Jackson. She works for the state as an examiner, evaluating claims for disability benefits. She lives with a roommate in a mobile home in Ridgeland, just north of the city. Suzanne tells me that although she is glad she no longer lives in Vaiden, she now goes home every weekend.

When I remind her how badly she wanted to escape from Vaiden, Suzanne admits, "It's ridiculous."

STEVEN

Steven's roots run deep in Dover, Oklahoma. His great-grandfather drove his homestead stake into the red clay soil of western Oklahoma in the Land Run of 1889, then became a farmer. A generation later and a quarter mile away, Steven's grandfather farmed the land, property which Steven's father farms today. And like the three generations that preceded him, Steven, too, is a farmer in western Oklahoma.

Steven, twenty-five, was raised on the family farm in Dover, a town of 600 people forty or so miles northwest of Oklahoma City.

Although most of the folks in Dover work for a company that makes oil pipeline, Dover is also a farming community.

Steven and his four brothers and sisters grew up in the same house in which their father was raised. It sits on 80 acres (an "eighty") of the family's property; the remaining 1,600 acres are scattered around Dover, parceled in eighties and "quarters." (One square mile of land contains 640 square acres; a quarter, or quarter-of-a-mile section, is 160 square acres.) Although Steven's father grows wheat, he is principally a cattle farmer. He runs about 310 head, a midsized operation for the area.

Steven explains: "What we do is we plant wheat in the fall and then, when the wheat pasture gets big enough, we run cattle on it. And whenever they eat the wheat down int'the ground, the grass comes up, and then they eat the grass all summer and we sell 'em, oh, here about two weeks ago, about August."

Describing his economic background, Steven says his family was, at different points, "probably rich, poor 'n' middle. Farming has been pretty sporadic. In the seventies we had four really good years back t'back, about from '76 through almost '80. Just unbelievable years. With this, you know, we had quite a bit of money. We bought a lotta land then, new vehicles, put a lotta work on the house, lotta stuff got done.

"Then from '80 to, like, '87, most of the farmers have—in fact, all of our neighbors—have declared bankruptcy. All seven of our neighbors but one within three miles of us have either quit and filed bankruptcy, or just quit and I think the bank just took it. Most of the farmers around where I'm at didn't make it."

Explaining why his father survived, even prospered, while his neighbors went into bankruptcy, Steven says, "My dad never missed anything. When cattle prices were good, he sold. He just never missed out on anything. There wasn't much money t'be made in the last ten years of farming, and he just hadn't missed it. If there was a little bit o' money to be made, he made it." And Steven's mother, who for the past six years has worked for the state as an ombudsman mediating disputes between nursing home patients and administrators, also has helped pay the bills.

Steven attended the local public school in Dover until sixth grade. After that, he says, "my parents wanted me t'have band and football, which the smaller schools didn't offer. So they took me on to Hennessey, which is twelve more miles on north of Dover."

Steven graduated from high school, then spent two years as an accounting major at Northwest Oklahoma State University before his father hurt his back and Steven had to return to the family farm. "It wasn't real serious," Steven says of his father's injury, "but it was just enough that he needed some more help." By that time, Steven's brothers and sisters had already left the farm, leaving Steven the only one able to come back and help their father.

During the first autumn when Steven was back in Dover, he attended school part-time at a community college about thirty-five miles away. The following spring he was too busy with the farm to go to school, but the next fall he enrolled at a small private college in northeast Texas. A year later, he had had enough of higher education.

"I could've went on into accounting, with a minor in computer science, but I hated it," he tells me. "I swore that I would never get up in the morning and hate what I'm doing again.

"I regret not having the option now of becomin' an accountant, because it just woulda been one more option," he says. "But I also regret goin' t'college because farming, you make lots of connections, and the connections you make are how you make your money. I regret not staying around those three and a half or four years and networking.

"You've gotta want the other farmers to want you to be around them. You want *them* to want *you* to farm the land next to them, 'cause they know that your fence is gonna be kept up. Your cattle, if they get out, are gonna be put back. If their cattle get over on your land, you're gonna put 'em back on theirs or tell 'em where they're at. You've gotta have them want you to be there, and that-away, whenever that land comes up for rent, the first one gets called is you. That is real important.

"Now, there are a lot of farmers that come in that've got a lot of money. But if you're not that way, where you're wanted, it costs you a lot more to farm because you're just not gonna catch the deals. Somebody else is gonna get the deals."

Religion played a large part in Steven's life when he was growing up. " 'Bout everybody out in my part of the country were Christians," he says. "We've always been Christians, quite a bit. I spent a summer in the Dominican Republic as a missionary. Thought I might wanna be a missionary once, but got that out of my system pretty quick."

For the past three years, Steven has not gone to church as regularly as he did when he was younger because he is away from home three and a half months of every year.

"Doing what?" I ask.

"Custom harvesting and buying cattle."

Steven still spends some of his time helping his father on the family farm. He buys cattle not only for his parents, but for his own cattle farm as well. Not even old enough to get a driver's license, Steven was only fifteen when he became a farmer in his own right. He says with a smile, "had t'make some money somewhere," so he rented a hundred acres and started his own wheat farm. He might have done better financially if, like other teenagers, he had simply taken a job at Pizza Hut or Burger King, because no matter how hard he worked, he could never manage to turn a profit by raising wheat. Then, three years ago, he turned from wheat farm to cattle. "I just put the cattle out on the wheat t'eat it, y'know, then the grass comes back up through it. And that was the first year that I ever made money farmin'," he says. And while cattle is his primary business, between the spring and winter wheat crops he also grows mung beans, most of which he ships to markets in San Francisco's Chinatown.

After ten years as a farmer, Steven recently tripled the amount of land that he rents. He also plans this year to increase the number of head he runs from forty-two to a hundred or so. "There's a lotta opportunity out there," he tells me, "lotta money t'be made in farming. But you can't mess around, you gotta do it. Mean you can't just hum-haw around about it. If you're gonna do it, you gotta really jump on it 'n' do it. 'N' you gotta know what the heck you're doin', 'cause there's a lotta little quirks t'it.

"If you're gonna buy cattle, you can't go down to the sale one day and buy your cattle. Last year, I got lucky and almost bought all my cattle, one time, one trip. Got real lucky. But the year before, I think I made a dozen cattle sales, three dozen cattle sales—no, probably twenty sales—tryin' t'pick up all my cattle. And I still didn't quite get all of 'em I wanted, but I was just at the point I didn't care anymore. I'd been t'enough sales.

"And buying equipment. You can't buy equipment from a dealer. You gotta wait till like a farm sale. You just gotta shop. You can't buy convenience at all, you just can't miss it. If somethin' is five hundred dollars cheaper over here, you can't not go look at it. I mean, that's a lotta money.

"The farmers that're really watchin' every little bit are makin' it. Either that, or I think they've got a gimmick where like the FHA [Farm Home Administration] gave 'em a bunch of money, or some way they were smart enough to somehow rip the government out of money. Cheat the government out of it is the only other way t'make it."

Although Steven describes Dover as a "basic farm community," he is the only one of his high school classmates—or, for that matter, of his siblings—to become a farmer. The rest, he says, all went to the cities. Explaining why he decided to remain in Dover and become a farmer, he says, "I like the work. I like the people. I like the people a lot. I like th'area. It's basically all I know. That's all Dad's ever done. It's what my grandpa did 'n' his grandpa. It's just a way of life.

"You pick your own hours. You're your own boss. You do have time off, y'know. At certain times of the year, you're not near as busy as you are other times. When there's work to be done, you can work sixteen, seventeen hours a day. And then when you're off, y'know, you might get a week where you've only gotta do two or three hours' worth of stuff all week. I like to work and get it done and then have some time off, instead of just working every day eight hours."

The only aspect of contemporary farming that Steven does not like is the government interference. "I'd like the government t'just get completely out," he fumes, " 'cause all they're doin' is they're keepin' the farmers who can't make it in. The federal government's price protection programs make the prices of stuff so there's no way when you plant your wheat, like right now we're plantin' wheat, I have no earthly idea next spring what that wheat's gonna be worth. It might be five and a half dollars, it might be a dollar a bushel.

"If the government would get out of it and let price and demand work together, the farmer would have some kind of idea how much t'plant, or if not t'plant, or maybe go t'a different crop or t'turn the land back into grass pasture. But the way they've got it now, with the way they do the prices on stuff, we have no idea year to year what we're gonna have at the end of the year."

In addition to cattle farming, Steven is also a custom harvester. When he tells me this, he asks, "Do you know anything about custom harvesting?", perhaps presuming that someone from Oklahoma would, or at least should, know what it is.

"Not even a little bit," I admit.

"Oh geez, how can I explain this to you?" Steven thinks for a moment, boils the concept down to its essence, then says, "Okay, custom harvesting is, you take your combine, you supply the combine and the truck, and you cut the grain and haul the grain t'the elevators for the people you're workin' for."

Not long after Steven started his own farm, he began working as a custom harvester in Oklahoma. He enjoyed the work and, three years ago, decided to join what is known as the "harvest run." This, he explains, is a three-to-four-month period when custom harvesters travel with their combines from state to state harvesting other farmers' crops. The run begins in late April in the South, cutting wheat in Texas, Louisiana, and Mississippi. It gradually moves north, through Oklahoma, Kansas, Nebraska, and, by August, into the Dakotas. Some harvesters even travel as far north as Canada.

"The harvest starts slow," Steven says. "One machine might get forty acres a day in an eight-hour day." As the harvest gradually moves north, into the wheat fields of Oklahoma and Kansas, the days grow considerably longer. "We might be able to start at like seven in the morning and get done at whatever time we wanna quit, one or two in the morning, or usually like twelve, because you don't want to put too big a day in 'cause you're liable t'wreck something. And those days, one machine might be getting a hundred twenty acres, a hundred thirty acres a day." By the time the crew begins to cut spring wheat, barley and oats in South Dakota, the harvest is winding down. "Usually we'll get started at ten o'clock in the mornin' and go t'ten or eleven [at night]."

Steven explains why he enjoys custom cutting on the harvest run: "I compare it to farming over four or five states. 'Cause I know people in South Dakota, who their kids are, where everybody in their family works. I know as many people there in Pukwana, South Dakota, as I do in Dover where I grew up.

"And I don't know if you ever went into a small area and you had trouble. Sometimes they won't accept you. Well, since I'm a custom harvester and I work for the farmers 'n' everything, you're immediately accepted. I know everything that's goin' on. I know all the backwoods stories goin' on. I know all the little things that people that live there for twenty and thirty years don't know, because I'm immediately accepted in. It's like having three hometowns. It's great, 'cause it's just like farming all them areas. You know everybody up there, 'n' everybody's happy to see you. It's just—it's neat. I've always wanted t'farm and farm different places, and that's the only way I know how t'do it."

Steven did not join a harvesting crew just because he enjoys the work, however. He says, "I'm tryin' t'learn the harvest run, which I have. I boughten a combine, and I'm planning on starting m'own harvest run." He envisions that within ten years he'll have "a pretty good-sized custom crew," with two combines, an eighteen-wheeler to haul them, two trucks for transporting grain, and three employees.

These days, Steven is quite happy. "I'm doin' what I wanna do," he says. Indeed, cattle farming is so much a part of Steven that, except for fishing, his cattle are his only hobby. "Just go out there and check 'em and chase 'em with the pickup. It's more or less playin'." And he cannot imagine enjoying any work more than custom cutting. "Like when you said, 'If you could do anything, what would you wanna do?' And I'd say, 'Be a custom harvester.' That's where I'm goin'."

Steven is also heading toward his vision of the American Dream. "I picture a farmstead," he says, "you know, a house 'n' a barn 'n' kids playin' in the front yard, 'n' probably the tractor workin' in the background." A few minutes later he adds, "I'd like to buy a fairly good-sized farm, close to where I'm at now, and live out my life there." Steven would also like to be married someday, when he can afford it. But, he adds, "I'd like t'have children almost more than I wanna be married."

Steven has an equally clear idea of what he would like to see done at the national level. In his opinion, exorbitant taxes are the country's gravest social ill. He says, "I know people have said that probably for a hundred years, but it does seem like taxes are unbelievable. Y'know, when I work doing my custom work, I make so much more money because I can deduct everything. When I work for someone else, I actually make more money, but I don't get home with anything. I think that we need to raise the personal deduction and lower taxes on the lower middle class and lower class. We just need t'get taxes under control is what I think. I think taxes are the big killer right now."

Steven believes that to bring taxes under control, we must decentralize governmental power. "We really need to break things down," he says, "because somethin' that's good for me may not be good for someone in South Dakota and may be *really* bad for somebody in San Francisco."

He continues: "Since Russia's went down, it wouldn't bother me t'see the United States kinda split up a little bit. Not so much different nations, but a lot more decentralized. Like the Plains areas all oughta be together."

Steven offers as an example the windfall profits tax. Congress imposed this tax to prevent gas producers from realizing a bonanza when price controls on natural gas were withdrawn in 1980. In the natural gas-producing states of the South, the tax was less popular than fire ants at a nudist picnic. Drivers in those states brandished bumper stickers that declared: "Let the damn Yankees freeze in the dark." Steven echoes this sentiment as he steams: "That really made me mad, when they put the windfall profit tax on Oklahoma. That was just stolen money.

"The eastern states knew they could get by with stealing from Oklahoma, and that was all that was. That was a flat thieving action, and that wasn't right. Then, whenever things kinda went down a little bit, we got it off. But y'know they still took—there's no tellin' how much—out, and that money just went away. That money went out of Oklahoma and was gone. I'd like t'see the money that is made in an area stay in the area."

Another thing that upsets him: "I think the American people have taken on the Southern Baptist idealism of 'We've got t'save the world from itself.' What I call it is idiot-proofing. They're trying to idiot-proof the world from idiots, so no matter what you do, you can't get hurt, no matter how *stupid* you are. You're not ever responsible. If somethin' goes wrong, it really wasn't your fault, a government agency should've been there and made sure that that didn't happen to you. With insurance and with this government attitude, people act like they're victims of their own lives. They're not responsible for anything that goes on.

"That's what we're trying t'do with everybody. We're just trying t'idiot-proof the entire thing where, when somebody falls down, somebody's gonna catch 'em. And y'know people think like Social Security, 'Why should I worry about my job? I've got Social Security.' People just are not responsible for what they're doin'."

Despite these problems, however, Steven is optimistic about his future. He says confidently, "I think the future's wide open. I think there's so damn much money to be made out there if a guy would just go do it. I'm actually kicked back from what I probably should be, but I'm making the money. From year to year, I'm making so much more money each year as I go that I don't see any reason t'really go out there and look for the dollar. I do work at it a lot. But I think the future's wide open. People're always talkin' about a recession and how bad things really are. I don't see it, 'cause everything really seems t'be working pretty good for me."

BRIAN and PENNY

When people bemoan the decline of the American family, the ideal they envision probably looks a lot like Brian, Penny, and their six-week-old son, Avery. Brian and Penny have been married just over two years. Brian is a first-year associate at a small law firm in Houston; Penny stays home to take care of Avery.

Brian, twenty-six, is black. He was born in Newark, New Jersey, and is the older of his parents' two sons. His mother was a teacher, his father a tax attorney for a major oil company. When Brian was five, the company relocated its headquarters to Houston, so Brian and his family moved to a house in a middle-class neighborhood in the southwest part of the city. Twenty-one years later, Brian's parents still live in the same house, which is just a few blocks from the house in which Brian and Penny now live.

Brian attended a private school through second grade. In third grade Brian transferred to the Houston public school system. After graduation he went to Howard University in Washington, D.C., and majored in accounting.

"I just never thought about going any other place besides Howard," Brian explains. "I had close black friends whose parents went to the University of Texas, and I did not see the same kind of connections with the university that I saw in my parents." Both Brian's parents went to black universities. "They still have friends from twenty years ago, thirty years ago, they talk about things they did on a Saturday night when such and such was there. Growing up, hearing how much they love their university, the friends they have from the university, the memories they have, I wanted to experience that. And I did. It was wonderful."

Brian graduated from Howard in December 1987, and took a job entering data (and reading the daily paper) at the Department of Energy in Washington, D.C. Eight months later, he entered law school at the University of Texas.

He decided to become a lawyer for two reasons. "One reason, I wanted to maintain a certain lifestyle, and I wanted to give to my kids what I was given, e.g., vacations, goin' to Grand Canyon or White Sands, New Mexico, or wherever the case may be. Also, I think you have to see yourself doing something in order to be successful, and I did not visualize me someplace doing accounting work. So I just decided to go to law school."

Today, Brian is an associate at a small law firm that specializes in civil litigation. He had offers from other, larger, more widely known firms, but he thought he would be given more responsibility more quickly at the smaller firm. He also believed that at the smaller firm there would be less pressure to stay at the office for unnecessarily long hours just to be seen by the partners, which would leave him more time to spend with Penny and Avery. On both counts, his instincts were correct.

Penny, twenty-five, is also black. The third of the four children in her family, she was born in Jamaica and spent most of her childhood there. Her father worked for an advertising agency on the island and wrote jingles and copy for commercials. Her mother was a seamstress. She worked at home so that she could take care of Penny, her older sister, and her two brothers.

Although Penny grew up in middle-class circumstances in Jamaica, by the time she was a teenager, the economic conditions on the island had so deteriorated that her parents decided to move the family to Houston. They hoped to provide a better life for their children, and they did. Says Penny, "When we got here, we started over from scratch, so we were poor I guess. Then my parents built things up and things got really good."

Still, for Penny, who was thirteen when she moved to Houston, the transition from Jamaica was difficult. For instance, she says, in the States, "a lot of importance is put on what you have and what you wear, and I just didn't have to deal with that before." More important, "people had to adjust to me being Jamaican.

"Then, I totally spoke with a Jamaican accent and I looked different, so people asked me all the time, 'What are you?' I had never heard that question before. And I never had to think about it, 'cause in Jamaica, you're just Jamaican. People are different 'cause there're a lot of races there, but you're not defined as a race. There aren't racial statistics like here in the United States.

"That's all there is in America, to me, racial statistics. Everything you fill out, you have to put your race on there. But I've gotten over that. I don't have a problem, you know, it doesn't bother me now. That's just the way it is."

In Houston, Penny attended public school. Brian and Penny met when they were students at the same high school.

"We were really good friends during high school for two years," says Penny. "We got closer and closer." During the summer after Penny's senior year in high school and Brian's freshman year in college, Brian was home for the summer. "We were just hangin' out as good friends," says Penny, "and we just couldn't get closer than to become intimate. That's when we fell in love and decided to have a relationship."

During Penny's freshman year of college, she twice visited Brian at Howard, and she "fell in love with the school. Besides education, there was just a great atmosphere that I couldn't get here. *And* he was here." So after her freshman year at a university in Houston, Penny transferred to Howard.

I ask Brian and Penny whether they lived together while they were at school. Penny says, "Sometimes I felt like we should because we could save on rent in college, 'cause we were both strugglin' with school bills. But I just believe that is something you should wait for, to live with your spouse or whatever."

Brian adds, "I think you can get a very good idea of how it is to be married to someone without living with that person. I think if you talk enough and spend enough time together, you're going to know that person."

In January 1990, eight months after Penny had graduated from Howard, they were married. Brian was in his second year of law school in Austin; Penny was working in Houston as a management trainee for a national hotel chain. Brian arranged his schedule so that all his classes were in the first part of the week, then he would make the two-and-a-half-hour drive to Houston to spend the second part of the week with Penny. In May 1991, Brian graduated from law school. The following February, Avery, or as Brian has dubbed him, "A-Man," was born.

Two months before Avery was born, Penny, who had left the hotel and had taken a job at a placement agency, quit working, and she does not plan to return in the foreseeable future. "I've known for some time now that I wanted to be at home with young Avery," she says. "I enjoy it and I think it's very important. If we were unable financially, I wouldn't have a problem working. But since right now I don't have to, I wanna be at home with the baby."

I ask, "Are you happy right now, at this point in your lives?"

"Yes," says Penny, her face lit up by a warm smile. "We've been looking forward to this for a long time. You spend all these years together, and you talk about what you want later down the road. So we've been talking about this for a long time, you know, marrying, starting a family. So we're happy."

"I'm very happy," adds Brian. "I am a firm believer in deferred gratification, and this is extremely gratifying. It was worth waiting for. I mean, I think when we first started dating, we were telling a friend of ours, 'Yeah, we're gonna get married one day.' At the time we probably sounded stupid. I can see that. But there was no doubt in my mind that we weren't. I never thought about us not being together."

"Had it all planned," says Penny. She and Brian laugh.

"We planned out a lot of this," says Brian, who is completely serious even though he is still laughing at Penny's mock certitude. "I mean, the birth of our baby was about on plan. Graduation and getting into the house was about on schedule. I guess this sounds pretty boring to some people, to tell you the truth, but it's quite okay for us."

He continues: "I'm not a planner on a daily basis. I'm not very organized. But I've always thought about my future. I mean, I've always had a thing, 'What do you wanna do five years from now?', simply because I was always asked that by my father when I was growin' up. That has always been a pattern of mine, to at least be aware of tomorrow and next week, and preparing for that. So when I say I'm gonna do X-Y-Z, you can bank on it pretty much. I'm gonna do it, if for no other reason than because I said it. I've no choice but to do it."

Many people would look at Brian and Penny—the devoted husband and father with a promising career, the loving wife and mother

who stays home to take care of their new baby and their home—
and say, "That's the American Dream." So it is ironic that neither of
them sees their life as the fulfillment of some uniquely American
dream.

Penny says, "I think the American Dream is—well, it's not just
an American dream, it doesn't just belong to America. It's just whatever someone wants to do, whatever they dream of, I think is the ultimate American Dream. It's probably labeled the American Dream
because you're supposed to be able to do what you want here and
achieve what you want here, have a dream, have opportunities for
that. So that's probably why there's an *American* Dream. But it's not
a picket fence and a boy and a girl and a dog or anything—to me—
anything specific like that. It's to achieve whatever you want."

I turn to Brian, who tells me, "Never really thought about it.
Hm, the American Dream." He reflects for a moment, then says, "I
guess the American Dream is aspiring to be successful, but I can't sit
here and delineate what it is to be successful and the trappings of
success.

"A lot of times, I believe the American Dream, whatever it is, is
imposed on people to make them feel"—he pauses again to collect
his thoughts—"less than average or less than normal. So in that
sense I agree with Penny. If people have certain dreams that fit for
them, that work for them, then that is the American Dream. Which
is what I think it should be. The American Dream is, theoretically, to
take people from all over the world, you have the freedom to think
and do what you want. And if that were the dream, that's fine. The
problem is, they've already defined what the Dream is, and they're
tryin' t'impose that on everyone."

"Who is 'they'?" I ask.

"I don't know. I don't know who *'they'* is, really. But the American Dream certainly has been defined. I think any child who
watches TV can see a certain definition of what the American Dream
is. So I don't like that aspect of it.

"The beauty of this country *could* be realized if they said, 'You
have the power to dream whatever you want to dream.' That's the
beauty of America. That's not, I don't think, realistic. That's not how
it is. You don't have the power to dream anything you want to
dream because your dreams are always compared to what the right
dream is supposed to be." Later, Brian tells me, "I wish people
would stop trying to impose on other people their lifestyles with

things they think are proper. I get tired of people berating or just lambasting other people for not being like they are. And I get pretty passionate about that.

"It's funny," he says, "our thinking appears disingenuous because we live what most folks would consider typical, normal lives. This is how you're supposed to live—grow up, fall in love, go to college, get married, have a kid. This works for us and I love it, but I would never tell someone that this is the only way or the right way or the best way. It's just our way.

"I agree with Penny, that the American Dream is what individuals want and dream for themselves, and having the right to do that in America."

So what do Brian and Penny dream for themselves and their family?

"That's real easy," says Penny. "Just have a long life together, and I don't care really a whole lot what goes along with it. I never dreamed or had wishes exactly, so maybe I'm not a planner like Brian is, after all. Really, just to be together as a family, and what goes along with it as far as job and all that, doesn't matter. I don't think about it much."

Brian's dream is less modest than Penny's. He declares, "There will always be a certain segment of the American population that does well. Always. My objective is to try to get in that segment." Brian laughs, but he isn't joking.

He continues: "I would like to be a very well-respected attorney. I would like to make enough money to live in the kind of house that I want. I would like to be able to take my kids on a vacation to Grand Canyon or Disney World or Petrified Forest, or just to expose them to things that a lot of kids aren't exposed to. I would like to raise my kids to be strong and confident people, and if they are confident and strong, then I feel that's a success. I would like to be a good husband, good friend. I measure success in small steps."

A few minutes later, he says, "I would do anything to anyone to save and quote 'protect' my family. Anything."

Chuckling, Penny says, "He sleeps with a baseball bat. It's under the bed."

"Louisville Slugger," says Brian, who isn't laughing, "a little small one, but big enough." He continues: "I'm paranoid. I feel I'm always on guard."

"He's a twenty-four-hour protector," says Penny.

"Why do you think that is?" I ask.

Brian answers, "Well, I don't know. I don't have any real reason."

Penny corrects her husband: "Your dad raised you that way. He's on guard."

Brian echoes Penny: "I'm on guard. I live my life, generally, always aware of my surroundings."

Penny: "You'd think he grew up in a bad neighborhood, or where the mob is gonna come in and start shooting or somethin' like that."

Brian: "But I didn't, nice little neighborhood not far from here. I like being aware of what's around me, being ready for anything. Pretty weird, I guess. Maybe that's the protector in me."

When I ask Brian what he thinks about the national situation, he says, "This country really is pretty polarized, and I don't see any end to it in my lifetime."

He explains: "As long as I can walk into a store and know that if I'm on an aisle by myself, that a security guard will quickly approach the aisle to make sure I'm not stealing anything, or if I'm jogging and someone crosses the street 'cause I'm running in their direction, to me, nothing's really changed. Because here I am, I have a law degree, make a pretty good living, and when I'm not in a suit—and even when I'm in a suit, sometimes—when I'm not in a suit, people only see one thing—six-four, two-ten, black man—and certain images pop in their mind. People take external differences—race is the most obvious one, even class to a certain extent, sexual orientation, what have you—and they categorize you and they define you.

"We're so separate. I mean, we don't really try to find the common ground that we do have, whether it's similar school, similar profession, similar religion, whatever the case may be. We find ways to separate ourselves. We harp on the separation and we somehow cloak ourselves in the quality that makes us different—which is fine, but it also polarizes us. So people don't see Brian Carmichael, someone who played baseball, played football, went to college with them, 'Hey, what's up?' They see a six-four black man. And as long as we continue to find ways to separate ourselves, I don't see this country getting any better.

"But I don't concern myself with the racism in this world. I really don't. I think it's been here, it is going to be here, and it will not stop what I do or what my son does. Just part of life."

Penny adds, "We don't let it play a big role in our lives, like complain about it, think about it, define things by it. Like a lot of people may say, 'Well, this didn't happen because I'm black.' It may be true, but we don't think about it. And we're not big on protesting, so you'll probably never see us. We just let it go by, say 'What the heck.' "

However, although Penny uses the collective "we," in this instance Brian does not agree with her. As he later says, "I have no problems with you saying whatever the heck you wanna say, but don't direct it towards me or my family."

"What would your reaction be?" I ask.

"Oh, we'd fight," he says. Both of them laugh, but, again, Brian is not kidding.

I reply half jokingly, "A somewhat unlawyerly response."

"Oh, it is unlawyerly," he admits as his laughter subsides. "I mean, there's a time to talk, there's a time to fight, and I think you have to know the difference. I am not gonna sit back and rationalize with you and get into a discussion. That's crap."

"I don't think that changes those people," says Penny, looking at her husband.

Brian agrees, "It doesn't. No matter what I'd say to somebody, they'd think a certain way. That's how they're gonna think. So I'm just letting them know from the beginning, 'You can say what you want to say, just accept the consequences.' And that's how it should be, accept responsibility for your action."

Although Brian and Penny do not allow racism to prevent them from accomplishing their goals and although they may not carry picket signs in the trunks of their Honda sedans, racism certainly affects them emotionally, especially the subtly racist implications of comments from people who describe them as "different."

"During the course of our lives," she says, "people have said to us, 'Well, you're different,' and they don't even wanna think of us as black anymore."

"That bothers me," says Brian. "I can just look on my wedding picture, fourteen people or so, I can look on there and I can know what everyone is doing. All graduated from college, a Harvard M.B.A., this, that, boom, boom, boom. They're positive people. They don't fit any kind of stereotype. But what's so unfair is that each one of those people up there in the picture will still be considered 'different.' "

When people tell Brian that he is "different," he responds by saying, "Listen, I can introduce you to ten of my friends and we're all the same way. So I'm not 'different.' I'm not one in a million. I mean, I'm different because of who I am, but not from any other reason. There are a lot of black people who are productive and positive, and, just like there are a lot of everybody else, a lot of bad people and a lot of good people. I guess it frustrates me, but I'm not a crybaby. I don't cry about it."

Penny says she and Brian would like to change people's images of blacks by being living counterexamples to the stereotypes, but she is not optimistic that bigotry will ever vanish. "Think it could be better or worse," she says, "but I don't think it will ever go away, just for the simple fact that there're different people in this world, different religions. I mean, ever since Adam was born, and that was a long time ago, people were prejudiced about this group over here, what color they were and what they practiced, you know. Hagar couldn't marry Abraham because she wasn't from his tribe or whatever. So I don't think it will *ever* go away."

Brian says, "America would be really a great country if we lived up to what we say and what we've written down in the Constitution or what have you. But between what we want to be, what we think we are, and what we really are, there's a huge gap. There is too much intolerance, whether it's religious intolerance, class intolerance.

"I think America stands for many different things to many different people. I would not want to live any other place besides America. I think there's a lot of opportunity here. There's also a lot of pain and oppression here. I don't think you can really say what America stands for. What it says it stands for is great—freedom, opportunity. That's just not true for everybody."

Toward the end of our discussion, Brian wonders whether he has given me a misleading impression of his own thinking. "Don't wanna give the idea that racism's the only thing that's wrong with this country," he says. "This country has problems that are as bad if not worse than race. There are too many people in this world who do not know how to dream.

"One thing respected leaders could do, somehow instill in kids the power of their dreams. I don't know how that's done, but somehow I think it was done in the past. I just don't understand how my grandfather, who could not go where I can go, could not do what I can do, could not eat where I can eat, could not do anything I can do, somehow instilled in his kids the power to dream of a better day for themselves and for their friends. Now, I can do anything I want to do, legally, anything I want to do, go where I want, be anything I want to be. But we are somehow crippled mentally, and I don't know why. I see this most in black boys, black little girls. It may apply to all groups, and I'm just not as aware of it. But I just don't understand. I just wish we could figure out—'we' meaning the country—could figure out a way to somehow inject in our children the power of dream and how important that is, to dream."

SAME CITY, DIFFERENT WORLDS I

NEW YORK CITY

ADAM

If I had enough money to need the services of one of Wall Street's most respected financial institutions, I would want Adam to be my banker. Though he is only twenty-five, and despite his somewhat boyish looks, he has the mature, sober bearing of someone fifteen years older. He dresses like a banker, too. Nothing ostentatious, everything well within the bounds of traditional good taste: midnight-blue chalk-stripe suit; heavily starched broadcloth shirt with a spread collar; silk tie, knotted in a half Windsor, with a subtle pattern of green arabesques against a slate-blue background. The only thing that does not look Savile Row is his Mickey Mouse wristwatch.

Adam's childhood was a model of stability, what Wally Cleaver's life might have been like if he had been an only child. Born and raised in Oklahoma City, the only son of a fifty-one-year-old oral surgeon and a forty-year-old homemaker and community volunteer, Adam attended the same private Episcopal school from age three until he graduated from high school fifteen years later. One of the only things about his childhood that Adam classifies as atypical is that he was raised as a relatively observant Conservative Jew in a state that is often described as the buckle of the Bible Belt.

Because Adam's parents had their son so late in their lives, they "were always a little bit behind the eight ball in trying to be a family." But, Adam tells me, "my dad was a great sport. He was the co-coach of the little league team. We did a lot of things together, fishing and repairing furniture around the house. He really made a super effort to be with me while I was growing up." Adam's father died when Adam was just seventeen. Adam still thinks of his father as one of his greatest role models.

As a teenager Adam loved science, so in his first two years at the University of North Carolina he majored in chemistry. He even spent one summer working with an analytical chemist in the Soviet Union. But one thing convinced him that he would not make his living as a scientist: money—or, rather, the lack of it. "I admire scientists more than anybody else," he says. "I think they are what makes America great and what drives the world. But unfortunately they're not well paid. They're not terribly well respected. They have to struggle for money. It's a fight on top of everything that they're fighting for in their professional life, which is trying to do good research. And as hard as *that* is, they've got to scrounge for everything." Adam decided "there has got to be more to life, and that 'more to life' is respect and wealth." So after he had completed most of the requirements for a chemistry degree, he began studying economics.

When he switched his focus from science to business, he discovered how much he enjoyed the world of banking and finance. During his sophomore year, one of his friends observed that commercial banks in North Carolina were charging university students too much money for too little service. So Adam, along with his friend and a group of eight other UNC students, founded a student credit union on campus, the first student-run credit union in the nation ever to become state-chartered and federally insured. Although the group had university officials and credit union professionals as advisers, all of its full-time operators were students. Adam was the founding vice chairman and vice president, and later became chairman and president. Before he left Chapel Hill, the credit union had $400,000-plus in deposits from over 300 members and employed sixty people. (Today, the credit union is even larger. Adam estimates that it now serves between 500 and 600 members.)

After graduating Phi Beta Kappa with degrees in economics and chemistry, Adam moved to New York to work for a prestigious Wall Street financial firm. He started as a generalist, running computer simulations and writing memoranda. Then, after two years of crunching figures and producing reports, he moved to the firm's private placement group. Adam explains that he and his colleagues help negotiate complex financial agreements between sophisticated borrowers and investors. In contrast with his previous job, Adam's current work involves less number-crunching and more negotiating, less math and more marketing, less calculating and more communicating. And he loves it.

Adam explains why he became a banker: "It's a very lucrative field. It pays very well. I think it's a very, very good learning experience and very exciting, which are equally important. And now I can walk into any industry in America and see what the 'drivers' are—what makes it work, what makes it a good industry, what makes it a bad industry—and get to see everything about business and what makes it exciting.

"One other very important reason is the individuals involved in this business. Being a bank, we generally deal with the CFO [chief financial officer] or the treasurer or the president or the chairman of a corporation. I mean, we're going with the top. These are very successful people, and it's interesting to see if these are good people, if they're bad people, if they're smart, if they're stupid. You kind of measure yourself up and you say, 'Can I do what he's doing?' Sometimes yes and sometimes no. It's interesting to see why people get where they are, how much they know, and what they're doing. See, these people in American society occupy a very special place. We place CEOs and chairmen on a pedestal, and it's interesting to see if that is justified or not. I find that very, very fascinating."

Adam believes that, for most Americans, the American Dream consists of "a nice house, a VCR, low fixed mortgage rates, three square meals a day, and a new car every now and then." But Adam wants more, far more—and most of what he wants is green. He says, "The premium that a smart person can command in terms of monetary wealth is max. If you're a smart person, you can write your own ticket—and the smarter you are, the more zeros you can put on your paycheck. It's absolutely incredible. It really doesn't matter what your background is like. I've seen people from all walks of life and any race, creed, color, anything, become fabulous bankers because they are fundamentally smart people. In this country you can magnify your intelligence, your creativity, to amass tremendous wealth.

"My American Dream—and I'm not kidding—is to be fabulously wealthy in dollar terms. I mean, I can be happy in a lot of things, but one of the things that would make me very, very happy is a lot of money. And I think that you *can* buy happiness. Just about the only thing you can't buy is good kneecaps because medical science hasn't quite caught up to that level yet. That's kind of a metaphor for health. But I really think that with everything else, you can achieve it through money. I don't mean that money automatically grants you happiness. But if you're a good person and you marry the right person and can get along with your spouse and things like that, money makes things easier. You can't be stupid and have a lot of money and be happy. But if you're smart and you have a lot of money, you can be very, very happy. That's what I'd like to achieve.

"I'd like to have a huge house and a yacht, play the stock market and just hang out. And I think that I'm on the way, that I'm on the path. I'm seeing things and doing things that hopefully will get me there someday. I don't think there's anything that makes me special. You have to be a smart person and a good team player—anybody can be that."

Adam notices that I circle the word "money" several times in my notebook. So I ask him what he thinks of the "greed is good" ethic that seemed to dominate the eighties.

"I don't think that greed is bad," he says. "Risk is bad, and the eighties were really a misvaluation of what risk was. Companies were basically buying very risky assets and they just paid the wrong price for them. It turns out those companies are not able to pay off their debt. I don't think the process was bad. They were just working from the wrong framework. They were trying to solve modern physics problems using Newtonian physics concepts. They were using the wrong paradigms. I don't think greed itself is bad. The maximization of value is ultimately what makes your society great.

"And there's a difference between greed and wanting to be terribly wealthy. The difference is the concept of justice. Greed implies that you're willing to have wealth at any cost and that you are willing to step over anybody to get there. That's clearly bad. There's never gonna be anything that's gonna make that right. I don't think it's a relative thing. I don't think it's a societal thing. It's plainly wrong. But the desire for money in a just way, and doing it through being creative and unlocking tremendous value, is not bad. If you're the one that comes up with the answer to society's problems, you oughta be rewarded. That's how you define progress in our society. So if I could come up with some sort of a pill that would end sickness, I'd sell it, and I'd sell it for a high price because there's a high value there. I don't think that's greed. I think that's progress.

"I would like to be *fantastically* wealthy, ultimately by creating as much value for society as I can. That sounds kind of trite, and one could dismiss that very simply by saying, 'Well, he wants to make a lot of money.' But that's not necessarily true. I would like to be well paid for creating tremendous value. I don't want anything that I don't deserve, but I want to create so much value that I'm just wealthy beyond all belief. That's not a bad thing. People have done it before. Look at somebody like Bill Gates of Microsoft fame. That guy single-handedly increased American productivity by multiples, and he's a very wealthy man. He's one of the wealthiest in America. There's somebody who created a lot of value and is paid very well."

Adam would like to get married someday, though he views marriage as a merger rather than the binding of two souls until death they do part. For Adam, marriage means "we can both do better in life through being together. If that means I'm going to stay home and take care of the kids, that's fine. I don't think that that's bad. I don't have any visions that I wouldn't want to stay home and scrub toilets or do whatever. I love cooking. I'd love to cook three meals a day for my wife. But she better have a real kick-ass job. Together, as a team, somehow we're gonna optimize. I just want to be on a winning team. I really want to be on a winning team. She's gonna have to be smart. She's gonna have to deal with a lot of issues and pull her weight. Housework's not the right answer. A hundred percent career is not the right answer. But the same holds for me as well." (When I ask Adam why he never mentioned the word "love," he says that was a given.)

I ask him to tell me his views about the national situation, and dire prognoses rush through his lips like water bursting through a crack in Hoover Dam. "America," he says, "is in deep, deep, deep trouble," and is "clearly headed on its way down." And the "root of the downfall," according to Adam, is the erosion of the concept of personal responsibility.

"Take something like preventable diseases. People know what causes these things. People just are not taking the personal initiative or responsibility to protect themselves against certain diseases, like AIDS. Sure, it's a terrible thing, but I don't think any amount of federal spending can cure AIDS at this point in time. It's a scientific barrier that's only gonna take time. Clearly, from a financial standpoint there's a lot of motivation there to solve the problem. I don't think money is the question. It's the fact that science is just not advanced to the point where we understand the disease and understand the virus enough to solve it. I'd spend all the money in the world to solve it, but it's not gonna help at this point. It's just a matter of time. People need to take care of themselves before they overwhelm all the resources of our society for having to pay for that."

Adam believes the decline of the ethic of personal responsibility is at least partly responsible for the crime that seems to be ravaging American society. As he sees it, if "a person messes up, you oughta punish them severely. [Then] let them out, that's fine. They mess up again, all right, you maybe don't punish them so much. But the third-time losers you throw away. I have no belief whatsoever that these people are recyclable, that you can reform them and let them back out into society. It just makes me sick every time I see juveniles have their slate wiped clean at the age of eighteen, or the age of sixteen, only to go out and kill and kill again, or when adults can go out and kill and kill again. That's an example of where personal responsibility has gone awry. We have to say, 'These people are responsible for their actions. Get rid of them.' The same is true of drug users. I'm willing to go the extra mile to get them the help they need, but until they take the personal responsibility to get cleaned up and hold a job and to make their lives work better, I'd say throw 'em away."

Adam advocates what I call the baseball theory of criminal justice—three strikes and you're out. He explains: "First of all you give them the opportunity not to mess up. Then you give them the opportunity to change. Then after that you say, 'You're through.' Don't give them more and more and more chances and spend resources on endless appeals.

"We coddle criminals. In other countries they shoot 'em. Criminals go in and out of the revolving door of justice in America. In South America they take 'em out behind the barn and shoot 'em. There's value in that. They've substituted the cost of a bullet for the cost of an entire criminal justice system, which ultimately the tax-payers pay for. That's value."

PAUL

It is 4:15 in the afternoon as I cross Mercer Street to enter New York City's Hebrew Union College. More than forty dirty, ragged men are already standing in line for the free supper to be served at 6:00. The men waiting in the line press their bodies close to the wall, hunch their shoulders, rub their hands together or cup them against their mouths—anything to preserve heat on this bitterly cold and windy December day in the West Village. Coordinated by the college's rabbinical students, this soup kitchen has been offering free dinners to 180 people every Monday evening for the past four years. Men begin congregating along the west side of the building as early as 4:00 because no one wants to be one hundred eighty-first in line.

Paul, twenty-three, eats at the soup kitchen every week. He admits that he is an alcoholic and that he drinks daily—not enough to get drunk, he explains, just enough to get high. He smokes pot, too, but less than he used to because it shows up in the urine samples he must give to his probation officer and to his court-appointed drug counselor. Paul also snorts coke or smokes crack three or four times a week.

Paul appears unnaturally bulky because he wears several layers of Army fatigues under an olive-drab jacket. He has fair skin; his head is covered with a thick mass of uncombed brown hair. His face and clothes look fairly clean, which distinguishes him from many of the others in the room.

Paul is a squatter in an apartment on Avenue B, a few blocks north of Tompkins Square Park. Because of all the broken windows, "everybody thinks it's an abandoned building, but it's not." Paul understands that, under the law, he is trespassing. But he believes he has a legitimate claim to remain in the building because his father once owned it. Of course, that was before the bank foreclosed on the property in 1989. That was also before Paul's father died and "everything crashed."

Paul was raised in a relatively affluent neighborhood near

Chappaqua, New York, forty miles northeast of Manhattan, along the banks of the Hudson River. He describes the folks there as "well-to-do and pompous kind of people."

As a child Paul had what he calls "distractions and behavioral problems" that prevented him from keeping up with the other kids in class, who were "bratty" and "snotty" toward their slower class-mate. Paul's parents were too preoccupied with their own lives to help Paul. He says, "Their concern revolved around me, but not their time." Paul is oblivious to the irony of his words.

Feeling isolated in school and neglected at home, Paul retreated into an imaginary world. "I just kicked back like a mule. I just said 'Fuck you! I wanna play with dinosaurs and I wanna be left alone.' "

For fourth grade Paul's parents sent him to a school that spe-cialized in helping students with learning disabilities and behavioral disorders. During his two years there, no one ever explained to him the precise nature of his problems. Paul believes that the school's administrators just wanted to get him "plugged into the system with-out offending my parents." The message Paul kept getting was, "The kid's all right. But," he says, "the kid wasn't all right."

Sixth grade was a watershed year in Paul's life. His parents placed him back in the Chappaqua public schools and hoped he would fit in. He didn't. The other kids knew each other better be-cause they had been together for the two years when Paul was away; consequently, Paul felt like a social outcast. And despite the intensive remedial education he had received at the special school, he still could not keep up with his classmates. If anything, he fell further behind. He thought, " 'What the hell am I doing back here? I'm being wracked around from one school system that's for people that got difficulties to a school system that's completely advanced.' That's a fuckin' total trip between two different worlds." And while he was still in sixth grade, his mother died—of alcoholism, he says.

Under the best circumstances, Paul is "a fragile person, strong as a wet cardboard box," and he was only twelve when his mother died. Her death sent Paul into an tailspin of excruciating despon-dency. He felt like a "person made of papier-mâché" who had been "gutted by a knife." His father took the death even harder. For a while he cried every night, and he needed many years to get over his wife's death.

Shattered by grief, Paul's father could no longer take care of his son. "He had to turn me over to someone who would look after me," says Paul, "and that would be the private school system."

Over the next six years, Paul bounced into and out of five different boarding schools, including one in Ireland. Drugs were part of boarding school culture, and Paul, only fourteen, feeling lonely and isolated, could not resist the pressure to try them, anything to alleviate his misery. "I wanted to alter the state of my mind," he says.

"Why?"

He responds, "Why do people have sex drives?"

Drugs—alcohol, pot, hash, LSD, speed—were directly or indirectly responsible for Paul's being forced to leave most of the schools he attended. One school expelled him because he repeatedly showed up in class stoned. Another school dismissed Paul after he came to class drunk and got in a fight with the math teacher. He was expelled from a military academy within four days because he shared a joint with one of the student advisers, who then turned him in to the headmaster. And even at the two schools Paul seems to have left of his own choice, he constantly took drugs to render himself temporarily oblivious to his pain.

Paul spent his last semester of high school at a private school in a Jewish temple on the Upper East Side of Manhattan. This school specializes in helping kids with learning disabilities—or, as Paul puts it, "kids who were bright but unable to function in the mainstream school system." While he was in school in Manhattan, he was seeing a psychiatrist to help him get over his depression. The doctor prescribed several antidepressants—Vivactil, BuSpar, haloperidol—that clouded Paul's brain and prevented him from concentrating on his classwork. Paul likens their effect to a wrecking ball swinging on a crane and tells me, "They fuck your brain up just as badly—even worse—than the drugs that you buy on the street." He said to himself, "You gotta learn how to survive without drugs." So he gave up the prescription medication—though not the recreational kind—and graduated in June 1987. He is very proud of his diploma.

Paul cannot explain exactly what he did for the next year and a half, though he spent some time in France and Germany. Meanwhile, his father was spending a lot of time in Ireland on business, and sometime between Christmas and New Year's Eve, 1989, Paul's father died there when an aneurysm in his brain burst.

Becoming angry, Paul tells me, "I don't know what the hell really happened. He died in another country. He died of what? I got a phone call. I got a letter saying he died in Ireland." Paul says "anxiety is what killed him."

Paul remembers his father as "very flexible, God bless him. He gave me the benefit of the doubt all the time, gave me all the slack I needed. If my father was a fisherman, he would've lost his reel and his rod. He would've let the fish take everything. My dad was a wonderful guy. He was so generous and bountiful. This guy, if he wouldn't give me what he had, he would give fuckin' the benefit of the doubt until the bottom dropped out.

"I had difficulties and emotional problems that he couldn't understand. I said, 'Dad, you gotta help me.' 'I can't do anything for you, son. The only thing I can do is the obvious. I can only change the circumstances. I cannot change your mind, and I cannot alter your depression. You have to do it yourself.' He tried to encourage me through his words of wisdom and his inspiration. I was very defiant, and I was very resentful, and I paid the price for it. And then when he died, it all hit me like a giant avalanche."

Paul could not cope with his father's seemingly mysterious death. "It was almost like a dream, like something out of *Twilight Zone*. I imagine that he might've been dead in one realm. In the other realm he was just faking that he was dead. He just wanted to get away from his kids and go off and marry some young woman and start a family and live his own life."

When his father died, Paul felt as if he had been deserted. He again turned to alcohol and drugs to dull the pain, taking speed, smoking marijuana, drinking heavily every night. But these only intensified his agony. "I was drinking enough for me to bring out closet things that were in me, in my past, that came to the surface—about hardship, and resentment that I harbor towards my father when I was in teenage years, being sent to my boarding school, felt like he was seeing me off and leaving me there with a bunch of asshole kids who I didn't like."

Paul sold pot to make money. He also used false names to order books and compact discs through the mail, which he then sold on the street. In 1990 he was arrested and convicted of mail fraud. He received five years' probation, which he thinks will be reduced to two and a half.

He currently receives public assistance—$168 cash every two weeks and $85 a month in food stamps—to help him get by. He abandoned the mail fraud after his arrest. Instead, he sells books that he "finds" in "secret places" that he knows of.

It is easy to forget that people like Paul have dreams, too. Paul's is to become a language teacher. He claims to speak Danish, Norwegian, Swedish, Finnish, Japanese, Chinese, Spanish, German, Italian, and "some old languages," including Old Norse, Icelandic, and Gaelic. I did not verify Paul's claim, but I did overhear him carrying on a brief conversation in Spanish with a janitor in the lobby of Hebrew Union College.

"What keeps you from becoming a language teacher?" I ask.

"My self-esteem problem," he says. "I'm really lacking self-esteem. I got a lot of potholes, a lot of potholes and pits in my self-esteem. There's a lot of holes, empty spaces.

"I'm a madman. I'm a crazy man. To me, life without craziness, a sane and quiet life, is not a life. But then the other side, I have to say a sane life is a better life than a mad life and a stressed life, and not havin' what you want, bein' pissed off at the world, feelin' like there's always an evil harpy, a bitchlike bird on your back with its venomous claws and its beak picking at your earlobes all the time." He imitates the harpy's screech and curls his hands into imaginary talons, picking at the air. "And that black cloud of depression that also hangs over you."

Paul explains that his heart often sinks into a "great pit," and his mind is like a "bright light" that says to him, "C'mon, bring your heart out of that pit. Bring yourself out of that pit. Bring yourself out of that fuckin' depression, and let's work together." But Paul tells me his constant depression, and the stress of always having to be out of his building and of never knowing when he might be discovered and evicted, prevent him from functioning as he should.

Paul says, "I have high ambitions to have an idealistic way of life, really wanting to make something out of my life. But I have to swallow my pride. Go around trash cans, pick out cans, having to go into nice neighborhoods, beautiful women walkin' by, pickin' out cans, lookin' for books, and embarrassing myself, swallowing my pride. I think that I'm in total disarray, jostled about, unfettered, just goin' from one way of lowlife living to another because I have all that past guilt and that depression. But what the hell's gonna help me if I don't get myself focused on just taking a bite out of the apple, instead of thinkin', 'Aw, it's poisonous. It's gonna kill me.' That's bullshit. That's just fear.

"I'm scared. But I'm gonna hafta try it anyway. I wanna remain in the trench. I know that the guy's not gonna shoot on the other side 'cause his bullets have all run out. But I don't wanna fuckin' get outta the trench 'cause I'm scared as fuckin' hell. I don't know what I'm gonna do."

If pain and fear are the warp and woof of Paul's existence, hate is the selvage that prevents it from unraveling. During our conversation the following week, he says, "I'm in an environment where I have to hate other people. I hate niggers. I hate spics. I'm a white supremacist. David Duke's my president. Blacks are lowly. They're mentally inferior. Spanish people are a bit different. They're of European descent."

Paul, who knows I am Jewish from a remark I made earlier, tells me that he also hates Jews. "I don't like fuckin' Jews," he says. "I grew up in a neighborhood with Jews. They treated me miskindly. The main thing is honesty, and the Jews haven't been honest with me. New York is the epitome of Jewish dishonesty. You don't have to read Hitler's diaries to know that." Paul tells me that one of his father's friends, who was Jewish, promised to loan Paul some money after Paul's father died, but he did not come through. Paul later qualifies his remarks by adding: "The only Jews I hate are the Orthodox and the ones who wear the yarmulkes. If you're of Jewish descent, why should I hate you. You didn't have a choice.

"I hate everybody," he says.

After Paul and I part, I walk north on Second Avenue, and I see Paul emptying the beer from a Budweiser can he has picked out of an open garbage bag sitting along the curb. As he shakes the last drops of liquid from the can in his left hand, he sticks his right hand out, palm up, and asks a passerby for change. The man politely refuses. Watching this, I move away from the curb, closer to the buildings on my left, because I do not want Paul to see me watching him. But Paul does glance my way, and our eyes meet for a moment. I do not know whether he recognizes me; neither of us acknowledges the other. Our worlds no longer overlap. We go our separate ways.

FREEDOM AND OPPORTUNITY

MARILYN

Marilyn, twenty-five, has lived her entire life in various small towns in central Oklahoma. For much of her life, Marilyn's father worked as a roughneck on oil rigs; today he works for a company that makes trusses for roofs. Her mother was a nurse's aide until a series of strokes rendered her unable to hold a steady job. Still, says Marilyn, her family lived a middle-class life, materially at least.

Psychologically, Marilyn's childhood was far less comfortable. Her father is an alcoholic and has "always been abusive" toward Marilyn's mother. Marilyn's father never hit her, but once Marilyn saw her father beat her mother so violently that he broke her arm. Speaking softly, Marilyn says, "Even when she had a stroke, the day she got out of the hospital, he like, pulled her hair. And I get really resentful towards that. I mean, I *love* my dad and I love my mom, but also I have like, not necessarily hatred towards them, but I have hatred for the way that maybe they brought *us* up."

When Marilyn was in sixth grade, her parents separated, then divorced. But, according to Marilyn, her mother believed she was not worthy of anything better than an abusive husband, and without his income she could not support Marilyn and her two older brothers. Six months after splitting up, Marilyn's parents remarried, though they had not reconciled.

"My mom used to not drink," says Marilyn, "but then she finally got to the point one day to where she was fed up, and she started drinking, too. She still drinks sometimes, but not as much as my dad."

At the beginning of eleventh grade, Marilyn, then seventeen, married Bob, a nineteen-year-old high school graduate whom she had known for six months. Marilyn dropped out of school later that semester.

She explains, "I hated school. And my parents had always fought. Always. I didn't like living with them. I hated it. I was ready to just get married. I thought, I was young, was ready to get married and move out of my parents' home.

"We did—I did—get married to move out of my mom and dad's, and we lived by ourselves for three months. But then we, like, moved back in with my parents. He was lazy and he wouldn't work.

"When we first got married, he had his own siding company. And he made good money. Then after that kind of went away, y'know, he didn't have very many contracts. It just gets real slow in the wintertime, but he didn't even try to find another job."

Marilyn and Bob moved in and out of her parents' house for the first three years of their marriage. Marilyn hated this. Indeed, she began to regret having married Bob soon after they said "I do"; they even discussed having their marriage annulled. But six months into their marriage, Marilyn learned that she was pregnant. "Then," she says, "I thought I would stay because I was pregnant. Then after that, because I had a baby, and then I had another baby" two years later.

During the third year of their marriage, while Marilyn supported the family, Bob learned how to drive an eighteen-wheeler. Because Bob finally had found steady work, she says, "it was getting much better."

Then one day, when her younger son was about one, Bob returned home from a trip to Dallas. "I thought I would let him sleep," says Marilyn, "and I was just gonna get some money and go to Wal-

Mart and get some diapers. Got in his wallet, and this phone number fell out. I picked it up, y'know—and obviously I would, anyone would have, I believe—but I looked, and it was this telephone number in Dallas. And I called it and this lady answered. Her name was Sally. And I asked her if she knew Bob Williams, and she said, 'Yes, he lives here on the weekends.' I said, 'He lives there on the weekends?' She said, 'Who is this?' And I said, 'This is his wife,' and she hung up the phone.

"He didn't get to sleep in anymore after that. No more." Marilyn laughs, then says, "That's the day I left, and I never went back." She was twenty-one.

Five months later, Marilyn and Bob's divorce was final. In retrospect, Marilyn says, "There were good days, but the majority of them were bad days. We didn't get along.

"I've thought about it a lot. I think it all really relates back to my parents, because my dad used to be real abusive to my mother. I always hated it—always. Never really said anything, I always kept it inside. And then when I got married, if Bob would, like, tell me to do something, I'd get really defensive, like, 'You're not gonna treat me like my dad treats my mom.' "

She adds: "He was real quiet. We couldn't relate to each other. We couldn't talk. And he drove a truck and he was always gone. He was a whole lot lazy, and I guess we just got married too young. He wasn't really *that* bad of a person. I could even look at him now—would have no feelings for him, but I don't hate him. Everything just accumulated and I'd had enough."

The same day that Marilyn left her husband, she went looking for a job. A friend of hers worked for a company that manufactures heat pumps in Oklahoma City, and Marilyn's friend told her that she made almost double the minimum wage. Marilyn, who had never earned more than minimum wage and had no job skills, thought, "I could support the boys and myself on that."

"So I went up to the temporary service, and they said, 'Marilyn, you wouldn't want to work out there. You get dirty. You just wouldn't like it.' I said, 'Yes I do, I want to work out there.' And they wouldn't put me to work out there, and they called my cousin to go to work out there.

"When I went up there, I'd been like a housewife, and I had on a dress and heels and pantyhose. They said, 'Marilyn, you wouldn't like factory work. It's just—not you.' But I was ready to do anything."

Marilyn was lucky. Her cousin had just received an offer from another employer. He called Marilyn and told her that he could not accept the job at the heat pump plant and that, if she still wanted the job, she should call the people at the temporary service. So she did. She told them, " 'You just called my cousin, but he's not gonna be able to report to work. But I'm ready.' And they said, 'Okay, Marilyn, you can try it.' " She reported to work later that day.

Of the 150 or so people who work on the assembly line at the heat pump plant, roughly 10 percent are women. Marilyn says, "When I first started, it felt real awkward. When we'd have breaks, the guys, they would talk about cars, and I was more into soap operas at the time. I could relate to that. And then they would talk about things, I had no idea what was going on. They talk about fishing. I'd never gone fishing before. And they'd talk about boats and mechanics and everything that guys would normally talk about. They even talked about women sometimes, when I'd be sitting there.

"A lot of people, when I first started, they used to ask me out. I'd just gotten out of my marriage. I didn't really want to have to deal with that. And I wouldn't go, like, tell anyone or anything, because I figured I could deal with it. Because sexual harassment, you get in trouble for breathing the wrong way anymore, and I didn't want to get anyone in trouble. But I did wish that they'd leave me alone so I could just work and get my job done and get my paycheck so I could go. Now I tell 'em I don't date much, and I definitely don't go out with people I work with. 'Cause that's how I make my living, and the two together just don't mix.

"I really didn't have a lot of trouble adjusting to the work though, because my dad, he's always taught us how to work hard, and we've always had to work hard. So he said, 'Gonna have to work no matter what.' 'Cause we came from just a middle-class family, you have to work, 'less you're born into richness and you can lay around, and be a bum or whatever."

Although Marilyn had little trouble adapting to the work, she struggled when she first became a single mother. She says, "Just having kids and working, it just seemed like a big responsibility. And I was havin' to do it all by myself. It was real hard, a real hard adjustment."

Marilyn finally chalked up too many absences. After five months, she was fired. She and her sons have lived with Marilyn's parents since Marilyn left her husband. Her mother takes care of the children, so that is not what caused Marilyn to miss work. Marilyn admits, "I used to go out partying, and I would be sick the next day. I'd have a hangover."

During those months of nightclubbing and drinking, Marilyn began to realize she was tumbling into the same trap of low self-esteem and liquor into which her mother had fallen. Then one morning, Marilyn's older son said to her, "Mom, are you sick again?"

"And then," she says, "I just remembered what I went through, and I thought, I don't want my kids to grow up like I did. I want my kids to have the *best possible life*. And in order to do that, I have to make it happen."

Four weeks after he fired her, Marilyn called her former boss. "I'm very sorry," she said. "I was just going through something. If you give me my job back, I'll be a lot better. I'll always be there." The boss rehired Marilyn, and she returned to the assembly line.

A year later Marilyn left the heat pump manufacturer for a job as a file clerk in the reservations office of a national airline. She was laid off six months later. Once again, Marilyn asked her former employer for her old job. Once again, he allowed her to come back.

Marilyn says, "That was the hardest thing, to go back for the third time. But I had to do it because I had to support my kids." I ask whether she felt as if she had to swallow her pride, and she quips, "A lot. I felt it in my feet." She says that "anyone that can go back to work at the same establishment—for the *third* time—can do anything."

When Marilyn started working on the assembly line, she earned $4.50 an hour. Today, she makes $7.30, 60 percent more than the current minimum wage of $4.25. And she loves her job.

"I like to work fast," she explains, "and production lines are fast. And I like to have goals to climb for, and if we have a quota, that's more or less like a goal, and you can reach that goal. And it makes me feel good when I do, because it makes me feel like I've achieved something.

"The management has always been good to me. Always. My boss, my plant manager, have always been real nice. And the people

I work with, my coworkers, they're real nice. I feel real involved with the people. It's more like a family out there."

But the people at the temporary agency were right about one thing. Marilyn shows me her fingernails. Her hands are clean, but the pink fingernail polish has been mostly chipped away, and there is a black semicircle of grime lodged beneath each nail. Marilyn tells me that she can never get all the dirt out from under her fingernails. She confesses, "I get dirty. I hate to get dirty." She chuckles.

Speaking quietly yet confidently, Marilyn says, "I don't always want to be just an assembly-line worker. I want to advance within the company and move up. Not only to prove to other people, but mainly prove to myself, that I can do it, y'know. That'll be the only thing that I haven't quit. I've quit school. I quit my marriage. I've always felt like a failure. But now I feel like I can—be someone. I'm going to be someone."

Marilyn always wanted to go back to school but never did. "I was scared," she says. "I was afraid I would be a failure and I couldn't do it." But she finally overcame her fear. For the past nine months, Marilyn has spent four hours a night, four nights a week, studying heating and air-conditioning maintenance at a technical school. She is the only woman in her program, and one of only two women in the entire school. But she's accustomed to this after nearly three years of working on the assembly line.

Marilyn will graduate in a month. After that, she plans to take some classes in accounting and business management at a community college. Her goals are to learn enough about heating and air-conditioning systems and business to become a salesperson for the heat pump manufacturer, and then to go to college to become a mechanical engineer. She anticipates that it will take at least another six years of part-time schooling to finish her degree. "But," she notes, "six years isn't anything compared to the rest of your life."

She is paying for her education with loans and grants. She predicts, "I'll be wealthy one of these days." She says, "I'd like to open my own business eventually. I have to make more money in order to do that, 'cause it takes money to make money, and I don't have any money." She does not know what kind of business she will establish, but she says it will be something that makes life easier for single parents.

During the week Marilyn is gone from the house nearly seventeen hours a day, but she does not mind. "I try not to look at unrealistic goals," she says. "Like with this trade school, I would think, 'Just make it today. Just do it today. Maybe you won't go back to-morrow, but just do it today.' And I thought that way every day. 'Cause people would ask, 'How do you work and go to school and have your kids and all this?' But that's how I do it, just one day at a time. I have long-term goals, but I set them aside and I put my short-term goals right here, to where I can reach them."

She adds: "Why I feel so strong and like I *can* go to school and be who I want to be, is 'cause I *don't* want to be like my mom. I don't want to live like my mother has lived. I *won't* live like my mother has lived. Everything I do, I feel as if I do for my kids. Be-cause I wish my parents had done that for me, so my life would've been better."

Although Marilyn now has a better relationship with her par-ents, living with them is the only aspect of her life she does not en-joy. She says, "I'm gone sixteen, seventeen hours per day. And it gives my kids a loving environment, 'cause my mom, she loves my kids to death, like, she thinks she loves 'em as much as she did us, and she's a sweet lady. But myself, personally, I'll be glad when I can be more independent and eventually get out of school, so the kids and I can be by ourselves."

Despite the long hours of hard work, and despite the fact that she must live with her parents, Marilyn says, "I'm happier now than I've ever been. Going to school makes me feel so good and so happy about myself. I feel like I'm achieving something."

And it is this opportunity to achieve that defines Marilyn's vi-sion of the American Dream. She believes it is "the freedom to be who we want. We can be whoever we want, and that's America's dream. That's why everyone wants to come to America, because of freedom.

"I used to take things for granted. I used to take people for granted, my job for granted, my kids. You never know what tomor-row holds. Never. But we have freedom, and we can be who we want, when we want, and how we want. It means a lot to me. I think I can be whoever I want to be now."

Marilyn believes her newly forged self-confidence flows from having transformed herself from the pantyhosed, high-heeled housewife who walked into the temporary agency four years ago to the working woman she is today. She says, "It's made me feel real good about myself because I've always felt kind of inferior when it came to a man. I felt like he knew so much more than myself, and they were always better. But now I feel equivalent, too. I don't think there's anything that was brought upon me that, if at all possible, I couldn't challenge it and then meet that expectation."

And whatever life Marilyn ultimately builds for herself and her sons, she will do it without a husband. "I don't plan on ever getting remarried," she says. "Once I get more financially independent, that will be a lot better. I like being single. I can go where I want, when I want, and I don't have to answer to anyone. And since I do have kids, then they won't have, like, a stepfather.

"I'm real close to my kids. I love my kids a lot, more than anyone in the world, and I don't think I would like anyone telling them what to do, except myself, in a parental aspect." Though Marilyn does worry about her sons growing up without a father figure, she says, "In today's world and time, I just couldn't trust many people with my kids. I have brothers. And we go to the lake with them, and they take my sons fishing. I feel as if they are missing out on a lot, but in the same way, I feel like I can make up for that. I play ball with them and we fish. We do everything.

"I want them to be brought up right, well respected and have manners. Kids are our tomorrow, and I want my kids to be a big part of everyone's tomorrow."

Just what kind of tomorrow her children will face is something that deeply concerns Marilyn. Like Suzanne, the woman from Mississippi, Marilyn believes we may be approaching the end of time foretold in Revelations. She says, "There's so many signs that are in the Bible that it says that're going to happen that are actually happening. That worries me a lot. Like, they say seasons will be to where you can't tell 'em apart—and you *definitely* can't, not anymore, at all.

"And I feel like people's lost their morals. Like AIDS, for instance. People aren't like they used to be because they don't have high morals for themselves as much. To go out to a club and if you meet someone, now people don't really think much about leaving the club with them. As of before, that would never be considered. And it worries me, because it says it in the Bible that things will get this way, and they have. And it says there will be a disease that was like the plague that will come out, and it will be nationwide. And AIDS, they have no idea how to stop it.

"I believe it all links back to morals. Because if everyone had high morals, then I don't believe this would have ever came about.

"It seems like everybody's out for themselves. They don't think about other people's considerations. They only think what it's goin' to take to get them there, and not who they're going to knock down along the way.

"I feel like our own people are cheating our own other people. Higher-up people—politicians, et cetera, et cetera—are basically ripping off the middle-class people. So the country as a whole, it does worry me because of our kids' futures. Because middle-class people just don't have any luck. We're always getting ripped off. And if the government keeps, say, messing with the middle-class people, then we don't have much of a today or a tomorrow.

"But what happens, happens. You can only control your own life. You can't control anything else. I'm tryin' to step up, step by step, in order to get to the top. I'll get there."

DIANA

The first evidence of Diana's political ambition is a twelve-foot-wide banner in front of her parents' home. It proclaims:

DIANA DAVILA

DEMOCRATIC STATE REPRESENTATIVE

DISTRICT 145

Inside the Davilas' home is more campaign paraphernalia. Hundreds of placards and lawn signs rest in neat rows and stacks against the walls of the dining room. A bouquet of half-deflated maroon and white balloons gather behind an armchair in the corner of the living room. To the right of the fireplace is a poster covered with articles about Diana—one of twelve Houston women to be selected as a Young Professional of the Year for 1991, and a member of what must be every civic club and community development board in the area. Hanging from the mantel is a blowup of the *Houston Chronicle* editorial endorsing Diana's candidacy. The article declares Diana (pronounced "Dee-ah'-nah") "the most capable candidate in the

Democratic primary for the District 145 state representative seat"—and she's only twenty-six.

Both of Diana's parents come from poor families in very small towns in northern Mexico. From the age of thirteen or fourteen, her father, an only child, had to work to help support himself and his parents. After he married Diana's mother and they had two children, Diana's father moved north to find greater economic opportunities for himself and his family. A year later he brought his wife, their son and daughter, and his parents to Houston. Diana's parents later had three more children—two sons, then another daughter, Diana.

The Davilas live in the East End, an area southeast of downtown Houston. For most of her life, Diana's family lived in a neighborhood known as the Second Ward, which Diana describes as a traditional barrio filled mostly with poor and working-class Hispanics. Diana's father was an upholsterer. Her mother stayed home to raise the five children and devoted what time she had left to community activities and to the church. (A small notice posted in the window of the front door of the Davilas' house warns would-be proselytizers: "This is a Catholic household. No other religious literature needed.") Diana's father is now semiretired. Her mother has become active at a local elementary school that was named for Diana's brother, Jaime, after he died in an accident four years ago. Today, Diana lives with her parents and her next older brother in a two-story home in Eastwood, a more affluent East End neighborhood, adjacent to the Second Ward.

Although neither of Diana's parents had more than an elementary school education—or, perhaps more accurately, precisely because of this—they continually stressed the importance of education to their children. "Education in my household was second to nothing," says Diana. "My dad has worked pretty much all of his life, and it is his opinion that if you start working without an education, then you have no choice. You will work your entire life, probably at something you may have grown to like, but certainly you didn't choose to do it. He says if you get an education, you have a choice as to what to do." Despite the financial strain of supporting a wife and five children on an upholsterer's wages, Diana's father would not allow his children to work during the school year. This enabled them to concentrate on their studies.

And study they did. All five went to college, and four obtained undergraduate degrees. Two of Diana's brothers became lawyers;

the third is a petroleum engineer. Like her brothers and sister, Diana attended a local public high school. She was the president of her class her junior and senior years. Then, after graduating second in her class, she became the second Davila to attend Harvard. (Jaime was the first.)

Unlike so many of her Harvard classmates, Diana did not remain in the Northeast. Instead, after she completed her degree in social anthropology, she returned to her parents' home in the East End, to her community. Except for her four years in Cambridge, she has lived in the East End her entire life. "I will never be removed from where I came," she says.

Upon returning to Houston, Diana worked as an English instructor at Houston Community College. For five months she taught English to Spanish-speaking immigrants who wished to become permanent residents under the federal amnesty legislation of 1986 and who were fulfilling the educational requirements of that act. Diana says teaching English to those people was one of the most gratifying experiences of her life; she felt as if she actually was making a difference in their lives. (An interesting parallel: during junior high and high school Diana helped teach rudimentary Spanish to local police officers, firefighters, and paramedics so that they could more effectively serve Houston's Hispanic community.)

Her teaching commitment completed, Diana applied for an internship with the Hispanic Congressional Caucus in Washington, D.C. She had asked her state representative, who is Hispanic, to write a letter of recommendation to the caucus. In tenth grade Diana had worked on his first campaign, and she had later volunteered in his campaign office, so she though he would help her get the job. Instead, the representative offered Diana a position on his staff, and she accepted his offer. Thus began her career in electoral politics.

"When I started working as an assistant to a state representative," she explains, "I had no intention of seeking political office. What made me now choose to seek political office has certainly been the incredible amount of influence one has as an elected representative of a community. Not an influence for myself, for my gain, but in terms of what you can do to make change. And not only legislative change, but change as a leader in the community." That's what Diana wants to be—a leader who advances the needs of her community.

Diana's chance to become one of her community's elected leaders arrived in the fall of 1991. Because of demographic changes reported by the 1990 census, the Texas legislature redrew the boundaries for the state's political districts. Diana's boss decided that instead of running for the Texas House of Representatives in a newly created district, he would run for a seat in the Texas Senate. This left newly created District 145 without an incumbent. Diana seized the opportunity. In December 1991 she took a leave of absence from her position on the representative's staff. The following month she began her first campaign for public office.

In the Democratic primary Diana was one of seven candidates—five Hispanics, two Anglos. Diana, the only woman on the ballot, finished first with 27 percent of the vote. In the runoff she defeated her opponent by a three-to-two margin. What makes her sizable margin of victory even more impressive, she says, is that her opponent in the runoff had raised approximately $100,000, while Diana's campaign had raised less than one-fourth as much.

Why did Diana win? Throughout the campaign she stressed her academic background and legislative experience, factors that may have swayed many voters. She also spent her days "doing the door-to-door" and "meeting the people." She says, "The work is tiring, but that is where you get your energy from, that the work is producing something. It's all a matter of seeing the results of your hard work."

Perhaps the critical difference was Diana's approach to campaigning and, more broadly, to leadership itself. She calls it "empowerment through participation." She says, "You've got to give people a sense of ownership in the process and make 'em believe that they will make a difference, that participation will make a difference. People have been involved in my campaign and they've seen the difference they can make. I will be successful when people start to realize that through my leadership their participation is making a difference.

"In becoming a state representative, or even in this process of being elected, I have touched a whole lot of lives, especially a whole lot of young girls' lives, who say, 'If Diana Davila can do it, I can do it.' I've gotten to a point where people are recognizing me. It's not that they recognize me that makes me happy. It's that they realize what I'm trying to do. It gives them a sense of hope that they can do it, especially in the minority community, where we have lacked role models. And certainly as a woman, as a Hispanic woman, there's a great deal of responsibility that I have in speaking to young women or in them seeing what I'm doing."

Diana does not consider herself a feminist, though she believes she represents "women's ideas and their needs, especially in areas where we haven't had representation." "Feminism" is not a relevant term for Diana. She's more concerned with "general needs," which she believes are genderless. She says, " 'Feminist' brings to mind radical movement, just for women. I think I can represent women's ideas and their needs and their concerns the right way, the way quote 'feminists' would want them to be represented. I think having a female perspective at the table is the important thing in my role, both in terms of personal and work.

"You might ask, what kind of opposition have I encountered in my field, especially one where very few women have been involved. In the legislature you certainly come up across some old-timers who don't recall women being in the capitol, who have some problems dealing with you. But certainly when they hear my educational background and see that I can do what any man can do in this role, things do change. I think there are very few people who are still resistant to having women involved in politics."

Diana believes that one of the gravest problems facing our nation is our children's future. "Children," she tells me, "are no longer dreaming."

She says, "As children in my family, we always dreamed that we would be successful. We knew that. We had the dream. But we knew that to become successful it was gonna take a lotta hard work. We saw that it had taken my parents a lotta hard work and we didn't think that it was gonna be easier for us. My family is the epitome of the American Dream because of my parents' immigration here and in what we've been able to achieve with their background. It didn't come true because they crossed the border and were in America. It became true through hard work and was based on education. And that education is the key to opening so many opportunities for today's children and their children."

Today, "you go into a classroom and you ask the simple question, 'What are you going to be when you grow up?', and very few kids will give you an answer. It didn't used to be that way. Children used to have ideas that they were going to be successful.

"I'm struck with children that I see who aren't like the kids that I was around or like me. There's almost a sense of hopelessness.

They're existing. They're doing what's required of them, but they're not looking ahead, and it's either because they don't have the support from teachers to make 'em do so, or it's not at the home. But they're just not seeing what it means to start preparing now so that their lives will be different. It's all a matter of choice, what you choose to do. And I talk to kids and I say, 'Sure, you need to be a kid. You need to have fun.' But at the same time, because things have become so competitive and because we have lost focus on education, somebody has to tell them that all is not fun. We can't just be concerned with wearing the right type of tennie shoes and watching TV all day.

"We're gonna need to make some drastic changes in our educational system. I always was amazed at those students—and it was definitely a majority at my high school—that came to school for eight hours and were only in a classroom. They had nothing to look forward to before school or after school. They weren't involved in anything else. High school meant coming to a classroom. Well, high school to me didn't mean that. I was learning just as much outside of a classroom, in my leadership roles and in my participation in other activities, as I was out of books from a class. So I think we're gonna need to expand the role of the school, open our doors a bit to the parents, to the community. I really think it's gotten to that point where we're gonna make some changes."

Geraldo Rivera once interviewed Diana for his television show. He was covering a story about the students of Austin High School, alma mater to all five Davila children. According to Diana, the students staged a walkout to protest the school's failure to provide them with the necessary books and materials even though they were already six weeks into the school year. Geraldo asked Diana why she is so successful when these other children are not.

Diana shied away from Geraldo's question. She does not think of herself or her family as exceptional. "I think more than anything we're *an example*. I sincerely believe there are many more Diana Davilas and Jaime Davilas out there, and the Davilas are an example of what can occur and does occur. We just happened to have a lot of little unique success stories—for instance, Jaime being the first from our community to go to Harvard—so we've gotten some attention. But I certainly believe there are more out there, and, as a leader, I want to be there to make sure that there are more Diana

Davilas and more Jaime Davilas. If proper tools are provided, the resources and the teachers, I think these kids will be successful."

Note: Diana won and now represents her community in the Texas House of Representatives.

WYNDHAM

Wyndham, twenty-eight, was born and raised in a neighborhood on the east side of Hollywood. His parents and three older sisters had come from China in 1963, a year before Wyndham was born. They had been members of the Chinese bourgeoisie, and they had made a somewhat belated escape from Mao's Cultural Revolution.

Although Wyndham is not certain about the details of his parents' flight from China—"kind of a touchy subject for them," he says—he understands the basic story. "Because they were capitalists," he explains, "because my dad owned his own company, he automatically was targeted as being not 'of the people.' So in order not to be too harshly persecuted, he gave his original company to the state and said, 'This is all yours. You guys can have it,' and was left with nothing.

"He escaped in '62, I believe. My mother had free access to and from China because of the trade company that her parents had owned, so she was able to kind of move freely throughout with my sisters. But my dad, because he really had no link except my mother to Hong Kong, he had no way of getting to Hong Kong legally through the Communist channels. He was smuggled in a boat from China to Hong Kong, where my mother was waiting for him."

Wyndham's parents, both of whom spoke English because they had studied at English-language universities in China and Hong Kong, brought the family to L.A., where his father's younger brother had been living for several years. Once in the States, Wyndham's father found a job as a foreman for a company that made essences—food flavorings—which is what his firm manufactured in Shanghai. He worked for fifteen years and saved enough money to establish his own food-flavoring plant, which he opened ten years ago and still operates today. Wyndham's mother went to work as an administrator at a convalescent hospital; today, she is the hospital's top administrator.

Wyndham attended public schools through junior high. Then his parents wanted to enroll their son in a Catholic boys' school. Wyndham took the admission test and did well, but he did not end up going to the private school.

"I had kind of a strange experience," he says. "The Father, who was the head principal of the school or the dean of the school, came up to me afterward and kinda gave me a strange comment. He said, 'All of our Oriental boys do really well here,' and that kinda made me feel a little weird, y'know, kind of this model-minority stereotype even in high school.

"I resented his remark. I mean, why is it that their black kids didn't do well? Why was it all of a sudden I was placed in this group of people that automatically was supposed to do well academically? It's like saying, 'Well, all our black kids do well in basketball,' or something like that. It is just as much of a putdown as it is a compliment. It automatically says to a group of people, 'This is the one thing you're pretty good at. If you're not good at it, then what are you good at?' It's just a subtle way of being racist."

One of Wyndham's junior high teachers convinced Wyndham's parents to allow him to continue attending the public schools. Wyndham says he had to "experience what it was like to be around females at the time. It was basically survival of the species." And, he adds, "I just had 'the urge' at the time. It would have been slow death for me to go through a Catholic all-boys school."

When he was a teenager, Wyndham did not behave like the stereotypical Asian adolescent, quietly deferring to his parents' wishes. Yes, he maintained an A-minus grade average, but he also sported a spiked hairdo, hung out in punk music clubs, and stayed out late. A typically rebellious teenager.

His rebellion continued into college at the University of California at Davis. "I had originally gone there as a biology major, 'cause there was a big pressure on me from my parents to take a real professional kind of path, become a doctor or something like that. It wasn't working out. There was this urge not to do anything that even had to remotely deal with science or anything like that, even though I had a really great interest in it and I still do. But so much of what I was doing in biology—I took a lot of biology and chemistry courses—so much of it was rote learning, and there wasn't a real building process or creative process that was involved in it at all. There wasn't a challenge there for me. I think a lot of it, too, was bucking what my parents wanted me to do."

While Wyndham was at Davis, he began to feel as if there was some part of him that he wanted to understand but could not. Wyndham, whose name is Teutonic, and sounds much like his Chinese one, Won Hai, calls it his "Asianness." He explains: "All the images that I've grown up with are white American images. I've always kind of based all my role models on what I guess would be the white American family image and white American culture. There is a whole side of me, I feel like it's missing in a lot of ways. How can I put this?

"My parents really didn't put a lot of pressure on me to learn very much about China or about Chinese culture. Like I never went to any sort of Chinese Sunday schools or cultural centers or anything like that. When we were brought up, my parents always lived in very white, middle-class communities, so all my best friends were always white. I mean, I even hated Chinese food when I was growing up, always wanted to have McDonald's hamburgers and stuff like that. I mean, I really didn't like Chinese food until I was about fifteen or sixteen. The extent of my Chinese experiences would be going down to Chinatown with my mom and shopping with her." Wyndham adds that he understands, but cannot read or write, Cantonese and Shanghaiese.

"When I started going to high school, it was the first time I really had friends that were Asian because my high school at that point had a pretty big Asian community there. I didn't really fit in with them 'cause they had grown up with each other."

In a "halfhearted" effort to learn more about his Asianness and to meet other Asian-American students who also were struggling to reconcile their own dreams with their parents' aspirations for them, Wyndham began attending meetings of the university's Asian students. But most of the other students in the group seemed just like the stereotype that Wyndham was actively rejecting. "They were all going to medical school. They weren't very interested in experiencing other things out there. A lot of them fell into a lot of these kind of roles that were allowed for them.

That really disappointed me," he says. "Where I saw the student union as kind of being a place where we could exchange ideas about our Asianness and our backgrounds and so forth, the rest of the students really saw it as kind of a place where we could throw a lot of parties. It was all volleyball and dances."

Wyndham graduated with a bachelor's degree in environmental design, which covers everything from textiles to graphics to interiors. He then moved to Berkeley, supporting himself by designing graphics, drafting blueprints, bookkeeping, and doing office work. A year later, he decided to go back to school to get a master's degree in architecture.

"I kind of came to architecture because it was the best way for me to pool my talents together," he says. "I like to draw, I like to make things, I like to create things. And I saw architecture as being a pretty good way of doing that."

Architecture was also Wyndham's way of reconciling his dream of doing something artistic with his parents' wish that he follow a conventional career path. He thought, "Architecture is a profession, yet it has an artistic component to it. So why not try that out."

Wyndham spent his first year and a half at the University of Texas in Austin, and a few of the good ol' boys in Texas provided Wyndham's first encounter with racism. He and his girlfriend, who was also Chinese-American, were leaving a fast-food restaurant in a little town in Southeast Texas. As they walked to the car, Wyndham heard "Chinese-sounding noises"—"ching-chong, ching-chong, bing-bong"—coming from two guys in a pickup parked in the lot.

Wyndham was stunned. "I was just like, 'Whoa! This is really weird. Here I am in America, and these guys are like kind of mouthing off.' It kind of slapped my face a little bit and kind of made me realize, 'Yeah, people don't really know who I am and what I am about.' "

Wyndham might have been more inclined to tolerate Texas's rednecks if he had found the education that he was seeking. But many of the professors whom Wyndham had considered the most innovative had left the faculty. "Architects have to go where the jobs are," he says, "and a lot of the jobs weren't there in Texas anymore."

So he returned to Los Angeles and transferred to the Southern California Institute of Architecture, SCIArc for short, to finish his master's degree. "They're really famous for being very off-the-wall. The professors there are kind of the new cutting edge in architecture. They're not afraid to explore new ideas and to really go out on a limb and try new things." Wyndham graduated in May 1991.

Unlike many of his classmates, Wyndham had a job lined up

before graduation. It was with an architecture firm that did mostly residential work for affluent white-collar workers who lived in Malibu and Beverly Hills. But the job only lasted three months because most of his boss's clients "were getting pinched by the recession."

Since then, Wyndham has built architecture competition models for one of his professors at SCIArc, helped design an exhibit for an exposition in Korea, and done "finish" work for a New York firm that was designing the new headquarters for a film production company in Beverly Hills. He completed the last job two days before my visit and is now looking for work.

"I've been very lucky," he tells me. "I haven't been unemployed for more than a couple of weeks at any given time. And it's been stuff that I pretty much wanted to do. I didn't feel like I was compromising myself at all."

Still, Wyndham is concerned about his future. He is fifteen years younger than the youngest of his sisters. He says, "I kind of see my sisters' generation and my generation as being very different. 'Cause they were pretty much in the middle of the baby boom, and I'm at the very, very tail end of it, if not the beginning of this other generation. And it's very frustrating to see them having a lot more opportunity. As I was growing up, I could see them going through the motions of landing a job that was a fairly secure job, and then moving up the ladder, or at least seeing some sort of procession that they could take. And I really haven't found that available.

"This last job was six months, which was like the longest job, and even at that one, when I was hired they said I was only going to be there for a couple of weeks. I don't feel like there's any security in a lot of the work that I've been able to find, even though it has been fairly good work, at least for architects.

"The economy now is just so unstable, architects are one of the first things that gets hit. People don't want to buy houses when they don't feel right about money. Architecture in general isn't a very stable job profession to begin with. Architects tend to not peak until they're in their fifties, and very few of them get the job status and available money in order to open up their own firms. So I picked this profession that, even in good times, it's very difficult to make money, and now it's near impossible to find any sort of permanent work. So it does worry me.

"But, in a way, I'm kind of glad that I came out of school in this really crappy time period. I don't have any really big financial burdens right now. And if I had been laid off of a job with a couple of kids now, you know, it wouldn't be only just me I'd be worried about. At least now it's given me kind of a new understanding of the importance of being responsible. 'Cause when I was growing up, my parents, even though they didn't really give me a lot of emotional support, they gave me a lot of financial support, so I didn't really feel the brunt of having to work for a lot of things.

"Since a lot of my friends who are architects are really struggling finding work, it's really put a lot of questions in my mind—whether the profession is right, whether my career path is right, whether there's a future in architecture for me right now. But I am still fairly optimistic about the whole situation. I feel like I have enough skills where I can do something else if it gets really tight. I'm just kind of seeing it as a time for me to explore other avenues and maybe diversify my talents."

There is one aspect of Wyndham's future about which he is confident. Within the next year and a half he will marry Charysse, his girlfriend for the past six years, his roommate for the past two, and his fiancée of two months. They met at one of the meetings of the Asian student union at UC-Davis. According to Wyndham, Charysse, too, was hoping to meet others with whom she could discuss her Asianness. "We had that in common," says Wyndham, who was friends with Charysse for a couple of years before they began dating.

Charysse moved in with Wyndham while he was still a grad student at SCIArc. "She was originally going to live in a place on her own," he says, "but we figured that time-wise and economically it'd be best if we just lived together. She stayed at my place for a while, then it kind of went from two weeks to two months and then from there on. And it's probably been like one of the best experiences, just kind of growing with the person and really learning what they are day to day to figure out whether this is the person you want to be with for the rest of your life."

Wyndham says that Charysse's parents have been more accepting of their daughter's living arrangements than Wyndham's parents have been. "I ran through a lot of hoops and a lot of shit with my parents, in terms of Charysse and I living together. At first I didn't tell 'em, and when they found out it was a temporary thing, that was okay with them. But then, as it stretched out, I had to kind of face up and tell them, 'Yeah, this is how it's gonna be.' It was really difficult for them to deal with." To make matters worse, Charysse has had a very tense relationship with Wyndham's parents, especially his father, ever since Wyndham's father found a condom packet when he once went through Charysse's overnight bag. "He thought it was fair game," says Wyndham. "But it's been very touch-and-go ever since. It's very hard for my dad to say even hello to Charysse."

Once Wyndham and Charysse are married, they would like to have children. "We're realistic about it," he says. "It takes money to have kids, and since I don't have a permanent position going anyplace yet, we're probably gonna have to wait a little bit longer than we might."

And, says Wyndham, once he and Charysse have children, if they can afford it, he would like Charysse to stay home to raise them. Wyndham explains that his mother was a workaholic. "I felt like a lot of time she wasn't there when I kind of needed her there. I think it's really important for parents to be with their kids as much as possible, at least for the first two years. To be there with 'em and at least build some sort of bond with their kids is I think a really good thing." Wyndham says Charysse feels the same way.

Given that Charysse currently earns more than twice what Wyndham does, he says he might consider being the one to stay home with their children. "Yeah," he says, "I think that would be okay, as long as I would have some of my own projects on the side to work with at home. I need to keep myself busy with more, I think, than just dealing with the kids and with the house. It's just an inner urge and an inner need in me to create, to produce things, to do things."

For Wyndham, the American Dream conjures two images. One is of "possibilities." "A possibility," he says, "to do a lot of things that wouldn't be possible in other countries, and that may mean financial possibilities or career paths."

The other vision is more "nostalgic," he says. "I see kind of this whole notion of two and a half kids and a white picket fence and two cars in the garage and living in a suburb. I don't know if that's true anymore—at least personally I don't see that as being true anymore.

"A lot of what the American Dream had held in terms of opportunity for people in the fifties and sixties is slowly dwindling away. A lot of resources have been kind of squandered away. It's gonna be a lot bigger of a struggle for people of my generation to fulfill their dreams."

In spite of this, Wyndham holds on to his dreams. He tells me, "I'd really like to own my own company eventually. I'm not sure exactly what, but I really want to be my own boss eventually. I want to have enough of a financial future where I can support a couple of kids through college. I think that could be construed as an American Dream in a real traditional sense of the word."

He adds: "I don't want to fall into a trap where I'm doing tract homes, and hopefully that won't happen. So career-wise, I think that my own view of success would be doing work that, I hope, would not only challenge me as an architect and as a person, but that would kind of better society in general, whether it be through public work or through some sort of programs, like housing shelters and stuff like that, which I have a great interest in, like, low-cost housing. Being socially conscious, I guess, is really important to me."

As upbeat as Wyndham is about his personal prospects, that's how cynical he is about the nation's future. "A lot of politicians have very short-term views on things. The way they make change is through very highly visible programs that tend not to do anything for people in the long run, and, if anything, sort of shortchange people in the long run, because it tends to lull people into a state of complacency."

Wyndham believes the solution to this problem lies not in the politicians' hands, but in their ears. "I think it has a lot to do with listening to people," he says, "listening to what the real needs are in society.

"I really think that the Reagan era and the Bush era, I'm still seeing so many bad signs coming out of it. I see those years as being steps backwards in so many ways. In civil rights and the economy. The way they have deregulated so many businesses and the onslaught of mergers and acquisitions, I see that as ruining so much of the economy, at least the stability in the economy. And their lack of feeling for social welfare, for people of the middle class and lower middle class. And also their total disregard for women's rights, equality, so forth. They've just really been dragging the country down in a really big way."

Wyndham says that if the nation's future is left up to politicians, he is not optimistic about its chances. "Because there's so much rhetoric and media hype, there's so much unchecked power that's

involved in the political process now, that, y'know, it's really difficult to believe anybody whenever they make any sort of political
stance. You don't know whether it's for personal gain or whether it's
for the needs of the people. I'm kind of waiting to see what happens, in a real pessimistic way."

Despite all this, Wyndham concludes our discussion by saying,
"I think that there are still opportunities out there for people and
that people need to remain optimistic about the future."

Note: Two months after I spoke with him, Wyndham accepted
a position at a firm that designs exhibits for conventions and trade
shows. He says that this kind of work is not what he really wants to
be doing; it is neither as challenging nor as fulfilling as he would
wish. "It's kind of a bill-payer," he says. But this job also pays 50
percent more than he would make at an architectural firm, which he
thinks is a "sad statement on architecture."

DIRK

Walking into Dirk's efficiency on Manhattan's Upper West Side, I
think, "Welcome to the Bohemian life, 1990s style." But as I look
around the room, I begin to realize there is an order underlying the
seeming chaos, almost as if I have entered a life-sized collage that
reveals the most important elements in Dirk's life.

Against the south wall there is a drafting table cluttered with air-
brushes, paints, unfinished paintings, and a half-empty bottle of
Bacardi rum. Strewn across the table and the chair are T-shirts on
which Dirk has airbrushed colors and patterns; the shirts are presents for Dirk's friends. Resting atop the radiator on the north wall
are other, larger works in progress. One of them asks in funky, foot-
high, sky-blue letters with an attitude: "Whats Up?"

An assortment of sound recording equipment clutters the east
half of the room. There's an eight-track recorder, a percussion machine, a voice compressor, and an effects box for creating reverber-
ation and echo. There are also microphones, cords, an empty mike
stand, and a variety of stereo equipment.

Behind the sound equipment, lining the bookshelves built into the east wall is Dirk's collection of martial arts videos, about fifty in all. Included are such staples as *Tai Chi Devil Dragon* and *Deadly Buddhist Raiders*. Dirk likes Bruce Lee's movies a lot, but his favorite flicks are the ones "where the old master comes and whips the young guy into shape, so he can beat up the bad villain that killed his brother or whatever," and "the classic Chinese Shaolin movies, the revolutionaries-struggling-to-overcome-the-oppressive-dynasty-type movies."

The younger of two children, Dirk, twenty-three, was born and raised on the Upper West Side. His father, who was Dutch, worked for one of the airlines as a purser; he died four years ago. Dirk's mother is a part-time teacher at one of the city colleges. She still lives in the apartment where Dirk's family has lived since he was born.

Dirk attended New York public schools all his life, including three of its high schools. First was the High School of Art and Design, a vocational school where students study commercial art, cartooning, photography, and the like. Dirk did not like that school, so he transferred to Music and Art High School, where he was not exactly a model student.

"I didn't go to class a lot," he says, speaking rapidly like a stereotypical New Yorker. "I smoked a lot of pot while I was in high school, and plenty of times I encountered a guard and I probably smelled like pot. Then they'd bring me down to the office and they'd search me and they wouldn't find anything, so then they would have to let me go."

But one day the school authorities did find some drug paraphernalia—"a couple of pot pipes and some firecrackers or something like that"—in Dirk's pockets. "Basically, me and the bureaucrats at the school had not been getting along for quite a while," he says. "I had problems with them and they'd been looking for a reason to expel me."

Dirk first tried marijuana when he was ten years old and began smoking regularly when he was fourteen. When I ask him to explain why, he replies: "I don't know. I don't know why. I guess I was a rebellious kid, I guess I always felt I was different than other kids. I didn't get along with everybody so well, and I was very hyper, used to get in a lot of fights and stuff like that. And I was angry with my parents. So, it was a way to get away."

"Why were you angry with your parents?"

"I don't know. Maybe not giving me enough attention or some-thing, I don't know. For not being understanding. I guess I just had a lot of resentment."

Dirk explains that his father's job kept him away from home much of the time. "My two memories of my father are either him just coming home from a trip or leaving for a trip. And then I re-member him doing taxes whenever he was home. All he was ever doing was trying to catch up with his taxes. So I didn't get to spend a lot of time with him.

"My mother pretty much made most of the decisions involving me and my sister because my father wasn't around all the time. But my mother was very stressful, a very disputatious, kinda depressive person when I was a child. And on top of that, she drank a lot. So I don't know what contributions that had to wanting the lifestyle I chose for myself at that time."

At one point Dirk was smoking as many as ten joints a day. Later, during the course of a serious relationship with a woman who was drug-free, he reduced his weed intake to as little as one joint a week. But he recently broke up with that woman, and he is back up to two joints a day. "I think I'm just kind of on a binge," he says. "I think I'll level off pretty soon."

After he was expelled from Music and Art High School, Dirk transferred to West Side High, an "alternative" high school described in a *New York Times* article as its students' "last chance to learn." Dirk describes it as "a school basically for kids who got kicked outta a lotta high schools, who couldn't hang in the regular high schools, so therefore if they wanted to finish up school, they could go here.

"I didn't belong there," he says. "I already knew more from my prior experience in school than that school would probably ever have a chance t'teach me. Because they have to teach me at the same level as the other students, and a lot of other students there re-ally never got a chance to get a decent education. They came from the Bronx or they came from the ghetto neighborhoods, and the schools that they were in were really just—they were zoos.

"It was kind of sad. I knew of very smart kids whose only view of ever fulfilling their American Dream was starting a crack business or something like that. And these kids were straight. They didn't use drugs, they weren't gangsters, but there wasn't very much opportu-nity for them."

During his junior year at West Side, Dirk's mother took a teaching job in Hungary. While his parents were living behind the Iron Curtain, they permitted Dirk to live by himself in a little pension in a ritzy area of The Hague. Although Dirk was enrolled in school, during the six months he was there he rarely attended class. Instead, he painted, rode his bike, smoked pot—which, he points out, is legal in Holland—and hung out.

The following school year, Dirk returned to West Side High. While he was there, he took the test to receive his high school equivalency certificate. But because he scored "very high" on the exam and because he had completed more than three-fourths of the required credits, the school's principal decided to award him a diploma.

Today Dirk is studying art at one of the city colleges. "Although he has been there for four years, he is only a junior. "I've been, uh, kinda taking the slow train," he says. He is carrying about twelve hours this semester, which leaves him time for other pursuits, such as studying kung fu and painting graffiti art.

"What's graffiti art?" I ask.

"That's a very complex question," he replies. "It's something I think about a lot. It's a kind of graphic-style art that people do where you have a name for yourself. My name [or "tag,"] is Waste. You'll be affiliated with a crew, or a group of other graffiti writers. My crew is CVC, which has a lot of meanings—Cool Villains Chillin', Crazy Vandal Criminals, Constantly Varying Coordinates, meaning like, if your tag is on a train, then the train is moving where you have tags all over the city. And I'm affiliated with other crews. I'm down—you say 'you're down' with a crew—I'm down with FCN, CPP, and One Fifty-Six."

Explaining why he and other graffiti artists choose this particular medium for self-expression, Dirk says, "A certain amount of it is rebellion. It's going and saying, 'I'm gonna do my art here whether someone else likes it or not,' and then it's there and they don't have a choice. It's also a way for other graffiti artists to identify you and recognize you and appreciate what you've done. New York City has ten million people. It's pretty hard to find an identity. But through graffiti, you can have an identity, you get recognized. You get recognition and you get what they call fame.

"To me, I see a big concrete wall someplace, that's not decorative. That wall serves a purpose—you have a bridge or whatever—it doesn't have to look unattractive, and a lot of it to me looks very unattractive. I think if I can go put my artwork on the wall, it makes me feel good. Other graffiti writers can see it and appreciate it. And I think that it needs to be appreciated. I think that there's no reason we should have ugly, uninteresting structures to look at. I think it's more interesting even if it's just written on, even if it's scribble.

"It's like almost giving your art, but to everybody. It's not like, if you do a painting, keep it and put in storage, and it's *your* painting. Graffiti is *your* work, but it's done for the public. It's making your statement of your views or whatever, in a public place where people can see how you're feeling. It's kind of a reflection of your views and the world you live in."

Although Dirk still occasionally produces "pieces"—graffiti slang for masterpieces—over the past three years he has devoted less of his time to graffiti art because he has become ambivalent about it. "There wasn't very many good writers out anymore," he says. "It was all what we call 'toy,' which is just someone with no style and with no technique. It just became boring, and I just didn't wanna be affiliated with it anymore, I guess. And on top of that, I felt like I was too old to go out, risking getting arrested for writing on a wall."

Less time spent spray-painting pieces leaves Dirk more time for his current passion: writing rap music. A devotee of rap since the mid-1980s, he has been writing his own "rhymes"—rap songs—for the past three or four years.

"I wrote poetry when I was younger, and I got into rap through the graffiti," he says. "I think it's a very politically rare art form. I think it's one of the few types of music that really is saying something today about the situation, about where we're living. I think that there's not enough sources of information for anybody, young people or anybody, in this country. The information that we're given is from too narrow a perspective. I mean, the media's owned by the rich corporations. Their interests obviously are making money, so they're gonna present the news in a way that helps promote their interests. I think that people need other sources of information from other places to find out what's going on, and I think rapping's a good outlet for that."

As a source of information, however, Dirk emphasizes that rap also has its shortcomings. "A lot of rap has a narrow focus. It's strictly people from the ghettos, and a lot of rappers, their whole experience is their life in the ghetto, and they haven't looked beyond that for other sources of information.

"I think a lot of rappers are focusing on the race issue and not realizing that the real issue is more of a class issue. For a black person to say 'the white man is taking from the black man' is just too narrow. White man is taking from the white man too. A lot of people are suffering.

"I have a different perspective. I grew up very middle-class, but I also grew up around a lot of people from lower classes and from higher classes. Also, my mother is a socialist, and my father is European.

"There's a lot of rappers out there who are fairly positive and incredibly smart, who are tryin' to enlighten people. That's the type of rapper that I wanna be."

I ask Dirk to perform one of his rhymes, and he raps from memory an unfinished piece titled "The One Solution." He bobs his head back and forth to the rhythm of his words as he speaks:

> *There's one solution: Destroy the institution.*
> *United together, we'll fight a black and white revolution.*
> *Overcoming, overpowering the source of oppression,*
> *Straightforward in this hour there will be no repression.*
> *Equally respected, equally protected,*
> *True equality means no one is neglected.*
> *Why should one have more food than he can eat,*
> *While others rob and steal just to get a piece of meat?*
> *'Cause that's the system, that's the way they made it.*
> *The great American Dream is the way they portrayed it,*
> *Equal opportunity in life's lottery.*
> *But if you can't get a ticket, tell me how could it ever be*
> *A truly equal system?*
> *It's not the way they say it is.*

The idea for "The One Solution" came from the bathroom walls of the college where Dirk studies. "People are always writing all over the walls, all kinds of stuff, political and otherwise. A white guy had written some white supremacist comment, and then a black guy had responded with kind of a racist black comment. And it just seemed to me so pointless, these two people fighting back and forth. So then I just came up with that beginning right there and wrote, 'There's one solution/Destroy the institution/United together we will fight a black and white revolution.'

" 'Cause I think that the institution *is* trying to keep people divided and separated into special interests so that they can't unite and actually get anything done. I think that's why the drug war—the so-called drug war—and the race issue and all that are fueled, to keep people divided. If everyone is focusing on their own special interest, they can't work together to overcome, to make changes. I mean, I'm not saying that you have to be radical revolutionaries and overthrow the whole system. I think that we can make changes that will work. And when people come together, changes *will* be made."

Neither spray-painting pieces nor writing rhymes will pay Dirk's bills. He says he is eligible for government assistance, but he believes welfare is "for people who need it." Besides, Dirk—who does not pay any income tax because, he says, he does not believe in the government's current policies, such as the Persian Gulf War and the farcical "war" on drugs—does not think it would be right to burden the taxpayers because of how he earns a living, which is by selling marijuana. Dirk claims that peddling dope earns him as much as $100,000 a year. "Which in New York isn't all that much, really," he insists. "It goes pretty quick."

Dirk explains: "One of the reasons I sell pot is because I don't feel like working within the system right now. I don't wanna work for somebody else, and living comfortably is something I enjoy and I kind of cling to.

"Me and my cousin had a funny joke, actually. Me and my cousin used to be partners, and we said that we'd never send anyone to their grave, we never gave anyone an O.D., but we mighta caused a couple of old people to go to Apex Tech instead of Harvard or somethin'. I know a lot of people who're pretty fogged out from smoking too much pot. But that's their choice. I don't think pot is a bad thing. I don't think I'm responsible for someone misusing it."

Dirk has his standards. He does not sell small amounts, he does not sell to anybody he does not know—"basically" just friends and friends of friends—and he does not sell to people younger than eighteen "or so." Most important, he refuses to have anything to do with cocaine or crack. "It's negative and it's very bad karma," he says.

But his apparent nonchalance belies his ambivalence about the source of his income. "Sometimes I don't feel good about the business I'm involved in. Not that I feel that I'm hurting people, because I don't. I think herbs should be legal. I think it's medicinal and I think it's not unhealthy. But I think there's a lot of bad stuff associated with the fact that it's illegal business, and I don't really like being affiliated with that sometimes. That can be a downer sometimes."

So what does this kung-fu–fighting, graffiti-painting, hip-hopping, left-leaning dope dealer think of the American Dream?

"Most people think that the American Dream means that everybody has an opportunity to get ahead and to do well for themselves if they just work hard at it. And I don't think that's true. I think that everyone *should* have that opportunity, and I think that a lot of people do. It's like that line in my song—'Equal opportunity in life's lottery/But if you can't get a ticket, tell me how could it ever be/A truly equal system?' Everyone has some slim chance at it, but a lot of people have a lot more chance than others. A lot of people have a lot more windows or doors to get in, and I think that in order to get started you need to get in through some window or some door, need to get lucky or whatever it might be. A lot of it is what you work for, but I think if you're white, in certain situations you have a lot more opportunity than a black guy. And there are other situations, a lot fewer, but there are other situations where a black guy might have more opportunity than a white guy. I believe in the American Dream, and it's a good thing to believe. But I just don't think that it's a reality."

All Dirk is looking for is "happiness and contentment and a nice girl who I can really talk to, who I won't fight with and who sees things in a similar way as me but who can teach me things." When Dirk finds this woman and marries her, he says he certainly won't be selling dope anymore; he hopes by then he'll be supporting himself with his art. Dirk's bottom line: "Basically to be able to live comfortably doing something that I enjoy and that makes other people feel good," whether it is as a visual artist or as a rapper.

It is as an artist and a rapper that Dirk hopes he might be able to address that problem which worries him most about the nation: our collective unwillingness to make the system work in our collective best interests.

He explains: "I think that a lot of people are being led astray. They're too lazy to think for themselves and to make their own decisions. I think that there's other people out there taking advantage of that and that concerns me.

"I don't think that the rich or the government are very concerned with the economy and with improving the situation. I think that their concern is that they get rich and their friends get rich. I think a lot of people are too lazy to say, 'Hey, these people are not working in our interest and it's our right to have them work in our interest.' So they pretend to believe what the media's telling them because they're just too lazy to go out and make a change, or they've been too discouraged or whatever to think that they can really make an impact. So they just let the other people make decisions for them that hurt them in the long run. I mean, I have friends, black friends, who spend a lot of time talking about how the system works against 'em and how they're not getting a fair shake. But then when comes election time, they don't vote."

"Do you vote regularly?"

"Yeah, I vote. If I know that there's a vote happening, if I know that it's time to vote on something, then I do. Occasionally I miss out on some of the smaller, more local things. Then I usually go to my mother, because there's a lot of times I'm too lazy to do the research and find out who to vote for. So I ask my mother about the candidates. My mom's pretty smart, pretty politically aware, so I take her word for it. But at least I put my vote in."

For a man who seriously espouses socialism just two days after the official collapse of what was the Soviet Union and who frets about our collective apathy, Dirk is peculiarly optimistic about the nation's future. He says:

"I think that what's gonna happen is that if things keep goin' in the direction they're goin', eventually people are gonna get smacked in the face. I think we're going to regress a lot. I think we have been regressing."

"Regressing? How?"

"Politically. We're losing our civil rights right and left. The government is putting these new little clauses in this and that, that are taking away rights that we've worked very hard to achieve—a woman's right to make a decision about whether or not to have a baby, a person's right to smoke pot, a person's right to an education, free speech. I think that these things are all being—they're not being eliminated, but they're being kind of shaved off. I think that's how the government is working right now, piece by piece, adding all these clauses and everything, so that they're limiting our rights. Rather than eliminating them, they're just limiting them. In that way, people don't notice it happening. But I think eventually the cumulative effect is gonna become so much that people are gonna realize that that's what's been happening, and there's gonna be a turnaround and kind of like a cultural revolution here.

"I mean, already there's a revolution happening, for instance, with the environment. Ten years ago, people probably wouldn't think twice about using paper cups or spraying aerosol, and if you told them all that aerosol screwed up the ozone, they'd say there's plenty of ozone. Whereas now, people are realizing that our actions are gonna have lasting effects and you have to be more aware of what you're doing and of the ramifications of your actions."

Dirk envisions a time in the United States when "people will realize that the culture, that the capitalistic culture that we're living under, is not advantageous to everyone. It works for the few. We've gotta change our views, our ideas about a lot of things, about the way that our society is. About what the American Dream is, for instance. I think people have to realize they have to change their view on that, to create a new American Dream, or at least find some new way to realize the American Dream that they have, because the way this country has been working is not giving equality of opportunity to people."

NATHAN

Nathan, twenty-five, is a sales manager for one of the country's largest consumer product manufacturers. He works out of an office in Westlake, Ohio, a Cleveland suburb filled with prosperous doctors, lawyers, and professional athletes who do not want to pay for homes in ritzier Shaker Heights. Nathan is busy this morning but agrees to squeeze me in before his 9 a.m. meeting. A secretary leads me from the reception area to a cluster of offices in the back. Nathan comes out to meet me.

He is of average height, with broad shoulders and the slightly sagging belly of someone who used to have time to play a lot of sports. Dressed casually in a navy mock-turtleneck jersey with a large golden crest on the left pocket, sand-colored cotton pants, and tasseled cordovan loafers, he looks more like a frat boy than a sales manager for a *Fortune* 500 company. He greets me with a confident, all-American-guy handshake and guides me into his boss's office.

Nathan's biological parents were teenagers—one black, the other white—and his mother gave him up for adoption. An African-American woman whose husband had died two years earlier adopted Nathan, then only nine weeks old. Nathan was not the woman's only child. She already had two daughters of her own, and she adopted another baby boy, Mark, at virtually the same time she adopted Nathan. She later adopted four more children, this in addition to the many children whom she took in over the years as a foster parent.

"My mom's a saint," Nathan says proudly. "She provided a lot of love to a lot of kids over the years."

Nathan grew up in the Lee-Harvard area of Cleveland, a predominantly black, working-class section of the city. His mother worked odd jobs to supplement the money supplied by the state. "We always had the bare minimum," says Nathan.

Aware of the deteriorating condition of Cleveland's public schools, Nathan's mother understood that for her boys to succeed they would have to grow up in the "appropriate atmosphere." So they attended Catholic Mass regularly; Nathan and Mark even became altar boys. And despite her modest income, Nathan's mother managed to send Nathan and Mark to a Catholic day school. Nathan later earned the chance to attend Hawken School, one of Cleveland's most prestigious prep schools, through A Better Chance, Inc., a program that sends bright inner-city kids to private schools.

By the time Nathan started at Hawken, in eighth grade, Mark had already been there for a year. Nathan loved Hawken then and appreciates it even more now. He explains: "Hawken opened up a lot of doors and gave me opportunities I would not have necessarily had if I went to other schools. It allowed me to interact with people who were overachievers. Folks who went to Hawken did not go there to screw around. Most of them went there to learn and to better themselves. It also allowed us to interact with people who were brought up in a different environment, more wealth. Some of our closest friends have parents or relatives who own some of the largest companies in Cleveland or are partners in law firms, et cetera. It gave us the opportunity to interact with these people. And I met a good group of folks, too, good friends." One of those good friends was Nancy, whom he married after their senior year at Miami University of Ohio.

After getting his undergraduate business degree in 1988, Nathan went to work in Pittsburgh as a sales rep for the consumer products manufacturer. While he was there, a friend approached him about opening a restaurant. Nathan, a die-hard entrepreneur who was looking for a business opportunity, eventually joined a couple of friends in opening an establishment that he describes as part restaurant, part art gallery, part nightclub, and part dinner theater. Although the operation has yet to produce a profit, it has generated sufficient income for Nathan and his partners to plow more than $100,000 back into the business.

After two and a half years in Pittsburgh, the company promoted Nathan and offered him the choice of remaining there or moving back to Cleveland. Anxious to return home after being away for nearly three years, Nathan chose Cleveland.

Given the circumstances of Nathan's life—given up for adoption, raised in modest circumstances in a working-class black neighborhood by a widow with more than seven other kids to care for, sent to prep school on a scholarship, married to his high school sweetheart, working for one of the nation's largest companies, and co-owner of a restaurant—Nathan personifies the American Dream. So I was eager to learn how he defines this concept for himself.

When he was younger, Nathan conceived of the American Dream this way: "Anyone who works as hard as they can, and does the best they can at what they're doing, they can accomplish anything in the world, anything that they want." He now adds one qualification to that dream, based on his "twenty-five years of experience." Certain individuals, he says, will have to work a little harder because society makes life more difficult for them. "So anyone can accomplish what they want as long as they work hard, but certain individuals are gonna have to work a little harder to face those barriers that society puts down."

To illustrate his point, Nathan walks over to a large sketchpad that is resting on an easel against the grasscloth-covered wall. With a blue marker, he draws two parallel lines horizontally across the pad. At the left end of each line, he draws a stick figure, which represents a runner in a race.

He explains: "There're two people who are running the same

race. This is the minority, or a white female, and this is a white male. The finish line is here." He points to the end of the runners' paths. "This is your goal, wherever you want to finish. They both have fifty yards to run. The difference is that society places these hurdles here." He draws three vertical "hurdles" on the minority runner's path, then continues his explanation. The only difference between the two runners, he says, "is that the minority must be a little quicker, a little stronger, to get to that finish line. But the outcome is still the same—they can accomplish whatever they want."

Returning to his chair, Nathan adds that minorities also have some opportunities that others do not. He recalls a talk he had with the father of one of his high school buddies. They were discussing affirmative action and other programs intended to assist minorities, and his friend's father told him, in effect, "Society is giving you every chance to fail by giving you programs and different things." Nathan sees things differently: "I think they're giving me every chance to try to succeed, and it's really up to me whether or not I fail or succeed."

Nathan was raised in an African-American community by an African-American mother, so he more closely identifies with black Americans. Yet because of his copper-colored complexion, people who do not know him are not sure in which racial pigeonhole to place him. Nathan says, "My wife's a dark Italian. When I'm with her, people assume I am a dark Italian. When I was in my predominantly Jewish fraternity, people assumed I was Israeli or Lebanese. When I'm with my family, people assume I'm light-skinned black. That has made life a lot easier for my wife and I because we don't face as many problems as other folks would if it was very blatant that this was an interracial marriage. But at the same time, I've been exposed to a lot of prejudice. There is not really one day in my life someone does not make a comment about minorities or blacks."

Nathan recalls a presentation he once made to a potential buyer, a white man, in an area where minorities own many of the competing businesses. The man responded to Nathan's presentation by saying something like, "Why don't you go present that to the niggers down the street." Mildly upset after recounting the story, Nathan adds, "If he knew what I was, he wouldn't have said that."

But, Nathan points out, blacks have often made the same mistake. For example, when he first joined the manufacturing company, he went to a meeting for minority employees. No one in the room knew him, and someone said, "I'm sorry. This is only for minorities." And sometimes blacks will carelessly spew hateful words about whites, unaware that Nathan's wife is white.

He says, "It used to hurt. It used to hurt real bad. But now I think I'm so used to it—it happens every single day—that I just kinda chalk it up as ignorance."

Though it would be understandable if Nathan were bitter or frustrated by others' insensitivity, he isn't. Instead, he uses his ambiguous racial heritage to his advantage. He tells me: "The good thing about it is you really get to find out a lot about what people are really like. For example, I might be with you out in the social sector. You don't know me, so you make an assumption. Down the road, if you're truly prejudiced, you may say something. So it gives me an opportunity to find out what type of person you really are. Now, do I get bothered by racial jokes or anything? No. I'm just as bad as the next person. I make ethnic jokes as well. If the intention was a joke, that's fine. But there are some people who are just truly malicious."

Sometimes others' inability to categorize Nathan as black or white works to his advantage in another way. He returns to his drawing of the runners, symbolically cuts one of the hurdles before the minority runner in half, and says, "If they don't know and you don't tell 'em, you may be able to move a little quicker because you reduced that barrier."

Yet with his next words Nathan says that his complexion often works to his disadvantage—with blacks. He tells me some blacks believe that his lighter-colored skin confers on him a special—and unfair—advantage. Consequently, "they put barriers up for you," he says, adding another vertical hurdle to the minority runner's path. Later, he says, "Certain individuals will do whatever it takes and work as hard as possible to succeed. I'm one of those people. Some people resent this. They don't understand. They're jealous."

"Who are 'they'?" I ask.

Nathan says "they" are people who believe that they have fewer opportunities than he does. "But the doors are open to them," he insists, "they just have to work a little harder."

Several times during our conversation Nathan likens himself to a chameleon. He is proud of his ability to blend into any social setting—black or white, rich or poor, simple or sophisticated. But, he admits, at times it can be very difficult being a chameleon. "In a corporate environment," he says, "people have to wear two hats—especially minorities. Minorities have to wear a very corporate type of hat to try to fit in with the corporate environment, and act in a certain way that they may not necessarily act when they are away from it. I do it. A lot of other people do it. It's unfortunate that you have to do that, but because of society nowadays, you're almost forced to, 'cause you want to succeed."

And Nathan is driven to succeed. Contentment is insufficient. "This is gonna sound real shitty," he says, "but I define success in terms of power and money. That probably sounds terrible, but that's the way I have always defined it. I know that a person can consider himself successful if he is content with what he's doing. But because my goals are a lot higher, I define success as something a little extra." As part of this "little extra," Nathan wants not only to take care of his wife and future family, but also to provide for his mother and his younger siblings—a house for her, college educations for them. He also intends to help other kids from the inner city so that they, too, will have a chance to succeed.

However, although Nathan knows how he wants to spend that "little extra," he cannot define when he will have attained it. He says, "My wife and I always talk about this. She asks, 'When will enough be enough?' I don't know if I will ever know. I guess you could look at someone like Donald Trump. You would think he had everything. Why wouldn't he stop? Why did he want more and more? I don't think I'm gonna be that bad, but my wife thinks I will be. I don't know if I'll ever reach a point at which I'm completely satisfied."

Nathan believes his nearly insatiable ambition comes from going to school with the children of Cleveland's wealthiest families. "There was some jealousy," he says, "oh, hell, yeah, there was a lot of jealousy, without a doubt. At Hawken there were some who made it very clear that their parents were wealthy, and if you aren't so wealthy, you are in the wrong environment, buddy. I think that's what drove my desire to become an entrepreneur, 'cause I saw what other folks had. The thing that bothered me most was there was some people whose kids still have it and never had to work for it. And I said, 'Someday I'd like to provide that for my kids.' That's really been one of the driving forces behind my aggressive behavior toward business."

Nathan's plan for a good life is straightforward. In your twenties, take chances. In your thirties, start a family. In your forties, earn as much money as possible. In your fifties, secure your hard-earned success. In your sixties, enjoy it.

"Except," he adds, pausing for dramatic effect, "take chances all your life."

As he sees it, he came from a poor black family in a poor black neighborhood. He did not have as many opportunities as many others have had. But with lots of hard work, as well as lots of love from his family and friends, he has made his life a success. He believes that no matter what happens, he could simply start over and do it again.

SAME CITY, DIFFERENT WORLDS II

HUNTSVILLE

SUSAN AND CARTER

Few people I've met have openly described themselves as elitist, at least not without a trace of ambivalence or a twinge of embarrassment. But Susan unabashedly declares that she and her husband, Carter, are elitists. "I don't mean snobbery," she says in her genteel Southern drawl. "It's just mainly education. If you've been educated and you've been exposed to things and you have a thirst for that, you wanna be exposed to more. You wanna travel, you wanna see more, you wanna learn more."

Born and raised in Huntsville, Susan, twenty-five, and her two brothers grew up in economic circumstances that Carter jokingly describes as "lower wealthy." ("We don't have a yacht," says Susan, tongue in cheek, "but just right under there.") Susan's father is a very successful businessman. Susan tells me that although her mother once worked as a fund-raiser for the girls' academy where Susan went to high school, her mother did that for fun, and for most of Susan's life her mother was a homemaker. These days, Susan's mother spends her time volunteering.

From grade school through college, Susan attended private schools, first Catholic day schools, then Emory University in Atlanta. "My parents, grandparents, aunts, uncles, everyone had always gone to Emory. My older brother [and, later, her younger brother] went to Emory, and it was just pretty much the only school I applied to."

She says, "It's a good school. I was fortunate it wasn't the tradition in my family to go to a lesser school, a community college or something. I mean, I don't know what I would have done if I hadn't been expected to go to a school of Emory's caliber."

Like Susan, Carter, twenty-eight, was born and raised in Huntsville in an economic environment he describes without reservation as "upper-class." Carter's father is a retired executive. He also sits on the board of the private boys' academy where Carter went to high school. Carter's mother has held a variety of jobs "for enjoyment" but, says Carter, has never had to work because of financial necessity.

Unlike Susan, Carter did not follow his father's footsteps to Emory. Eager to get away from the South and Southern culture, he went to a private college on the West Coast. But he was unhappy there; he was, he thinks, "too young" and "too far away from home." A year and a half later, he transferred to a public university in the South. It was a good school with a good program in interior design, and equally important, "it was in the South."

I ask Carter to explain why the South and "Southern culture" are so important to him. He tells me, "Family. A sense of family is important in the South."

"Where you're from, who you are, who your people are," adds Susan. "Not socially important, but because people have a—"

"Sense of belonging," says Carter, finishing Susan's thought. "My identity is very much tied up in being from the South. And I didn't even realize that, I don't think, until I had gone away."

During the summer after his junior year, Carter designed the interior for a house in Huntsville and discovered that that was what he really wanted to do for a living. Yet by the time he finished college, he had decided he should instead find a "real job in the real world." Through one of his friends, he landed a position working for a manager of private trust funds. But, Carter soon realized that he did not want to be a financial adviser or banker, so he returned to Huntsville to begin a career as an interior designer. That's when Carter and Susan met.

Carter knew who Susan was because they had grown up in the same social circle, but they had never met. Then one night, Carter saw Susan at "a sleazy bar" (Carter laughs at this irony). Carter had one of his friends introduce him to Susan, then a junior in college. A couple of years later, Carter and Susan were married.

Today, Carter and Susan live in a beautiful stone house, which they are remodeling. Susan works as a fund-raiser for a non-profit organization. Carter is an interior designer who specializes in high-end residential.

Susan enjoys her work. "I'm being paid to be nice to people," she says. It's also "very challenging because there's a lot of psychology involved in asking people for money when you have nothing to give them in return, except for goodwill." But she misses the idea of working for profit. She thinks someday she may open her own business, or she may just become more involved in Carter's design firm.

As for Carter, he loves his work. He cannot envision himself doing anything else, except his current work on a larger scale; indeed, his goal is to become the premier interior designer in Huntsville, then in Alabama, and ultimately in the South. Though he admits that his family's social connections have given him an "in" to jobs, he is proud that he went out and did "somethin' on my own."

Perhaps thinking that I might not be giving her husband sufficient credit for his achievements, Susan adds that clients who know their parents "expect a lot more" from Carter than others might. "Every job matters," she says, "because if Carter does it wrong, everybody's gonna know."

But being your own boss comes at a price, namely, peace of mind. "It's very frightening," says Carter, whose company did not earn "a dime" the first six months. "The more I learn, the more I realize how much I don't know."

"We lie in bed every night and talk about the business," adds Susan.

"And that's the hardest part about my job," says Carter, "I take it home. I mean, my office is in my house and so I take it home with me every night."

Still, Carter and Susan think the sleep they lose is not too high a price to pay. As Susan proudly points out, Carter is one of those "rare birds" who earns his living doing what he loves to do. And Carter enjoys creating his own destiny.

Educated at some of the nation's finest schools, owning a beautiful home, getting paid well to do what you love to do, creating your own destiny—for many people, it's the stuff the American Dream is made of. And so it is for Carter, who defines his American Dream as "having a wonderful life with a wife and children and bein' able to provide for them." For Carter, the only missing piece is two or three children.

Susan sees things a bit differently. It's not that she rejects Carter's American Dream; on the contrary, she wants the life he describes. What she dismisses is the *concept* of the American Dream. "I think nationalism is outdated and dead," she says, "so I don't really have an attachment to the American Dream." When she hears the phrase, she does not think of herself. She thinks instead of the "Republican party, and everybody having a car, everybody having a house, everybody having a job, every child has an education."

"Why do you think of the Republican party?" I ask.

"Because I think of the flag and I think of elements that are, I don't know, Bush, Reagan."

"You're not a Republican in the least," says Carter.

Susan replies, "That's what I said. I don't think of me when I think of the American Dream. I mean, I'm a Democrat."

Susan also rejects one of the assumptions that many people feel is implicit in the very notion of the American Dream—that society owes you a chance to achieve that dream. "I think if you work, you get what you deserve," she says. "I'm all for the little guy, and I think there's a lot of injustice, but I don't think that everybody should or will achieve the American Dream. I don't think of America as having to be somewhere that provides for everyone or provides an opportunity." She later adds that the government is "obligated to provide a healthy environment where opportunities can create themselves," which, in her mind, requires the government to "maintain a healthy capitalistic system," nothing more.

Carter disagrees. "I think the country needs to provide an education and provide the opportunity to achieve the American Dream if you want it. You ought to have that chance to achieve whatever your personal dream is, and that's what the American Dream is."

Just as with the concept of the American Dream, Susan and Carter have overlapping, but not identical, definitions of success. Although she does not think success is "tied up in material things," Susan still sees money as a sort of yardstick with which to measure success—the more you earn, the more successful you are. Money is less important to Carter. Of course, like most people, he would prefer to earn more money rather than less. However, the quality of his work and the well-deserved esteem of his professional colleagues are as important to him as his income.

"Whether this is old-fashioned or not," adds Susan, "Carter's success is tied up in my success as well. I feel like his success has something to do with me."

"It does," agrees Carter. "My business, it's not one person. She's very much involved."

Noting that he and Susan are building a marriage that seems very similar to those their parents had, Carter continues: "I'd say we're far more traditional in our relationship than most of our generation. Far more. In the sense that I think that, you know, Susan will play a more supportive role in my career, maybe even more of a supportive role than our mothers would have played, do y'know what I'm saying, as opposed to just being in the home. Susan'll be involved in my career."

"It's a partnership," says Susan.

Carter turns to her and says, "I don't think you'll work when you have children, and I think that's unusual for our generation."

Susan does not immediately respond to Carter's remark, so I ask her whether she plans to work once she and Carter have children.

"Y'know," she answers, "I don't plan anything, but I'd say no, at least when they're young."

Carter echoes: "At least when they're young."

Susan continues, "I'm not writing off ever working again at all, but—"

"Fact," interjects Carter, "I think you will again."

"Right," says Susan, not missing a beat, "but I'd only go back to work if I had to *and* if I found something that I really wanted to do. 'Cause I think there's a lot to give in the community without having a paying job. I think I could attain as much self-esteem and goodwill doing for others without being paid, if I could afford to do that. Which is another reason why money's important."

Carter picks up Susan's thought: "Success is what you leave in this world for other people. I mean, family's important, but it's only important as a base from which to go out and help others." At the end of his life, Carter wants to be able to say to himself, " 'Somebody else has benefited by me being here.' And," he says, "I think that's a strong point with us." Susan agrees.

Although Carter and Susan are committed to making small-scale improvements in the world they live in, Carter thinks that the country as a whole is "so horrifically boondoggled on a humongous scale" that the United States, just like the Roman Empire, is beginning an irreversible decline. He says, "Our generation will not see the United States of my parents' generation. I think that we've lost a generation that has come through without any support, no families to back them up on what they're doin'. I think that you'll be in the top ten percent of the country if you have someone who *cares* for you, someone that really gives a damn about what you're doing. But can we get families goin' again who are gonna be supportive to that next generation? I think that's idealistic. I don't think that it will happen, especially with the way Congress and everything goes."

Carter sees a glint of hope, however. He says, "There is a chance if someone, some grandmother somewhere, is holding that kid and goin', 'You make it, dammit!' That kid may get up there."

Carter also doubts whether his generation will be able to achieve the material prosperity that its parents and grandparents enjoyed. "I think that we expect a hell of a lot more," he says. "We expect a lifestyle that two incomes can afford. Whereas my grandparents did not expect that at all, and came through the Depression and achieved a high level of material prosperity but did not expect it growin' up. We've grown up in total prosperity, an up, up, up cycle, and I do not see that that will happen for our generation at all."

After Carter observes that members of his and Susan's socioeconomic class might escape the gloomy future he forecasts, Susan says she does not believe the picture is as grim as Carter has painted it. "I think Carter is talking about us being rich or us being, you know, driving three cars or something like that. I think that, generally, even the uneducated, even the factory worker, isn't havin' it so bad. I think their quality of life is terrible because they don't enjoy intellectual pursuits, or their value system is so messed up, or their family situation. But economically, it's not gonna be *that* bad."

Curious about the source of Susan's impressions of life for the contemporary factory worker, I ask her how many factory workers she actually knows. She admits that she does not know any—though, she says, she once worked at a bank, and some of the women she worked with lived in trailers.

In Susan's opinion, if people today are having trouble making ends meet, it is because they choose to live beyond their means. "You don't see people choosing not to have a car and riding the bus or something and choosing health care instead. Their priorities, I think, are totally screwed up. They expect health care to be paid for, or they expect X-Y-Z to be paid for, by the government, and then they also spend their money. Now I'm not talking about the homeless person, but the middle class wastes money."

Carter chimes in: "I think the upper class wastes its money, too."

"But," says Susan, "they've got more money to waste."

"Well, that's true," says Carter.

Susan continues: "My father sees these people [who work for him] every day, and he'll tell me what they're spending their money on and what they do. And the people who work for him are these people, who have debt up to their ears because they spend their money on—"

Carter jumps in: "This is true. The people that work for me, like I give a bonus to somebody, and they'll go right out and buy a third car and don't have water, running water. Literally, this is a true example. I know a guy—he's a little nuts, and this is an extreme example"—"It's not," insists Susan—"and he has three trucks and does not have running water for his kids at his house."

"See what I mean," says Susan. "The middle class in this country—or the lower middle class—their value system is not save, not plan. It's spend and it's debt.

"I don't feel that sorry for 'em. I mean, we're educated and so we *choose* things. We made choices, and I don't think they are. I mean, Dad, my father, sets up profit-sharing plans for his employees that are not educated, as a way to set them up to save money. They can withdraw it after five years, and inevitably they come to him and they say they want to take the money out because they owe money on their credit card, where they've bought, y'know, a minibike or something they can't afford. They aren't living within their means. They're living by debt. The whole country has been sold this debt idea, and it's damaged the country."

Susan goes on to tell me that she remembers always hearing that her father had surrounded himself not with people in business suits, but with blue-collar workers. "I've heard stories about it all my life," she says. "He's very cynical about it, and I guess I am too."

Carter and Susan agree that there's one critical element in any solution to these problems. "Values," says Carter. "It's all in values."

He believes that many children today are growing up without any role model from which to gain a good sense of values. "What I see in the news is all, you know, the black male youth, all he has as a role model is predominantly a drug whatever, you know." Carter thinks these kids need as role models parents who are honest and hardworking, who provide for their children, and who "have some kind of American Dream."

Like Carter, Susan sees the disintegration of basic values as one of the root causes of the problems confronting the United States. After telling me that she grew up in a home without television ("We were never distracted by some of the things I think people are distracted by"), she says that these days, the TV, not the family, inculcates people's values. For example, people used to buy a house with a mortgage and then work hard for twenty years to pay it off. "Now," she says, "people would rather buy the minibike *now* and rent the apartment." But, she says, until access to credit, especially credit cards, is tightened so that "people who have no business having that credit" no longer have it, until people reject the acquisitive, consumption-oriented ethos of the tube, and "until people value things like savings and delayed gratification—which they're not gonna do"—the United States will never solve the problems it currently faces.

Despite Susan's stern condemnation of people who live beyond their means, she and Carter are not wholly unsympathetic to those who, unlike themselves, did not have the good fortune to be born into wealthy families. "I don't feel guilty," says Susan. "I feel obligated." Susan and Carter each sit on the board of a different charitable organization. Carter notes, self-effacingly, that he was asked to sit on the board, so it is "not as virtuous as it may sound." They also say they would be willing to pay higher taxes so that members of "the general public" could have access to certain basic services, such as health care and education.

However, Susan says she and Carter will not risk their children to the local public schools. Susan believes that if she and Carter send their children to "a lesser school, they may not make the friends that can get them the connections t'be able t'do something else, you know what I mean. It's all wrapped up with community."

She continues: "I want my children to have the opportunities I did, and I want their children to, and I'm gonna do everything I can to channel them in that direction. Because I can't give everybody the same opportunities."

With admirable candor, she says, "The fact of the matter is, like I said, we're elitist. Once you've got it, you do everything you can to hang on to it."

DARRELL

Darrell, twenty-two, is a corpulent, taciturn Southerner. He wears blue jeans and black concert T-shirts, and spends his weekends "fishin' " and "huntin'," usually for deer or turkey or squirrel or rabbits, but "just about anything" will do.

Born and raised in a rural county about thirty miles west of Huntsville, Darrell lived with his parents and his two younger sisters on his parents' farm along the back roads of the county. His folks raised feed grain as well as a small herd of cattle, about fifteen head at a time. In addition, for the past twenty years Darrell's father has been a supervisor at a plant that manufactures shower curtains and bathroom rugs and tiles. Darrell's mother is a housewife.

Growing up, Darrell and his family regularly attended the local Church of Christ, though Darrell "just kinda got out of it" once he graduated from the public high school and moved out of his parents' house. "Started workin'," he says in his laconic fashion, "never had time."

An "about average" student through high school, Darrell never seriously considered going to college, a decision he does not regret. "Just didn't care nothin' about it," he says. Once he graduated from high school and moved out of his parents' house, he went to work full-time. He was eighteen.

Darrell worked for a year for a company that builds swimming pools. Then he went to work at a county water processing facility. But he was "just sittin' around all the time. I couldn't handle that," he says, and there was "not enough money in it." So he went to work as a laborer for a home building contractor in Huntsville. He earns $6.50 an hour running errands, picking up trash, and doing "just whatever."

Darrell is divorced. Darrell was twenty-one and Tina, his ex-wife, was seventeen when they met at a party last year. They began seeing each other steadily, were married six months later, and were divorced eleven months after that. I ask him to explain why they decided to call it quits and he says, "Her mother kept on buttin' in an' I just got tired of it after a while." As he sees it, the moral of this chapter in his life is "get to know somebody before you go through that again."

Although Tina and Darrell did not have any children during their marriage, Darrell tells me that she is now two or three months pregnant. He says he is "pretty sure" the child is his, though his deadpan expression makes it difficult for me to tell whether he is being sarcastic or serious. Tina and Darrell have not yet worked out any custody arrangement, but, he says, "I guess it's mine, so I'll support it."

I ask, "Are you happy at this point in your life?"

"Yeah," he says, though he tells me he has no idea why.

He offers a straightforward definition of the American Dream for himself and for everyone he knows. The American Dream, he says, is "bein' in debt the rest of your life."

"Why do you say that?"

"That's about how it is for everybody."

How deeply in debt is Darrell? "Not a lot," he says, "but enough." He owes about $15,000 on his two pickup trucks; that's "about it." He considers himself a success as long as he is able to keep up with his bills and "keep everything goin'."

Ironically, the only aspect of the national situation that worries Darrell is "how much money we're in debt." Other than that, he believes the country is moving in a positive direction.

"Aw, I think it's gettin' better," he says. "I just think around here, where I live, everybody's always tryin' t'help everybody else. I don't know how it is anywhere else, but it's that way now."

PART TWO

NONBELIEVERS, SKEPTICS, AND DOUBTERS

LAVONDA

Although most of the people I met during my journey believe in the American Dream in some sense, there were many who told me they do not. Take Lavonda, for instance.

When I met Lavonda, twenty, she was sitting in the lobby of a building at Washington University in St. Louis. We were both waiting to meet John Singleton, who, at age twenty-two, wrote and directed the critically acclaimed movie *Boyz N the Hood,* and who earlier that day had told his life story to a standing-room-only crowd of more than 400 students in Graham Chapel, a hundred yards away. Decked out in a crimson tunic that hugged her short but slinky figure, fishnet stockings, shiny black above-the-knee boots, and a black suede jacket with fringes, Lavonda looked nothing like the other denimclad, down-jacketed students waiting to meet the young director. Sitting in a massive chair that looked as if it belonged in an English lord's country estate, Lavonda was engrossed in a Joan Collins novel when I interrupted her.

Lavonda has cocoa-brown skin and looks directly in your eye when she speaks. She shines shoes for a living, working as many as thirteen hours a day. Daytime, she works at a posh athletic club in downtown St. Louis. "We're talkin' a lot of old money and a lot of new money," she says. At night, she works at PT's, a relatively upscale strip joint across the Mississippi River in East St. Louis. She calls her shoe-shining business "Shining Star Shoe Shine." Lavonda currently lives with her boyfriend, Tiger.

"Are you in love with Tiger?" I ask.

A few moments pass before she says: "Yeah, I do love him. I'm going through this thing right now—I don't know if I want to stay with him or venture out and find somebody else. I don't know. I mean, I know no one else would put up with my shit. I know that. I'm just very moody and bitchy and picky and I want everything now. I'm very impatient. I've done a lot of *bad* things—I played around on him several times—and he's willing to stick it out. These days, I meet a lot of guys and I don't think there's anything out there anymore. And if there are, they're gay these days. I guess I will stay with him for now. I'm just so bent on my career, it doesn't really matter what happens. I *do* love him, but I just don't know if I'm *in love* with him."

"What's the difference?"

"If you are *in love* with 'em, it's fun. If you *love* 'em, it's work."

Despite her ambivalence about Tiger, Lavonda would like to get married—in four or five years, perhaps—and Tiger is likely to be the man. But she is terrified by the idea of having kids "because of the pain you go through at childbirth. And I don't wanna get fat—I don't want my body to go out of orbit. And then after I have a child I won't be able to use sponges anymore. You can't use sponges after you have babies 'cause the hole gets bigger. Then I'll have to go on the Pill or something. I mean, we're talkin' major body changes goin' on here, and I can put that on hold for quite a while."

"Does it bother you, working at a strip joint?"

"It's just a job. Matter of fact, for a couple of months I just had it in my head, 'I wanna dance, I wanna dance.' Finally I did it. I got up onstage and danced. I was jammin' onstage, but I realized I just can't grind my stuff in some guy's face. I danced one set—three songs—and just got off."

"When I say the term 'American Dream,' what do you think of?"

"I think of people striving to be more liberal, striving to break

out, to stop being so narrow-minded. I think that dream about owning a house and a white picket fence is kinda gone because of so
many divorces and so many illegitimate children being born. It is
just not a dream anymore, with AIDS going around. I don't think
there is any dream. There's just a dream of you, yourself, trying to
do for yourself. It used to be that everybody had a dream which
would include everybody. These days I think the American Dream
is individual."

Lavonda thinks it is important that she make something of herself. "If you're gonna be a ho', if you're gonna be a prostitute," she
says, "be a thousand-dollar-a-night prostitute. That's what my grandmother always say. If you're gonna do anything, be good at it. Don't
do something and be bad at it. Then you're really messed up."

Although Lavonda likes shining shoes—many of PT's regulars
are white-collar workers who tip well—she dreams of someday becoming a filmmaker. She intends to bring a black woman's perspective to the American cinema, a viewpoint that she thinks is missing
today.

"The black movies they're making now are all from a male
point of view, and I'm gettin' real tired of it. Black women have totally different problems from black men. Like the oral sex thing.
That's a problem. Black men have a hangup about it. They have to
wait three or four weeks before they do it. Then there're the ones
that don't do it at all. I mean, they got big dicks, but we get tired of
that. Give us somethin' else. They make vibrators these days, so they
gotta get with it." Lavonda confronts black men's passion for oral
sex and their simultaneous reluctance to return the favor in her first
screenplay, *Sex in the Nineties.*

She continues: "We have lots more problems than black men
do, like getting pregnant and being abused. It seems that Hollywood
just wants to stick on the gangs and all-black this and all-black that
kind of stuff. They don't want to venture out. They always want to
deal with race and drugs and gangs when it comes to black movies.
It's all from the male point of view." Lavonda also has ideas for another two dozen scripts, not all of which involve black people. "Half
are mostly based on black characters," she says, "and the other half
are mostly based on white characters."

I ask Lavonda whether she thinks that race relations are a problem in this country. She says, "You know, if you were to ask me that
question two years ago, I woulda told you, 'Oh, I think America is

much better about race.' I mean, I really believed that back then. But in the last two years it just seem like it's just goin' back to the drawing board. It just seems like it's reverting to worse."

She tells me about one of the dancers at the club where she shines shoes at night. This woman, who is white, was performing a "private" (dancing directly in front of a patron who's willing to pay $20) for one of her regular customers. Lavonda explains that this man, who is also white, is not a big tipper. "He just kinda sits and talks to her. She thought of him as more of a friend. Anyway, these days she doesn't look so hot. She hasn't been makin' a lot of money lately. She's been telling me she's only taking home fifty dollars a night. Anyway, there's this one black guy who wanted a private from her, so she gave him a private. Twenty dollars. No big deal. But her regular said that he will never ever come see her again because she gave the black guy a private. I just felt sorry for her. I'm not gonna try to get mad. I'm not gonna form some kind of riot or somethin'. I just feel sorry for people like that.

"You gotta make money. And if you're gonna be a dancer 'n' you're gonna be picky, then you're not gonna make any money. 'Cause you get all kinds of guys who're gonna come in there for privates. 'N' if you're gonna be picky about race, then you're not gonna make any money 'cause that'll get around fast. She just couldn't believe that her regular thought like that, that he had a hangup. And apparently he had another regular dancer he liked, too, and she was the same fee. So he stopped coming to my friend. So sometimes I feel sorry for people.

"I don't know how race got started back up. Because like I said, two years ago it seemed like everything was just peachy keen. I never really find racial prejudice directed *at me*. It just seems like it's just gotten worse over the last two years. 'N' I don't know where it started. I don't know where it's gonna end, or if it ever is. Kinda sad."

Growing up, Lavonda lived with her father and stepmother. When she was nine, she says, they "started gettin' religious. First they were Jehovah Witness for about a year. They didn't like that. And then they were Jesus freaks—Jesus this and Jesus that. Then they were nondenominational and we was goin' to church seven days a week." Consequently, Lavonda has no use for organized religion. "My parents burnt me out on it, goin' to church seven days a week. Let's just say I've taken a three-year break. I know right from wrong.

"These days there are so many reverends out there that are so wicked anyway. I was shinin' this priest's shoes and he was tellin' me how he was in Vegas gambling. *He's a priest.* So it makes you wonder, 'What the hell's going to church for?' These days you've got to take religion in your own hands. Talk directly to God. I used to write God letters. I would just conversate, just write it out, 'cause I can't sit there and say prayers out loud. I was like about ten or eleven, and I would just take pen and paper and write him a letter, 'cause I figured he knew what I was doin'."

Although Lavonda has almost always lived in predominantly white, middle-class suburbs and has never so much as seen a gun except on television, the rise in violent crime caused by the drug trade and by gangs concerns her more than any other issue. She explains: "The reason why these kids are goin' so bad is 'cause their home life is so messed up. Everybody wants to be cared for. Everybody wants somebody to care about them. And gang members realize, 'This is my boy. This is my partner. He cares about me.' And you know they are going to go out and do that 'cause that's their family. That's what it is—that's their family. The gangs is their family 'cause they have no home to go to.

"That's why this country is so messed up. Everybody ignored it ten years ago. These kids were ten years old back then. Now they're my age and they're gone already. Seriously, they're gone. There's nothing you can do. It's way out of control. L.A. waited too late. They're gone. St. Louis might still have a chance. It's not nearly as bad as L.A., but it's gettin' there. It's rising. It's a lot of drive-bys goin' on now that used to didn't be maybe two years ago.

"They oughta do what they do in Turkey. Get caught stealin' somethin', cut their hand off. Get caught with drugs, they shoot 'em. This country is way too lenient on criminals—*way* too lenient. And that's the problem. Sometimes I think in America you got these people that are just too open-minded." Lavonda affects a tony, intellectual voice. " 'They have rights. They're criminals, but everybody has rights.' You know, like they're tryin' to say that the criminals have rights to a bed and stuff like that. Please."

THE HUMAN
DREAM

EILEEN

Eileen was seventeen when she visited Manhattan for the first time, and she immediately fell in love with the city. She says, "I knew two days after I was here this was where I was gonna be, and this was where I was gonna be a hairdresser, and this was where I was gonna live." Of course, there were ten years and a thousand miles between the life Eileen imagined for herself in Manhattan and her real life in Red Wing, Minnesota.

The second of six kids and the oldest girl, Eileen, now twenty-nine, was born in Ames, Iowa, while her father was completing his electrical engineering degree at Iowa State. Her father then went to work for a company that builds and operates nuclear power plants. When Eileen was little, her father was transferred several times to different locations throughout the Midwest and the northern Plains. Eileen was ten or eleven when her father was sent to a plant built on an Indian reservation in southeast Minnesota.

When her father took that job in Minnesota, Eileen's family settled in Red Wing, a town on the banks of the Mississippi River, fifty miles southeast of Minneapolis, just across from Wisconsin. Fewer than 12,000 people live there. "Everybody knows everybody," says Eileen. "It's a small kinda place." Her folks and two of her siblings still live in Red Wing. Her father is "pretty much the bigwig" at the nuclear power plant. Her mother, who was a housewife until Eileen's youngest brother went to college, now works at a shopping mall.

After graduating from the public high school, Eileen did not want to continue her formal education. "I just went because my dad wanted us all t'go to college," she explains. She went to school at St. Cloud State because it had a good program in special education, and she thought she might someday like to teach.

During her first year at St. Cloud, Cory, Eileen's "first boyfriend and only boyfriend," was going to school in Ely, Minnesota, a few miles south of the Canadian border. Every weekend Cory was making the four-and-a-half-hour drive south to see Eileen. Eileen eventually decided "that was ridiculous," so during her second year she transferred to Ely. Figuring her parents would disapprove of the move, she did not bother to tell them about her decision until she had rented an apartment there. After Cory finished his two-year program, he and Eileen returned to Red Wing so that he could accept a job working for the city.

Despite the fact that Eileen had received nothing but Cs and Ds ("barely") and that taxidermy had been her favorite course ("I got an A in it"), Eileen gave college one more try. In the mornings she pumped gas at a truck stop; in the afternoons she commuted forty-five minutes to a school in Wisconsin.

Two months later, she had had enough. She came home and told her father, "I can't do it anymore. I'm going to hairdressing school."

Eileen's parents were not enthusiastic about her choice. Her father told her, "You'll never make any money. What are you thinking?" But her parents just shook their heads when they realized they were not going to change Eileen's mind.

"This is something I always wanted to do," says Eileen, "so what were they gonna do?"

She enrolled at Hastings College of Hair Design in Hastings, Minnesota, a small town roughly halfway between Red Wing and St. Paul. To earn money to pay for school ("My parents have always

been supportive of me—always. But they've never paid for anything. I've never, ever taken money from my parents"), Eileen
tended bar at Annie's Bar and Grill, "the jock bar where everybody
went and drank" in Red Wing. She also cut hair to make a few extra
bucks. Ten months later, she graduated and became a full-time hair
stylist.

Eileen started her career with Joyce. Cory introduced Eileen to
Joyce, who had been a hairdresser in the salon at the local discount
store where Cory had once worked. When Eileen met Joyce, Eileen
loved her immediately. "She was, like, my idol," Eileen tells me.
"She was, like, 'This is what I wanna be.' "

By the time Eileen started working with Joyce, Joyce had
opened her own salon in the basement of a house owned by two
old ladies. Soon business was so good that Joyce and Eileen moved
to a prime location in downtown Red Wing. They even hired another hairdresser to work part-time.

To finance her share of the move, Eileen needed a loan from
the bank, which her mother had to cosign. Eileen's father did not
trust Joyce and suggested that his daughter get a written contract
from her. But Eileen wouldn't listen. "Don't worry, Dad," Eileen told
her father, "Joyce is cool. She's my best friend." ("You know, we
partied together even though she was older than I was. We were on
the same wavelength.") Eileen repaid the loan within a year. She
was now partners with her idol.

While Eileen was establishing herself professionally, her relationship with Cory was becoming more and more like a marriage.
They had been dating for six years. They had slept together "all the
time" when they were up in Ely. And once they returned to Red
Wing, Cory would sleep with Eileen at her parents' house, then get
up before her parents awoke and drive home to his parents' house
so that he could change for work. This bothered Eileen's parents
("My dad's like so old-fashioned it's ridiculous," she says), but they
eventually grew accustomed to the situation. Cory "was part of the
family," she tells me.

Cory and Eileen were so devoted to each other that they decided to build a house together on a piece of property about fifteen
miles south of Red Wing, near Lake Pepin. When Eileen told her
parents about their plans and that she had already obtained another
loan, her father asked her why she was borrowing more money and
building a house to live with a man to whom she was not married.

Eileen replied: "Because we wanna live together. We don't wanna pay rent. It's stupid. We know what we want."

Eileen now admits she should have listened to her father. Both times.

The first thing that collapsed was her "partnership" with Joyce. With anger and hurt in her voice, Eileen tells me, "I go t'work one day and everything's gone. Gone. Cleaned out. Joyce has left town. She's gone. She took everything. Everything. Her apartment's cleaned out. It was like overnight, they left. Her and Pat [Joyce's boyfriend]. Left town, no sign, nothing. I was like, I went t'work and there was my salon, empty. I couldn't believe it."

Fortunately, one of Eileen's acquaintances from hairdressing school had her own salon in town, and she invited Eileen to join her. "Just like that I was in another salon," Eileen says proudly.

Meanwhile, Eileen and Cory finished building their house and moved in. That's when "the pressure started," Eileen explains, "when the last piece o' wallpaper was hung in the house and it was like there was no excuse left t'not get married or have babies." This pressure—" 'Why don't you get married? You got the house. You've got great jobs. You're makin' good money. When are you gonna have kids?' "—came from both families, but especially from Cory's mother, who, according to Eileen, wanted grandkids from her oldest child.

"Panic set in," says Eileen. "I always knew I was never gonna marry Cory. He never knew that. Nobody ever knew that. But I knew that since I was seventeen, when I came to New York for the first time."

She goes on: "In the back o' my mind, the whole time that I was with Cory, I always knew there was gonna be an end—even though I knew that if I were to get married, if I were to have children, he would be the man it would be with. I always knew that because there was nobody like him. He was like the perfect person in my eyes to be with, to grow old with, to have kids with, that whole thing. But that's not what I wanted.

"And the bad thing was, like, all he did was hunt, fish, trap. That's Cory's life. He was Joe Outdoorsman. And like I grew up with that—fishing, trapping, hunting, everything. That's all we did. We were just outdoors people. He wouldn't even get on a plane. Lay on a beach—are you kidding? Go to Europe? Forget it.

"And I kept saying to myself, 'This isn't gonna work.' It's

great—if I wanted to have kids. 'Cause all my girlfriends got pregnant at like seventeen, eighteen. Now they have three kids. They're married. They have the house. Their husband works at Red Wing Shoe and he goes bowling on Monday nights and he's got a beer belly. An' they're miserable. They've never seen anything. They're never goin' anywhere, and I didn't want that.

"An' a lot of it was, like, my mom—the same thing happened to her. All growing up, my mom always said to me, 'See the world. Don't get married right outta high school.' She always told me that. 'You're wrong for staying with Cory. You should date other people. You're gonna regret it.' An' I was like, 'Shut up.'

"You don't listen to your parents. If you just would, everything would be fine. 'Cause everything they said was right. Everything. Now, ten years later, I'm doin' what I shoulda been doin' then. I'm like behind, y'know. When people are in college, that's when they date 'n' they go out 'n' they screw around 'n' they have parties. But I was like married from the time I was fifteen." She later admits, "I've learned a lot of lessons, but it's always been the hard way."

Though she had decided to leave Cory and to leave Red Wing, Eileen still had one problem: "How am I gonna tell these people that I'm not gettin' married, I'm goin' to New York?"

She left Cory a "Dear John" letter and moved out. Two years later the couple finally sold their house. "An' I was so relieved," she says. "I sold my car, an' I got on the plane and left." Eileen was finally moving to New York.

For a week.

Eileen could not find a job as a hairdresser at any salon in Manhattan. Everywhere she interviewed, the management told her she'd have to serve an apprenticeship shampooing—for a meager $200 a week—before she would be permitted to cut hair, and it was more of a "we'll see how it goes" than any kind of promise. Eileen figured, "I can't live in this city for two hundred dollars a week." So after seven days in Manhattan, she decided to try Boston, where one of her brothers was living. She reasoned, "It's not that far away. It's still the East Coast."

Eileen worked in Boston for two years, first in a salon next to Faneuil Hall in downtown Boston, then at the salon in Saks Fifth Avenue. After that, she transferred to the Saks in New York City. Manhattan at last.

A year and a half later, Eileen is still cutting hair in the salon at

Saks on Fifth Avenue. Although a salon in a ritzy department store is "a great place to build a clientele 'cause there's a lotta traffic," she says, "where you wanna go is to a smaller private salon and get like fifty percent commission, an' then maybe after, like, five hundred dollars, get the rest like cash under the table or somethin' like that."

Like Darrow in a courtroom, like Perlman on a Stradivarius, Eileen sees herself as having a special gift that makes her an extraordinary hairdresser. "It's not the cutting of hair," she explains. "It's the people. I have this ability to meet somebody for the first time, just look at them, put them in my chair—I don't even have to talk to 'em if I don't want to—and I can immediately read that person just from their mannerisms, the way they're dressed, if they're scared or if they're open. I can read people immediately. An' there's so many hairdressers that don't have a clue. They can't read people at all, an' they'll give 'em this hairdo. That's why there are so many bad hairdressers, because they may be a great *artiste* and can do a great cut, but they don't know the person, an' that's the key to the business. I can tell what a person's like when I meet them. It's like a scary thing."

She goes on: "I don't wanna sound like a psychic or anything, 'cause I don't believe in any of that shit. I'm very skeptical. My girlfriend goes to these 'readers' all the time. She lives her life through Ann the Tarot Card Reader. That's bullshit. I don't know what it is. But I know that it makes me a great hairdresser, more so than anyone that I work with. I just know that I can go really far with this.

"An' I love working with people's vanity because I love watching somebody who, like, doesn't like the way they look, an' they come in and they're feelin' really bad an' they had a shitty day an' they hate their hair, an' they're fat, an' their husband's fuckin' somebody else. And they sit in my chair, 'n' just because I made their hair look exactly how they wanted it, because *I knew* how they wanted it, they leave my chair and they're a totally different person. They forgot about all that stuff. They look in that mirror and it's like, 'God, I look good.' An' then they leave and it's like, 'Eileen did that. She made me feel this way.' "

Eileen absolutely loves her work. She can't wait to get to the salon and have someone sitting in her chair, and she pities those who work only for money.

For Eileen, the ultimate goal is not money, but the opportunity to travel, "goin' to other countries and seein' how other people live." Her means to that end, she believes, will be her skill as a hairdresser. She soon will leave Saks and move to a private salon. She figures she'll need ten, maybe fifteen years there to establish a great name for herself in Manhattan. After that, she'll be able to get a contract with a fashion magazine, such as *Elle* or *Vogue,* or with a top-flight fashion photographer and go to shoots in exotic locations.

According to Eileen, most of the hairdressers who are in the position that she wants to be in are in their late thirties. So, although she wishes she had left Red Wing sooner, she feels as if she's "on the right track, at least."

Eileen is doing the work she has always wanted to do, in the city she has wanted to be in since she first visited it twelve years ago. One might think her dreams have come—or, at least, are coming—true. But Eileen does not think in terms of dreams, and the phrase "American Dream"—"like the apple pie and all that stuff"—doesn't really pertain to her. She says dismissively, "Dreams are individual. America—is America. If you're an American and you have a dream, that's the American Dream."

Rather than dreams, Eileen thinks in terms of goals. "So far in my life," she says, "I've set a pattern—where I wanna be in what amount o' time, and have gotten there." As she said, she's on the right track.

On a personal level, Eileen's goal is to be "self-sufficient, always." She explains: "I have a real thing with that because most women that I meet, all they're looking for is somebody rich to support them. My girlfriends that I've met here, they're just out there looking for the rich man, looking for the guy who's got the great job and can get them an apartment in the city an' a country home an' have three kids, an' they don't have to work, an' they can have a nanny an' go shoppin' on Madison Avenue. That makes me sick. It disgusts me. To me, it's more important to be able to do that yourself.

"An' I know that that stems back to my mom and my dad always fighting over the checkbook. My mom was constantly begging my dad to get her a checkbook. An' she used to rip checks outta the back of the checkbook without him knowing, and then when he would come to that number, that was when the fight broke out.

"I never wanna be like that. I always wanna be in control of my own money."

I ask, "Do you consider yourself a feminist?"

"No," she says, adding, "Women will never be equal in our society, even as much as I want them to be. But they never will be. In my eyes, men are always gonna be the dominating one, sad as it is.

"Maybe I'm just one of the few that's tryin' to prove that women don't have to be—or shouldn't be—dependent on men. So many women are dependent on men, but they don't have to be. They think they are, an' our society wants them to think they should be. But that's not the way it should be."

Note: Two months after I spoke with Eileen, she moved from the salon at Saks to a private salon in midtown Manhattan. Just as she had planned.

MIKE

Mike, twenty-seven, works two jobs, as a police detective and as a part-time security guard in his apartment building, to be able to afford his apartment—but it's worth it, because the view from his living room is like a postcard. Looking southeast from thirty-six floors above Chicago's North Side, I can see Lakeshore Drive paralleling the contours of Lake Michigan and Belmont Harbor. A frigid, implacable November wind dapples the lake with whitecaps. On the inland side of Lakeshore Drive, the softball diamonds in Lincoln Park are barren. To the southwest Wrigley Field sits quietly hunched in the bitter cold, patiently waiting for spring and the return of those hapless Cubbies.

Mike's place is well decorated, especially for a bachelor's apartment. Portraits of Billie Holiday, Miles Davis, Count Basie, and Dizzy Gillespie hang on the wall above the couch. Against the opposite wall stands a bookshelf filled with fine stereo equipment and stacks of jazz CDs. There's also a small but varied collection of books, including several biographies—of jazz musicians; of professional athletes; Eldridge Cleaver's *Soul on Ice* and the sequel, *Soul on Fire* (the latter written to make a buck, comments Mike); Malcolm X's autobiography, which Mike has read five times (he admires Malcolm's intelligence and his ability to ceaselessly educate himself yet still retain his "street slickness")—as well as books about jazz and national politics. The only room that looks as if it belongs to a young bachelor is the kitchen, the counter of which is littered with boxes and bottles that have been left open, possibly for days.

Preppily dressed in a baby-blue-and-white-striped shirt, khaki chinos, and well-worn cordovan penny loafers, Mike rocks back in his chair as he tells me about growing up on Chicago's West Side, in a working-class black neighborhood known as Garfield Park.

"Some people say it's always been rough," Mike tells me, "but it's changed—I would say a lot—in the last ten years. It has gotten a lot rougher."

As a child Mike did not realize how tough a place his neighborhood was. "You know, to me it was just where I grew up. I knew there were things that went on around me that not everybody's exposed to. But I didn't know the difference. You don't know the difference, sometimes, until you see other things. Then you say, 'Wow, the people who're living where I live don't actually have to live like they do.'

"But everybody's not like that. Most of the cats that I grew up with were pretty straight. Everybody basically has jobs now. They're not working at *Fortune* Five Hundred companies or anything like that, but basically they have jobs. A lot of people are supportin' families. One of my best friends that I grew up with, he just joined the police department."

When Mike was a kid attending Catholic grammar school, his mother stayed home to raise him and his two younger brothers. His father was a police officer. By the time Mike was a student in public high school, his mother had already begun working part-time at an investment consulting firm. Between Mike's sophomore and junior years of high school, his parents divorced. Shortly thereafter, his father, by that point a sergeant, resigned after fifteen years with the force. Mike's mother is now an equity trader with the investment firm; she still lives on the top floor of the "two flat" in Garfield Park where Mike and his brothers grew up. Mike's father is a self-employed handyman. He lives on the city's South Side in the house where his father used to live.

After high school Mike bounced from one university to a junior college to another university. He felt as if he should be going to school, but after a while he was not sure why. Finally, he asked himself what he really wanted to do, and he said to himself that he'd always wanted to be a police officer. That's when he decided to join the Chicago police department.

Mike's father tried to discourage him from joining the force. "I think if it had been up to my dad," Mike says, "I probably would have gone to law school, eventually become a judge or somethin' like that. He used to say that all the time when I was little. My mother just said, 'Hey, do what makes you happy.' If I hadn't been a policeman, if I'd been anything else, I would've always said to myself, 'Man, I wonder what it would have been like to be a policeman.'" Although Mike regrets not having finished college before joining the force—he is only a semester away from completing his bachelor's degree in criminal justice, which he'll eventually finish—he says, "I wouldn't trade the experience of the last five and a half years for anything in the world."

For three years Mike answered routine calls and responded to emergencies as a uniformed officer in a blue-and-white "beat car." Then, after he spent a year as a plainclothes officer, the department promoted him to detective. He investigates violent crimes.

His experiences as a police officer, along with "just growing up," enable Mike to put life's difficulties in their proper perspective. He explains: "I see people who live in dirt all the time. I see people at their worst. Like you see people cryin' on TV a lot, bitchin' and moanin' about stuff that, you know, to me has absolutely nothin' to do with nothin'. Even stuff that I see that bothers me, you know, I can say, 'You could be worse off, *a lot* worse off.'"

Mike is seeing two women steadily—one of them has been "real off and on" because of his "philandering ways"—but he is still happily single. He has never been married; he has no kids. Of course, this might change. Someday. "I kinda like being single," he says, "but I do want some kids. I want t'watch somebody else grow up like I did. But I don't want to have any kids if I'm not married. It's kind of hard to try and raise kids when the mother's here and the father's there, jugglin'.

"I really don't plan on gettin' married anytime too soon. There's a lot more to marriage than meets the eye, and I see a lot of people who I don't think are really prepared for it. There are only a few people who I've seen before and after they got married and I could say, 'Hey, these two people're meant for each other. There's no bull-shit in the game. This woman actually loves this man, this man actually loves this woman. There's no ulterior motives here.'

"A lot of people get married because they feel like they should be married, as opposed to ' 'Cause I'm in love and I want to spend the rest of my life with this particular person.' I'm a little naive in that respect. I honestly think people should live happily ever after. And they should work *hard* to live happily ever after."

For Mike the phrase "American Dream" does not conjure images of "happily ever after." When Mike hears those words, he says, "A lot of negative things come to mind—phoniness, hypocrisy."

He continues: "The American Dream that other people speak of isn't really reality. It's not what's goin' on. I think you have to know what *you* want, as opposed to living *the* American Dream. And then you can say, 'I lived my—*my*—American Dream.' But it has to be up to you. I don't think you can say what the American Dream is because everybody's ideas are different.

"The term 'American Dream'—for me it doesn't apply. I can't see it applying to me. I just live for me. I'm not looking for th' pie in th' sky. I know that just because I could end up with a house, two-point-five kids, and a coupla dogs and two cars, my life may not be complete. So I don't live my life *for* the American Dream. For the most part I take it one day at a time.

"I do want to be successful. But I feel like I'm pretty successful because I'm happy in my heart with what I'm doing, and I think that's what matters most of all, more than anything else.

"My parents brought me up to be the best that you can be at whatever you are. And if you do that, then you're a success. If you half-ass and it doesn't work out like you want it to work out, then you're the one that loses. I do think I do give it my hundred percent, so therefore I'm never sad. I know that every day that I go to work, I'm doing the best that I can do with the hand that I've been dealt."

Mike defines success not only as always giving your best effort, but also as doing what makes you—not other people—happy. But before you can be happy, he says, you must know what it is that makes you happy. "I see a lot of people who don't know what they want. And by them not knowin' what they want, they're never really gonna be happy. Success comes from inside. You have to decide what makes you successful."

Mike's work, which so often exposes him to life's ugliness and despair, has given him a sense of the irony implicit in our national myth of the American Dream. He says, "There're a lot of people that I have to deal with that don't have any concept of an American

Dream. All they see is—nothin'. I don't know if it's despair, and I don't know if it's by choice, but they don't see anything positive, you know. Is it the responsibility of other people to make their dreams come true, or is it up to them? I see a lotta people placing a lot of blame on people who it shouldn't be placed upon, that their American Dreams aren't bein' fulfilled."

A bit later he adds, "The way people view life, all they see's what goes on in their block. And what's goin' on in their block is nothin'." Some people, he says, "the day that they're born, they're doomed." He relates two stories from the period when he was assigned to work on Chicago's South Side.

The first is about a little boy named John. "For three nights in a row," Mike says, "we picked him up after curfew. Curfew's at ten-thirty. We picked him up at eleven o'clock comin' out of a fast-food restaurant with a order of french fries. Three nights in a row, 'cause this was his dinner. It got to the point by the third night we didn't write him up. We just took him in the car and took him home. I mean, that's what he knew, though, bein' out late at night and his dinner was a order of french fries. How he got the money, I don't know. I don't know whether his mother gave him seventy-five cents for the french fries or what. But that's what his life was about. 'N' by the time I left over there, he was turned into a gang-banger. He was gettin' into trouble with the police. I started seein' him at the station, you know, bein' in trouble, as opposed to thinkin' about school or thinkin' about something positive."

Mike tells me another story, this one about a thirteen-year-old. "He had about five grams of heroin on him. The thing was, he knew the juvenile justice system—not only the juvenile justice system, the criminal justice system—as well as we did. He told us what we could and couldn't do to him. The worst thing about it was he had the smugness of an adult, of somebody that was older than me. What we could and couldn't do to him, what kind of case we had against him, what was wrong with the case, what we did wrong with it, and how he was gonna be out in a little while anyway. That's strange. If I saw a policeman when I was thirteen years old and he said anything to me, I would almost start cryin' because [Mike affects the voice of a weeping little boy] 'I didn't do anything wrong. Please don't do anything to me. I'm gonna get killed.' Whereas now you got this little kid, and he's like, 'Hey, here I am.

There's nothin' you can do with me.' That's kinda sad. That gets to be kinda depressin' after a while.

"Some of these kids, they're just startin' off in a hole. They're startin' off with not a chance. I chose to be a policeman. Could I've been other things? Yeah, if I'd wanted to. These kids probably won't even get that chance.

"Sometimes you hear a lot of stuff about how people end up in prison and they're gonna end up dead one day. And you wanna say this is not true, and you wanna not believe it. You wanna say, 'That's a bunch of nonsense.' But sometimes it's true. A lot of these kids, they don't stand a chance at all. Not at all. It's really sad, I mean, seein' little kids dealin' dope, runnin' dope. But then you have to keep your perspective. Sometimes you have to back up off it. If you lectured them, you'd almost be wasting your breath, 'cause that's not what they want."

Mike believes that, regardless of their circumstances, people ultimately must take control of their own lives if they want their visions of the American Dream to come true. Yet Mike is also highly critical of those who are unsympathetic to people, especially the poor, who must surmount greater obstacles than others do before their hard work can pay off, before their dreams can come true. Mike says that people who are more fortunate often criticize and judge those who are not as lucky as they are, but then don't do anything to help.

"Part of the American Dream is giving back," he says, "and a lot of people don't."

STACY

"I guess I'm, like, at peace and I'm happy," Stacy says diffidently. "I am happy, I think. But until I start doing something about what I wanna do in the future, I don't think I'll feel like, you know, fulfilled. Until I start knowin' that I'm getting close. Because I feel like right now I'm just kinda hanging. I'm not exactly sure what I'm gonna do. I mean, I'm not worried, or I'm not, like, anxious and nervous about it. I just don't feel—I don't feel balanced.

"I'm kind of, like, stuck in a transitional thing."

Although she is twenty-one, Stacy is nervously frozen in adoles-
cence. At times, she seems as vulnerable as a little girl waiting for
her parents in the lost-and-found at Disneyland. Part of this comes
from Stacy's big brown eyes, which look as if she is just about to
cry. Part comes from her voice, which is edgy with self-doubt. At
other times Stacy seems like a typically rebellious teenager. When I
meet her, she is wearing a black bodysuit and threadbare blue jeans
that are three sizes too big, cinched at the waist by a two-inch-wide
black leather belt. Three bracelets and a watch jangle on her right
wrist as she smokes her Marlboro Lights. And when she isn't smoking, she is conspicuously chewing Day-Glo green spearmint gum.

Born and raised in California's San Fernando Valley, Stacy is an
only child. Her mother, only twenty when Stacy was born, divorced
Stacy's father when Stacy was a few months old. Stacy has only one
memory of her father. She was three or four, and her father had
taken her out for the day. "I don't even remember what we did that
day," she says. I just remember him dropping me off, my mom
wasn't home, and him leaving me on the steps. And I just remember
being hysterically crying and him telling me it's gonna be okay. I
mean, I don't even remember, like, if he stayed with me until my
mom came home." Stacy's father eventually stopped paying child
support and, except for a handful of brief reappearances, vanished
from her life.

When Stacy was five, her mother married a man Stacy describes
as a stern disciplinarian. "Their marriage was really pretty awful,"
she says. "They were always arguing and fighting all the time. Used
to go outside of the house 'cause they were fighting so loud." Stacy
was in fourth grade when they finally divorced. She says, "I was really happy, actually, 'cause it was such a nightmare when he was
here."

Without a husband's income to help with the bills, Stacy's
mother "had to work really hard," says Stacy. "To raise me and
work full-time was really a tough job." Yet despite the financial
strain her mother faced, Stacy grew up in "middle-class" economic
conditions. "I think my mom struggled," she says, "but *I* got everything that I wanted. I was kinda spoiled."

Stacy's middle-class upbringing resulted from her mother's
diligence—and her maternal grandparents' willingness to help Stacy
and her mom. "My grandparents have always been there for my
mom," says Stacy. "She was lucky 'cause she had people to turn to,

so it's not like she had her back up against a wall and didn't have anything." According to Stacy, her grandparents arranged for Stacy and her mother to remain in their house in North Hollywood, the house where Stacy has lived most of her life and where Stacy's mother still lives. Stacy's grandparents also paid for most of her education at two local prep schools and, she says, still provide her and her mother financial help whenever they need it.

After high school, Stacy's grades were not good enough to get her into a four-year college. So the autumn after she graduated, she enrolled in a local junior college to try to boost her record. She did not enjoy her first choice of institutions. "It's all just everything I learned in high school, but even more drier," she says. "And there's a couple of good teachers, but not many at all." Two years later, thinking that a different school might offer her a more satisfactory education, she transferred to a junior college in Santa Monica. She didn't like that, either. "I'm not an early person," she says, "and I had to wake up at about six o'clock and sit in that hour of traffic. I started out okay, then over the course of the semester I just kind of burned out, I guess." After one semester, she transferred back to the local junior college and took an art history class. Now she doesn't go to school at all.

"But I wanna go back," she insists. "I mean, I really do wanna go back to school. The thing is, it's such a pain in the ass having to go. It makes me not wanna go, when I have to go to a JC [junior college], when I feel like I have to go through high school all over again."

Stacy tells me that, although she genuinely wants to go to college, she is not a studious person. "I read all the time and stuff on my own. But I don't know if it's 'cause of my nature, that somebody says you have to do something and I rebel against it even though I don't want to. It's not that, y'know, I'm not into learning, 'cause I very much am. It's just that I don't wanna be told what I have to learn and have to learn it. I have a very hard time, I think, with authority. It's like, anything that would pose opposition or a threat, instead of, like, overcoming it, it's just like another reason for me not to wanna do it.

"I did good in the beginning. That's always how it starts—I do well in the beginning, then things start, you know, kinda snow-balling. You have to turn more and more things in and I just kinda start slacking off. I really don't wanna sit down and have to write this paper, or something like that. I just don't. I mean, I know people who feel that way too, and they'll go and they'll get someone else's paper, or they'll go and copy out of books in the library or something. But I can't do that. I feel like if I'm gonna do the work, *I'm* gonna do it. So instead of, y'know, just finding an alternate way, maybe like cheating or something, I just don't do the work."

Today, instead of going to school, Stacy works four days a week—about twenty-eight hours—at a little gallery that sells handmade jewelry, ceramics, glass, and wovens. On her three days off, she runs errands and hangs out with her friends and family.

Despite feeling "tremendously guilty" about it, Stacy has not bothered to tell her family that she quit school. She suspects that her mother may know, but Stacy has been able to avoid confronting the issue because she has been living in an apartment with a friend since last October. Stacy explains that she has not told her family about dropping out partly because she was supposed to have been the first person in the family to get a college education, and they would be "really disappointed." And she does not want them nagging her about the subject because she plans eventually to complete her education.

Sparing her family needless disappointment is not the only reason Stacy has not told them about her decision to take a break from school. To be covered by her mother's insurance, she must be a full-time student. If she isn't—rather, if she tells her mother that she isn't—Stacy then must find a job where she can get insurance coverage. But, she says, "I'm not ready to go and work a nine-to-six job as a secretary or something like that. That's not what I wanna do. I just don't wanna do that."

"Why not?"

"Because I think it's very depressing. When I see other people, I mean, maybe that's okay for them, but I think I'd be really depressed having to go into a place and just, like, sit there and type or just do something that I don't wanna do."

Actually, although Stacy enjoys working in the crafts gallery, that is not what she wants to do, either. She says, "There's just a feeling that I'm just, not passing time, but I'm not on the road to, like, what I wanna be doing.

"I might wanna do something within, like, designing clothes. I'm not sure that I would love to do that. But if I majored in English, I'd wanna do something, like maybe start writing or teaching. I don't know if that would make me happier than—I mean, I would love to design clothes, but I think that, like, helping, you know, like teaching children or something like that, I think that would be really a satisfying experience."

Whichever she decides to pursue, she says, "It's not gonna be an office job, where I'm gonna just leave at the end of the day and my work's done and then I don't think about it until the next morning. 'Cause if I'm doin' something like designing or if I'm teaching, it's gonna be part of a lifestyle. It's gonna be, like, what I'm about. I wanna just have something that I really, really like doing and I enjoy and that I can get excited about."

I say, "You've mentioned fashion design, you've mentioned writing, and you've mentioned teaching. Why not pick one and go?"

Stacy responds: "Why aren't I motivated enough, and why don't I just go out and do something? I don't know if maybe it's, like, I'm scared, and that might be part of the reason that's holding me back. 'Cause maybe that means like you are gonna be grown up now, you are gonna be an adult. No more, not carefree days or anything like that, but you're an adult now, you have to do these things. I think that *does* have something to do with it, a little bit.

"When I see my mom and I see other people who are older, I think, God, I don't want my life to turn out like that if *that's* what happens when you grow up. And you know, it's like I'm rebelling against, like, myself. I'm rebelling against, like, growing up. I say, I don't want my life like that, and I know I have the capabilities to not make it like that. But I guess when you grow up somewhere and you see that all the time, you start thinking that, well, maybe it's inevitable, maybe *that is* what happens. 'Cause it seems like so many people are just like—it doesn't seem like they're so happy. I don't wanna be stuck doing something I'm not happy at.

"When I was young, I was spoiled. I got everything I wanted. My mom always, like, managed to shelter me and make sure everything was okay for me. But I guess I felt like life, not that it was owed to me, but this is just how it should be. And then all of a sudden you start realizing, Well, it's not how it's gonna be." But, she says, "I'm not blaming anybody except for me."

Not only is Stacy frightened by the prospect of growing up and having to accept adult responsibilities, she is also scared of failing. She says, "I think that scares me a lot. I guess I'm just scared that somehow I might not cut it, or I might not be good enough, or something like that. I guess that part scares me. But I'm never gonna know if I don't try. And I don't know if it's 'cause I don't wanna disappoint, y'know, the people around me, so I just think that, 'Oh well, if I don't do it, I'm not disappointing anybody.' But it shouldn't be about that. It shouldn't be about disappointing. It should be about, 'Yeah, I know I'm gonna do it because I know I'm smart enough, and if I'm interested enough, *I can.*' "

So what does the American Dream mean to Stacy, a girl who openly describes herself as sheltered, a little spoiled, uncertain of the direction she wants her life to take, afraid to accept adult responsibilities, and scared of failure? (Stacy says this characterization is "totally correct.")

"I don't think the American Dream exists," she says. In her mind the phrase conjures unrealistic images, "kinda like a *Happy Days–Brady Bunch* type thing. I don't know if my dream would be an American Dream. I think it would be more like just of a universal type, just wanting to be happy, wanting to find somebody who I'm in love with, wanting to have children, wanting the world to be a good place where your children are gonna grow up in. Something along those lines. Financially, yeah, of course, I want a comfortable life. To me, I would rather have personal happiness than, like, financial."

For Stacy, satisfaction and happiness are easily defined: "Just to enjoy doing what you're doing, being around people who you wanna be around, who you love and you like, and, you know, like, doing something that makes you feel good." A moment later she adds: "To me, that would be, like, a great feeling knowing that I didn't have any fears and I just went for everything that I wanted to do."

This summer, Stacy will travel to Europe with a couple of her friends. She hopes that this trip, a present from her grandparents, will inspire her and that, upon her return, she will begin to embrace adulthood.

"I don't know what I'm really looking for," she says. "I'm just thinking that, y'know, when I go away this summer, for some reason, I really think that this will be kinda like my last little thing of, like, still having my carefree days, where I'm not serious about starting on a career or school. I feel like this is gonna be the end to it, 'cause after this my future and adulthood is gonna be staring at me, like, in the face."

According to Stacy, she has already taken her first tentative steps across the threshold of young adulthood. She told her employer that when she returns from Europe she will not be able to work during the day because school will come first. She also plans to move back home to reduce her living expenses.

I ask, "Do you think maybe you're expecting too much from this summer?"

"No," she says, "I just think that I'm kinda viewing this as I'm saying goodbye to the days where I don't wanna have to face growing up. This is kinda like the kiss-off, like, 'Okay, I wanna get serious now,' and this is gonna be like my last blowout of, I guess, being a kid still. Because it's not gonna go on forever like this. It can't. I mean, I'd go crazy if it did, 'cause I feel like I'm being pulled in, like, so many directions. Part of me just wants to be taken care of and still be that kid. But that other part, I wanna go out and I wanna start making *my* life, y'know, and taking care of *myself* and not being dependent on someone like my mom for things to fall in place like they normally do.

"I mean, that's a hard part that I have to deal with, 'cause I've always been taken care of, and my mom's really overprotective and she just makes sure that everything's okay for me. So, when I have to try t'go out and make things work for me, it's so, I guess, scary, because if I've always had somebody else doing that for me, I'm gonna have to do it myself. I guess it's hard to let go of that."

Note: I spoke with Stacy after she returned from Europe. "I came back with a really great feeling about myself," she said. "Feel like I learned a lot about myself." With her newfound self-confidence, she began implementing the plan she had described to me three months earlier. She has moved back home and is about to begin classes at a local junior college. She intends to fulfill the requirements for acceptance to a fashion design school in Los Angeles. As we say goodbye, she tells me, "I have a lot more in me than I acknowledge."

DAVE

Dave, twenty-six, grew up in Calabasas, a suburb of Los Angeles. "It was pretty much upper-middle-class," he says, describing the community, "but I grew up in a middle-class family." Dave's father has worked in the movie industry for nearly thirty years. For most of that time he was a color film technician. But today he works for a video company. Dave's mother does clerical and administrative work for the pharmacy in a local hospital.

Growing up, Dave was a jock. He played basketball and ran track, but his best sport was football. In fact, he was good enough to attract attention from a few college football coaches. During the autumn of his senior year, however, when college football recruiters were evaluating prospects, Dave's parents got divorced.

"It was pretty tough," says Dave, " 'cause I was graduating and, y'know, it's s'posed to be my time of the year. The weekend my dad moved out of the house was the weekend that I broke my collarbone. It was my senior year and I was supposed to be looked at for college scholarships. So it was kind of tough. I think it was tougher on my younger sister. She had a rough time with it. I pretty much had to be the mediator of the whole family, y'know, keepin' everything upswing, beat tempo, y'know, just keep my sister going, keep my mom and dad happy. So I'd kinda be like a referee."

Dave admits that the distraction caused by his parents' divorce was not the only reason he did not earn a football scholarship. He explains that, when he was young, he was diagnosed as dyslexic, and he used his condition as an excuse not to take math in high school. "That was probably the main reason why I didn't get any scholarships," he says.

But he still wanted to play college football. So, after graduating from high school, he enrolled at a nearby junior college and spent a year as a redshirt freshman on the football team. The school disbanded its football program before Dave's second year, and he transferred to another local junior college, where he played for two more years. He also earned an associate's degree in criminal justice administration.

Once again, Dave's performance on the field attracted interest from at least one college football coach, a man from Sonoma State University. Although he could not offer Dave an athletic scholarship because the conference in which Sonoma State competes prohibits it, he invited Dave to visit the university's campus in Rohnert Park, which sits twenty-five miles west of Napa Valley.

"He sold me on the place," says Dave. "I came up here on a re-cruiting trip, fell in love with it, y'know. It's kinda different com-pared t' Southern California. You got a change of weather up here, 'n' it's a lot cleaner air. It's a lot safer place to live, and it had my ma-jor."

Perhaps even more important than the consistently beautiful weather, fresh air, and a bachelor's degree in his chosen field of study, Sonoma State offered Dave the opportunity to finish out his college football career, as an outside linebacker and defensive end for the Sonoma State Cossacks. Dave tells me, "I always had a dream when I was little, to play college football. And even though this place wasn't a scholarship school, y'know, I still got to complete my dream of playing college football.

"I have terrible shoulders now. It was just somethin' that went kinda hand in hand together. So when the two years were over, it was almost a blessing, 'cause the shoulders was just getting abused."

Being a member of the football team required that Dave take "a lot of B.S. classes. You took weight lifting and football—advanced and all this other stuff."

I laugh. "Football what?"

"Advanced football," he says, a bit embarrassed. "Yeah, it's cheesy, but y'know." A minute later he adds, half seriously, "Got an 'A' in it."

Dave could count only a limited number of those "cheesy" but mandatory courses toward his degree. Consequently, he took longer than average to earn his bachelor's degree. His parents paid his tu-ition and rent; he held a variety of part-time jobs to earn spending money. Finally, after seven years, three schools and three football programs, he received his bachelor's degree in criminal justice ad-ministration. He graduated the weekend before our visit.

Although Dave is happy that he has at last finished school, he is also frightened because he is now entering what many people say is the worst job market for college graduates in twenty years. He says, "There's hardly any jobs out there, unless you work at a fast-food restaurant, and work doin' that is an ego killer. Y'know, I think for a teenager, I think that's a great job to start out with. But a college graduate with a degree, and working at either UPS or a community center, making five seventy-five an hour, I think that's just—it makes you kind of wonder. It makes you a little worried about what the future has in store for you."

But Dave remains confident about his future. "Because I don't want to quit," he tells me. "I'm not a quitter. I know what I have in store for me, and I know what process I gotta do to get my goal. It's kinda like my senior quote in my high school yearbook—'Obstacles are only what you see when you take your eyes off the goal.' It was anonymous, so I don't know who wrote it. It was one of those posters, y'know, it was a cool poster. I don't know what beach it was, but the poster had a huge rock with a huge hole in it, y'know, and that was supposed to be the obstacle and the goal was the hole. But I feel pretty optimistic about my future, 'cause I won't quit. I'm gonna do whatever I can to get in."

What Dave wants to get in is a pair of firefighter's rubber boots. "I've wanted to be a firefighter since I could talk," he says. "I remember birthday cakes with firemen on 'em. My parents took me down to our local fire station for my birthday with all my friends and we got t'walk around the station and put on the turnout coats and everything and sit on the truck. Aw, God, I was prob'ly about eight.

"It's just a great job. It's a rewarding job. It's a lot of satisfaction in it, t'help people out, 'n' I've always wanted to help people out. I've either thought about joining law enforcement or firefighter, but I think firefighter is the key. It's been like my long-lost love to do.

"People always say, 'Why in the heck you wanna be a firefighter? It's crazy. It's scary.' I'm going, 'Yeah, but it's not a monotonous thing.' Each call's different. Each fire's different. Each medical aid is different. Everything. So it's just a great job. It's a long hard process to get into. Realistically, about two, three years."

Dave is "applying everywhere in the world right now" for a position with any fire department. He explains that there are a couple of reasons why it is so difficult for a would-be firefighter to find openings. One is the amount of training people must complete before many communities will accept their applications. Dave just completed his training to become certified as an emergency medical technician, or EMT. He will have to work full-time for six months as an EMT before he can enroll in paramedic school, which is nine months long. After that, he has to apply for official firefighter training so that he can obtain his "firefighter one" certificate. Then he finally will be eligible for a job as a paid firefighter.

Of course, that does not mean he will find a position any time soon. "A lot of it also is your race and your gender," he says.

"How so?"

" 'firmative action, and just a quota," he says without any rancor. "It's just hard, y'know. I'm not just goin' by what I know, I'm just goin' by what a lot of my friends are saying. Like if I was a female or if I was a different race, oh, if I was black or Hispanic, I'd prob'ly have a better chance, because they have to meet these kinda quotas for affirmative action. So it just makes it harder for a male Caucasian to get into a job as a firefighter."

I ask Dave how that makes him feel, and without any sharpness in his voice, he says, " 'Bitter' I think'd be the most appropriate word, because I think it should be that who's ever the most qualified for the job should get it. Like, my girlfriend's dad's a captain in the San Francisco fire department, and he's had a few probationary firefighters who have been women who can't do any normal operations that a firefighter is asked t'do, y'know, raising ladders, lifting ladders off trucks, manning a hose, doing any kind of ventilation work with a saw or an ax. It's just an abundance of things, 'cause it's a physical, demanding job. And if you're not capable 'cause of your size and your strength, then y'know, that's gonna limit you.

"That's why. That's what makes me bitter. Because, I don't know, I feel that I'm qualified. But of course, everyone thinks they're qualified. But I'm also goin' t'school. I've gotten my degree in criminal justice. I've also gotten through my EMT. I'm gonna go through my paramedic and I'm goin' through my 'firefighter one,' so I consider myself pretty much qualified."

I ask Dave why, if he is bitter, there is no hint of it in his voice. "Well," he says, "there's nothin' I can do about it, y'know. Laws have been passed. It's goin' on 'n' it's not changing and it's not gettin' any better.

"But you're right, I don't have the hatred bitter. I just have the bitter because I just don't think it's right the way it works, the way the system works. I just don't agree with it."

On weekends Dave usually spends his time with his girlfriend, Kirsten. She will be a senior at the University of California at Davis, which is seventy-five miles east of Rohnert Park. Dave and Kirsten met at a party two and a half years ago, they've been dating ever since. Dave loves Kirsten and hopes someday to marry her, though he is not yet ready to make that commitment, " 'cause right now," he says, "I just have too many things to deal with."

One of the things Dave must achieve before he marries Kirsten is financial independence. His two part-time jobs, as a fitness instructor at a local community center and unloading boxes for UPS, provide him with enough income to pay about two-thirds of his monthly expenses. His parents give him the rest. Hoping that the hands-on experience will help him land a job with a paying fire department, Dave also serves as a volunteer firefighter for Cotati, a little city south of Rohnert Park. He says, "I wanna be financially secure, so I can be able to, y'know, stand on my own two feet, and if I had to support Kirsten, I could be able to do that."

Money is not the only thing keeping Dave from the altar. He says that although both of his parents have remarried, he believes that their divorce left him wary of marriage. "They were married for almost twenty years and I just can't understand, after twenty years, why? It's like my mom's always said, 'You can never go into a marriage thinkin' that you can change somebody.' But I think their divorce has made me a little hesitant about gettin' married—the pain that they both went through. It just seems like everything's so monetary. I'm not saying that that was the reason why they divorced—y'know, I'm sure it's 'cause they fell out of love—but God, marriage just means so much, in so many ways. Right now, I just don't have—"

Dave stops midsentence, then says, "Y'know, I've still got a lot of growin' up to do."

I ask him whether, once he and Kirsten are married and have children, she will stay home to take care of their kids. "I don't know," he answers. "She's a pretty independent girl. I know she would want to work. She realizes that in a marriage, especially this day and age, you're gonna need two incomes. So I'm sure once the kids get old enough to go into whatever, child care or can be baby-sat, I'm sure that's what would probably happen, and then she would prob'ly go back to work."

A few minutes later I ask Dave about the American Dream. "Like, whenever I think about it," he says, "like whenever I hear it on TV, like these immigrants comin' from other countries to get the

American Dream, I ask myself, 'What do they think is the American Dream?'

"I think there is more of a struggle, survival of the fittest, y'know, a struggle to keep your head above water. Sure, you do have your rich people, and that's probably their dream. But I don't know, I just find that phrase really hard to understand.

"As I see it as a whole, we got a lot of people in poverty. We got a lot of homeless people. I thought the American Dream consisted of no one'd be homeless, everyone gettin' a top-notch education. For the majority, I don't really think there is a dream. It's a dream, but I don't think it'll ever become a reality. I just think it's gonna be a dream for them because, you know—I'm not the type of person that stakes everything on money, and you know the phrase 'money doesn't buy you happiness,' but I don't see too many homeless people that are happy not havin' any money.

"I just think that, sure, everyone has their dreams and their goals, but a lot of people that are in poverty have a hard time seeing their dream come true. I don't wanna sound like a pessimist, but I just think the American Dream is words. I look at it like, just basically, I have a dream, this is the way I want my dream to come out, and I'm gonna work as hard as I can to get to see that dream become reality."

And what is Dave's dream? "To be happy, healthy, successful. I think happiness has gotta be one of the major things t'have in life. Friends, oh God, 'n' just family. I just think that all goes kinda hand in hand together."

Dave also has set certain goals for himself. "Professionally, be a firefighter. Personally, t'be the best boyfriend, the best husband, the best father, the best friend. Be successful, I wanna be successful. I wanna be able t'hold up my head high, m'shoulders back, y'know, just say, 'Hey, I'm Dave and I've done this and this and this and this.' And I think that's successful."

He says, " 'Success'—God, that's a big word, means a lotta things. I don't know, it seems like I kinda hit on being the best a lot, but I think being the best goes hand in hand with being successful."

Dave is so committed to becoming a firefighter, I wonder whether he could be happy doing anything else. "Yeah," he tells me, " 'cause I'd work my hardest to be the best and to do what it takes for me to be happy in that job. I'm not that person that's gonna sit back on my heels and be miserable and not make anything happen. I'd kind of like to consider myself a person, like a—what is it?—a playmaker, who makes things happen."

Discussing the national situation, Dave tells me he worries about "where we're headed in the future." Noting that he earned spending money during college by looking after grade-school children during lunchtime and recess, he explains: "One reason why I'm kinda scared for the future is because I've seen what some of the younger generation looks like. It's gonna be frightening.

"There's some things that just come out of these kids' mouths. Half the kids at the fourth, fifth, sixth grade have done more stuff than I did when I was their age, whether it's drugs or sex or the language. I swear t'God, there's a kid, I'm not gonna mention any names, he was in sixth grade, and he had a condom tucked inside the headband of his hat. He took off his hat and it fell out. I said, 'What do you have in there?' He goes, 'My rubber. My stepdad gave it to me.' No way. 'Well, do you know what you do with that?' and he explained the whole thing to me. I *never* knew what that was until like ninth or tenth grade. I was a major jock. I guess I was naive to that stuff. But it just blew my mind. I could not believe it. I just went, 'Oh God, I feel for the next generation.'

"Where we're gonna be, how we're gonna be, an' how is this world gonna be, y'know, with the environment, the deficits, the budgets. Y'know, we got a huge hole in the ozone layer and it kinda makes me a little nervous. Crime, I'm worried. I think about crime and how that's always rising and there's really no answer for it. The drug problem, the gang problem, all that concerns me."

"How do we solve these problems?" I ask.

Dave laughs for several seconds, then says, "If I knew that, I'd be President of the United States." More seriously, he adds, "God, I don't know. I think it has to start with the communities. I think it has to start with people in the communities. First of all, we have to end this racism problem. I think that's what hurtin' a lot of this, y'know, because blacks are killin' the Mexicans, the Mexicans are killin' the whites. It's just a chain reaction. It has to start with the schoolkids, then it has to start with the parents, and it has to be dealt with in the communities."

To straighten things out, however, Dave believes the government will have to spend more time on domestic concerns and less on world affairs. "I think we're too worried about these third-world countries takin' over. I think we should butt out of a lot of situations that happen outside of our country. I think we should worry about what's going on in our country before we go elsewhere."

I ask, "Are you optimistic about the country's future?"

"Yeah, I am. You know this can only be shitty for so long. It's gotta change. Someone's gonna come in and just clean house and set this country right. I think someone's gonna come in and just take, y'know, take control. I do believe that it has to do with the communities, the community representatives, everybody. It's just— somethin's gotta happen, and I think it will. I think it'll be in the next three to five years."

I point out to Dave that he has offered two very different views of the nation's future, one democratic, the other autocratic. Wrestling to reconcile these inconsistent perspectives, he says, "I think that it's gotta start with us, each individual, and then because we do have one person as president, he's gonna have to, y'know, he's gonna have to be the leader, 'cause that's how this country's run."

PAULA

Paula, twenty-seven, is a rabbinical student at Hebrew Union College in New York City. The oldest of three children, she was born in New Jersey and grew up mostly in a small town called Long Valley. According to the AAA road atlas, it is thirty miles due west of the "Welcome Center" in Newark.

Paula's father was born in Poland and came here with his family when he was four. For most of Paula's life, he was the principal at a public elementary school. He retired two years ago. Today he teaches Yiddish once a week at a community college. He also supervises the student teaching program at a teachers' college. Paula's mother was a homemaker until Paula was in junior high, then she went to work as a librarian in one of the public schools. She later became the director of Long Valley's public library and served for ten years on the school board. She retired this year.

After graduating from public high school, Paula attended Rutgers and majored in English. During her senior year, she decided that she wanted to become a rabbi and applied to Hebrew Union College. Her application was rejected. Two years later, after working for Planned Parenthood in New Jersey, for a liberal political action office in Washington, D.C., and for a Jewish community center in Queens, Paula again applied to rabbinical school. This time, her application was accepted.

Paula's religious background is not what you might expect of someone who has decided to become a rabbi. Although both of her parents are Jewish, they did not raise their children in a traditionally Jewish environment. For most of Paula's life, her family did not belong to any synagogue or temple, so on Jewish holidays they did not attend formal religious services. Instead, for instance, during one year's High Holidays, Paula's parents kept their children home from school and took them to a park. "We walked around the park and we talked about God," says Paula. "That was High Holiday for us."

Paula and her younger brother and sister received almost no formal Jewish education or training, and what schooling they were given was highly unconventional. Paula's parents, along with eight or ten other families, established a sort of "cultural Jewish school" for their children. The children did not study Hebrew, but they did discuss Bible stories and celebrate the Jewish holidays.

During her senior year of high school, the parents asked Paula to become the teacher of their alternative religious school. "I remember the first day I went in to observe the teacher who was leaving. I remember sitting in the classroom, watching her teach, and thinking, 'I don't know how I'm gonna teach this stuff because I'm not sure I even believe any of this stuff.' And I walked out of there and I started reading and I started trying to prepare what I was gonna teach, looking at the textbooks they were using, looking at the curriculum. And I realized that this was really something that I could teach and there was a lot more there for me than I had ever thought. I taught there for a year. That's when things really started.

"It was very, very satisfying. I really enjoyed the kids. I really enjoyed teaching. And what was probably most ironic of all was that the woman who had taught me in that same school, I was teaching her children now. That was really nice."

Looking for a summer job at the end of her freshman year at college, Paula saw an ad from the directors of a Jewish summer camp. They were looking for a music teacher. "What could be more perfect?" thought Paula. "I played guitar. I loved music." Paula, who has played the cello since she was eight, tells me, "Once you can play the cello, guitar is easy."

As preparation for the summer camp, Paula attended a week-end retreat, sponsored by the Reform Judaism movement, for camp song leaders. "At the time I really didn't feel affiliated with any Jewish movement, with Reform or Conservative, because we hadn't been affiliated as a family in so long, and I didn't really know where I belonged. I don't think I understood enough about what it meant to be a Reform Jew or what it meant to be a Conservative Jew to be able to say even what I was.

"I knew like eight Jewish songs that came out of the shtetl with my father. All of a sudden"—Paula becomes effusive, the joy of her initial discovery coming into her voice—"the Reform movement was full of this music, of folk and Jewish music, that I had never heard of in my life."

After an "okay" summer at camp, Paula returned to Rutgers without having saved any money. She says, "My deal with my parents was that they paid my college expenses, but I had to make my spending money. So I thought, 'What am I gonna do now that I have this great skill? I can teach Jewish music.' " She picked up the phone book, opened it to "synagogues," and started with the A's. The first one she called offered her a job.

Paula became increasingly involved in Jewish activities. By the end of her sophomore year, she had become the leader of the Reform Jewish student group on campus. She led its religious services and planned its social activities. By her senior year, she was teaching at three synagogues, running a youth group for Jewish teenagers, and still heading the campus organization.

"I did a lot of learning along the way, about what it meant to be a Reform Jew," she says. "For the first time, I felt, Jewishly, that I knew where I belonged." That's when she decided to become a rabbi.

She explains: "I never became a musician because I could never focus on just one activity. Being a musician meant giving up a lot of things that I was not prepared to give up. But being a rabbi allowed me to hold on to a lot of those things, and I could still use my music and the teaching, which I loved. I mean, my father was an educator. For a long, long time, from the time I was ten, I wanted to be a teacher, and he *always* discouraged me because he thought I would have a better life if I did something else. So I found another way to be a teacher. That's what a rabbi is. There are just so many opportunities as a rabbi to be there for people at the high points and low points of life, to watch kids grow up, teach Judaism. It's just not a boring, one-kind-of-thing job, that's for sure."

I find it ironic that, among Paula's reasons for becoming a rabbi, the last one she mentions is religion. I point this out to her, and she says, "When I first decided to apply to become a rabbi, that's how I really looked at it. I didn't know enough about Judaism to call myself a teacher of Judaism. Now, the music has sort of fallen by the wayside even though I still sing. And some of the other things have taken second or third priority to teaching and studying Judaism.

"But I'm still a very big social activist. I almost thought that if I didn't get into rabbinical school the second time, I would have gone back to Washington and gotten into politics. That's what I would have done." Explaining the connection between her social activism and her Judaism, she tells me, "I feel commanded by God to feed the homeless and to do the kind of work that I do."

Paula is currently in charge of the college's weekly soup kitchen. She explains that after the soup kitchen had been running for a year, "they were looking for a student to oversee it 'cause a few students had divided up the work and it wasn't working out. So I decided that it was something that I really wanted to do, and I took over and ran it for the last two years. I'm back in charge temporarily. The person who's running it this year is away."

Before her work with the soup kitchen, Paula had done a lot of advocacy for the homeless. "I almost got arrested demonstrating at City Hall in New York for a piece of housing legislation that the New York City Council eventually killed by sitting on it for months and months and months." The soup kitchen provided Paula with "this wonderful opportunity for me to become involved right here in my school with a terrific project, and I just never thought twice about it. And people say to me, 'How do you find time?' I just don't think about it. It's just scheduled into my week like anything else is. I don't stop and think, 'What else could I be doing with my time?' because this is one of those things that gets me through the rest of the week. It really does.

"Rabbinic students do a lot of studying, and the studying is really important. But I'm not a real good studier. I'm real hands-on. 'Let's stop talking about theories of education. Let me get in the classroom and teach already.' I have my days where I say, 'Okay, enough of this studying stuff. I need to *do* now.' I've always been a real *doing* person, and that's why the soup kitchen is so important to me. I'd go crazy in the library if I wasn't in here a few hours a week doing what needs to be done. And it's still not enough. I could be doing that full-time."

"So," I ask, "instead of becoming a rabbi, why not become a social worker or an advocate for the homeless or something like that?"

"Because I have a lot more power in the Jewish community," she replies. "There's a lot more potential in terms of educating other people and getting other people involved. A homeless advocate only has a certain amount of reach." As a rabbi, Paula has "an opportunity to teach values that I think are inherent in Judaism."

Her time with the soup kitchen has taught Paula many lessons. "I've learned that when I pass someone on the street who is begging, and I don't have any change to give them, I can still say something nice to them instead of being embarrassed and then turning my head and walking away. I've learned the value of every human being who eats at the soup kitchen.

"There are guys who come up to me and say, 'I'm a trained electrician, do you know of anywhere that I can get a job? I would do anything to get a job and get back on my feet.' One guy was one of those bicycle messengers. He got hit by a car and was in the hospital for months and lost his apartment because no one was there to pay the rent. He had no health insurance, nothing to cover him. I mean, we tried to get him into a private shelter, so that as he started to work he could save enough money to then get a place again. I've had people come up to me and say, 'Tonight's gonna be my first night on the street. Do you know of any private shelter I can go to, because I'm terrified to go to public shelters. I'd rather sleep on the train.' I have heard so many people's stories, and I would take each one of them home with me if I could."

Paula is married to Jordan, who is also a fourth-year rabbinical student. They have been married three and a half months. They met seven years ago at a reception that the college sponsored for people who were interested in applying to the rabbinical school.

"Do you want to have kids someday?" I ask.

"If I could afford them now, I'd have them now," she says. "But we're racking up those student loans, so it'll be a little while."

"Why did you choose to become a rabbi instead of something a little more lucrative?"

"I'm not very practical," she replies with a laugh. "I've always been more of an idealist than a realist. My dad and my mom both chose professions that weren't what you call lucrative, and they just always seemed to be happy. They liked their jobs, and I guess that was the value that was taught in my house, that it's much more important to do what you are happy doing and what you are good at than what makes money. My dad always joked that anytime I went to med school, he was ready to foot the bill. But money never really entered my thinking."

Not that becoming a rabbi is the only profession Paula considered. "I thought about becoming a professional musician for a long time. I thought about teaching music. There's still a part of me that thinks life would've been much simpler if I had gone into music education. I wouldn't have to spend five years in graduate school. I would have fairly normal hours."

"Rabbis have abnormal hours?"

"Very abnormal hours. First of all, meetings are at night. We work on weekends. There's no such thing as a nine-to-five rabbi. No such thing. Rabbis have to be workaholics or they don't even let you into the school. I put in twelve- to thirteen-hour days on a regular basis—and then I go home and study. We have a friend who was just ordained who was telling us he's putting in about eighty hours a week."

"Are you happy now?"

"I don't know. I don't know. I've been asking myself that question a lot lately. I don't know. I'm very, very overworked, and I'm not sure. I have a real issue with the amount of work that this career demands and whether I'm ever going to be able to give my children the kind of time and attention that I think children deserve, if I'm ever going to find a comfortable balance. Being a workaholic is really being a something-aholic. It's an addiction, what drives me forward is work. But I also resent it at the same time when it leaves no time for anything else, including spending time with my husband or other things I like to do."

I ask Paula how she will solve this problem. She says with a sigh, "I don't know. I'll write a book when I come up with the answer, 'cause there are a lot of women who really, really struggle with that problem of trying to find a balance and trying to do everything. I want a house, full-speed-ahead career, and I want to have kids. And I want to give my kids the kind of time and love that kids need. I haven't solved this problem. On a moment-to-moment basis, I'm happy. When I look down the road, I'm very uneasy.

"To my grandfather the United States was the Golden Land. Everyone thought he was crazy. He left a fairly good business in Poland. He was better off than many. Jews were very poor in Poland. But he wanted to go to the—in Yiddish it was *Goldeneh Medinah*—the 'Golden Land.' And he thought he could make it here, and he did make it here. I mean, every generation of my family—until now—certainly has done better than the last.

"But then again, my parents' goals were always just to live comfortably. They never felt that they've been lacking in anything that they really needed. And to them *that's* what's important in life, not having more and more and more. I think now, though, things have changed a lot economically, especially in this recession that we're in now. I think a lot of immigrants still come expecting to find streets paved with gold. I just don't think it's like that anymore. I think it's very hard, and I see it every week when I come in here. There's no 'American Dream' for the hundred and eighty guys who come in here to eat every week."

Paula believes the American Dream is "an illusion. It's something that a lot of people chase that's not so easy to come by anymore. People are chasing success and money and things that don't really make you happy anyway—getting 'somewhere,' becoming 'someone.' I don't think how much money you make or how much success you find in life makes you anything, necessarily. It's what you do with it, how you use it, how you treat other people.

"I'm not even sure I would ever use the term 'American Dream' because, as much as I'm an American and it's important to be an American and it's important for me to participate in the American political process, I think of myself first and foremost as a Jew. So I'm not even sure that I would even use the word 'American Dream' to describe what I want out of life.

"What do I want out of life? I want to live comfortably. I want my children to have what they need, not always necessarily what they want. The kids who get too many Nintendo games don't appreciate what they have. That was one thing, as kids, as soon as we were able to work, we were out working summer jobs and we were taught to appreciate what we have. I want to have happy, healthy kids who somehow end up somewhat sane despite being the children of two rabbis, who learn to love Judaism as much as I do, who marry other Jews and continue having Jewish families. And that's no small thing in this world, there's so much intermarriage. I want my kids to marry Jews, I want to have Jewish grandchildren.

"What else? I'd like to have a satisfying career. I'd like to find fulfilling work. I'd like to feel that I've made a difference in people's lives, that I've had some impact. I'd like to feel like I can leave this world a little better than I found it. That's what I want.

"My success is certainly not defined with a price tag. I define success as us being able to help other people and have an impact on people. To be a successful rabbi is to be there for people when they need you, for people to say, 'Wow, I've really learned a lot from Rabbi Feldstein. She was really there for me when I needed her.' That's what being a successful rabbi is about for me. That's what I hope to be."

Paula adds, "Because every generation of my family lived better than the last, I used to expect that I would live better than my parents did. At this point I just hope that I live the same. I mean, I'd be happy to live at the same standard of living, but at this point I'm not even sure that I can expect to live at the same standards that my parents do. God knows *when* we'll be able to own a house. It just doesn't look real good for a long time. I don't know. I used to expect that I would find a job as a rabbi real easily, but the way that market has been going, I'm not sure that I can expect that either. I have a lot of trouble with what to expect."

Paula is equally anxious about the nation's future. "I'm really worried about where the Supreme Court is gonna go on eroding a lot of our rights—minorities, women, abortion rights, religious freedoms, speech freedom. I'd like to see a liberal swing again. I'd like to see us go back to Democratic presidents and good liberal politics and a liberal court. But the days of Justice Brennan are *long gone.*"

Paula is also concerned about "the homelessness, the hungry, and more and more unemployment and more and more people are going to be at the soup kitchen's door." She says, "I am convinced that we could serve a thousand meals and we would have a thousand people at our doorway. There's no end to this in sight. I live for the day that we close our doors 'cause there's no one left to feed.

"I keep fighting for things," she says, "but I don't know if I expect to ever see them occur."

ANDY

"I wouldn't say I was an extremely happy child," says Andy, twenty-five, in his deep, gravelly voice as he exhales the smoke from a Camel Light. "When I was younger, it took my mom a long time to get over her divorce. My image of my mother after she was divorced was laying on the couch in her waitress uniform with her hand over her eyes, saying, 'Leave me alone.' She was very depressed for a couple of years after she divorced, and I didn't get along very well with my brother. So for me there was the TV.

"I was allowed to watch a lot of TV. My parents and my grand-parents, there was sort of like this complicity, 'Go ahead. If that's what you wanna do, that's fine. It'll get you out of our hair.' And as a result, TV affected my world view.

"You begin to think that the real world is out there living in their homes, y'know, happy and eating pork roast and then sitting around and playing UNO together, and then they all go to bed happy that they've spent the evening together. You look at *The Brady Bunch* or any one of those sort of serendipitous situation comedy shows, and you think, 'Every family on TV seems to work so well, and my family is so fucked up.' "

Andy's own childhood was anything but *Brady Bunch* perfect. "When I was four," he says, "my parents were divorced 'cause my dad—well, my dad's gay and he came out of the closet." Andy was eight when his father explained this to him. "It never really bothered me," says Andy, "and I think it was because I was young enough when I was told that it just was kind of, 'Oh, well, that's the way it is.' Although it took me till about age sixteen before I could openly admit it to anybody. And that was just because you don't tell a fourteen-year-old kid, 'Oh yeah, my dad's gay.' It's just not a very popular sort of move."

After the divorce, Andy, his mother, and his older brother moved in with Andy's maternal grandparents. They lived in Yorkville, Illinois, an hour's drive west of Chicago. Andy's mother waited tables for a while, then went to work reviewing employees' benefit claims for a company that makes cold cuts and deodorant soap.

When Andy was nine, his mother married a man who owned a successful plumbing contracting and supply business. Andy's mother and stepfather had twins, and his mother began designing kitchens for her second husband's remodeling business.

During the recession of the early 1980s, work for Andy's stepfather dried up. As the business soured, says Andy, so did the relationship between his stepfather and mother. They separated when Andy was sixteen, but they have only recently started divorce proceedings.

By the time his mother and stepfather separated, Andy had grown desperately bored with life in Yorkville. It was "a classic small town," he says. "Life was work and school and church. You knew everybody from those three things. I just kind of realized that I would go crazy if I stayed home and worked the family business and whatever."

After graduating from the public high school, Andy attended the University of Illinois at Champaign-Urbana. He majored in journalism for two years. He then decided he wanted to study film, so he transferred to Columbia College, a small fine arts school in Chicago. By this time his mother had closed her kitchen remodeling business and had gone to work doing the same thing for someone else.

Andy quit school before he finished his degree. He explains, "I'm in keeping with a theme in my family—dangerously close to graduation. I ended up being six credits short. I took all the course work and I had two incompletes. I started working, I never went back to finish, and I doubt I ever will.

"I figured this out very shortly after I was out of school, that any job that I would really want, the degree would just be sort of arbitrary. I don't really ever see myself applying to a large corporation for a job to sit behind a desk, so I don't really worry about it.

"Depending on what you want to do, a college degree doesn't hold the same weight as it used to. It really meant something years ago to have a college degree. It was a very big dividing line between those who had and those who didn't. And now, I think colleges are businesses in the business of making money by handing out degrees. It's just sort of like another service, and you can go there for four years and spend lots and lots of money and have a degree, and pretty much be the same as anybody else who is out looking for work."

During his college years in Chicago, Andy began freelancing for various film and video production companies. He did a little bit of everything, but eventually settled into building sets "because it was the job where they left you alone the most."

While he was working in film, he began thinking about becoming an actor. "I'd always wondered about performing," he says. "I'd taken a few acting classes and always liked it and, y'know, always felt like a funny person. And so I started taking improv classes and then just started performing with little groups around Chicago."

For a year or so, Andy tried working on film sets during the day and performing at night. But it became impossible to do both. "When you get hired on for a two-week film job," he explains, "that means *two weeks*—not two weeks of office hours, two weeks of working from when you wake up until when you go to sleep. If I had a two-week film job, my performer friends wouldn't see me for two weeks, except for on Saturdays and Sundays when we weren't working. And if I had a weeknight show, it was really hard to do. I was really lucky to get off of work early, like by seven, in order to make an eight o'clock show." Faced with a choice between remaining in production and becoming an actor, Andy decided to try acting.

"When I first quit work," he says, "I lost thirty pounds in about four months without even trying just because I didn't have enough money to eat. I was probably living on maybe, *maybe* a hundred dollars a week, if I was lucky.

"There was about two years where I was always broke, where I was always having to borrow money and then trying to pay it back. Y'know, coming home and having to avoid the landlord because I was ten days late with the rent, never picking up the phone because of all the bill collectors that called me. I got tired of being called by bill collectors, people earning seven dollars an hour to treat me like some sort of petty criminal. The reason I was poor is because I was trying to follow and do in my life what I wanted to do."

Toward the end of his starving-artist period, Andy began performing with the players at Annoyance Theatre, on Chicago's Near North Side. "As a group," says Andy, "the Annoyance Theatre is loud and rude and fun, and that's what the shows are, loud and rude and fun. They enjoy shocking people." Some typical Annoy-ance productions: *That Darned Antichrist, Manson: The Musical, The Miss Vagina Pageant,* and *Tippi: Portrait of a Virgin, an Afterschool Special Gone Bad.*

"Through design or not," says Andy, Annoyance is "completely TV-baby theater. Most of the shows in some way reflect TV sensibil-ities." For example, in *The Real Live Brady Bunch,* adult actors per-form actual episodes from the television series. They play their parts straight; they do not lampoon the show by overplaying their charac-ters. There's no need. As Andy, who saw the show on opening night, says, "It was about as hard as I've ever laughed at a show, 'cause it was just so absurd to see adults doing this thing that as chil-dren we just accepted as some form of reality. And to see adults doing it, it just makes you think about it. 'Cause I remember looking at this production and thinking about how *The Brady Bunch,* whether or not I liked it and without ever really thinking about it, was in some way almost ingrained on my DNA. It sort of just had been sucked up into my brain."

Andy's break came when the producers of *The Real Live Brady Bunch* took the show to New York. Andy had been playing bit parts in *The Brady Bunch* and other Annoyance shows for about a year and a half. The man who played Mike Brady in Chicago could not travel with the cast to New York, so Andy went in his place.

In New York *The Real Live Brady Bunch* was a sleeper hit off-Broadway. The show's original six- to eight-week run was extended to six months. Now the show is in Los Angeles in a theater across from the UCLA campus. If the show is successful, says Andy, it could run as long as a year.

He says, "The show I'm doing right now, I enjoy because it's fun. I'm making seven hundred dollars a week for doing basically two hours of work a night." He chuckles at the thought, then con-tinues, "It's a fun job, but it is a job. It's a job, but added in to that, my bosses are my friends, my coworkers are my friends. I get to be onstage, and I get to have people laugh and cheer for things that I do and for things that everyone else onstage is doing. I feel like if you have to make a living, this is a pretty good way to do it. It's the best job I've ever had.

"But the reason I'm pursuing acting, quite frankly, is because, well, I don't really have a lot of skills. I can't run a computer. I'm lousy with money. I mean, I *could* be a good salesman, but I don't think I would be because I would be just nasty and mean, probably. I kinda just feel like I have to make this work. This is my one marketable skill.

"And I want to make this work, because I can't picture doing anything that has the same amount of fun. You know, the fun-over-money-earned ratio is pretty damn good in acting. And it's important to me to have fun." The only other work Andy thinks he'd enjoy as much is being an heir. "That would be a good job," he says.

There is not much that Andy does not enjoy about professional acting, except that "show business is all based on bullshit. L.A. and show business is just not honest with itself, and I have a very low tolerance for personal dishonesty. Show business does not say, 'We are crass. We are money-grubbing. We are power-hungry.' Show business says, *'We're the maker of dreams.'* You know, there are so many things in people that I can take. People can be complete assholes, but if they're just sort of up-front about it and unapologetic about being assholes, they're so much easier to take. Just the insincerity and the dishonesty of show business really tends to bother me. It's almost expected that you be someone other than who you are.

"It's important for me now to not become entirely full of shit, which is a distinct possibility when you start into this business. I just don't want to lose my soul somewhere on one of the streets of L.A. I want to keep some sort of sense of perspective about show business and about acting and about all of this, y'know. That's important to me. I mean, I could see myself becoming a complete prick, y'know, just becoming everything that I hate about actors and show business."

Despite all this, Andy is pleased with the direction in which his career and his life are headed. "Which is saying a lot for me," he says, "because I tend to be kind of a bitch and kind of a curmudgeon. But I'm very, very hopeful about things. I've been going on auditions that seem to have been going well. There seems to be some real momentum moving. The show is doing real well. I'm excited about L.A.

"The last year of my life has been a really nice sort of period of progress. I really feel like I'm makin' some headway on my career. But it's strange. I feel in a way it's just all kinda dumb luck."

Because Andy feels that so much of his success comes from luck rather than hard work, he believes that the idea of the American Dream does not apply to him. The American Dream, he says, means "Do well in school, do what the teachers say, get good grades, get out, get a job, do what your boss says. And after thirty years you'll be a boss, and you'll be able to have kids and a car and a house and a lawn mower, and you'll die with an insurance policy that will provide for your kids' college education or their kids' or whatever." But, he observes, "I haven't worked very hard in terms of the American Dream, plugged away for thirty years at a job and did what I was told. I haven't worked that hard. I've kinda, y'know, dicked around and been in these goofy little shows, and not too much further down the road, I could be making lots of money."

Andy also dislikes the idea of a uniquely *American* dream. "I hate the idea of thinking in terms of 'us' and 'them,' in terms of America versus the world," he says. "One of the problems with this country is that we don't have a world view. There's still a lot of xenophobia, there's still a lot of insular thinking. I just don't think it's a question of the American Dream. I think that we'd all be better off if we started thinking of the human dream to have a good life."

Andy also rejects the materialistic ideals symbolized in the American Dream. "To me, it's all based on money and creature comforts and sort of equating those with happiness. That's what I think it's originally meant to be, but there's too many nebulous factors like happiness and fulfillment that aren't really factored into it.

"I just want to have a nice life, y'know. And I don't mean rich. I don't mean hugely rich with huge cars. I just mean, like, be able to have a nice place to live, have a family, have children and be able to send them to school.

"Everything else, every other kind of anxiety that can enter into your life, you can figure out some way to change your behavior to fix. But money, you can change your behavior to try and fix it, but there's a certain point where money is just a problem, an unsolvable anxiety problem that you just have to kind of stare in the face day to day. And I learned this from my mother. I mean, I'm from small-business owners, basically. When the recession hit in the seventies, they all took beatings and they still are taking beatings.

"But, also, my family is of the same temperament as I am, where they don't want to work very hard, y'know. I've talked to them about it and they feel like, 'Well, why should I kill myself for fourteen hours a day so that I can keep creditors happy?' I'm from a very sort of lazy, hedonistic background, y'know.

"It makes me happy to be able to wake up when I wanna wake up and dress the way I wanna dress and go where I wanna go and say what I wanna say. And I think that a lot of people don't have those luxuries. I don't have to worry about a boss overhearing me say something on the phone. I don't have to worry about people in the office thinking that I don't look professional in the way I'm dressed. I have a lot of freedom, and that's as important to me as having a nice corner office is to some people.

"If I could do it as a living, I would hang out with funny people. That's what matters most to me. And so I need to find a job that I can make good money at that allows me to have lots of time to be able to do the things I want to do and that is fun. And I know it can sound terribly childish, but I really am not concerned with business. I just don't care. I don't want to be viewed as a responsible citizen."

Nor does Andy want to be a star. He says, "I don't understand why you would want to do that. Not being able to go for a walk would be awful.

"I love character actors. They're my favorite actors, different people that play a hundred different roles in a hundred different movies. To me, that seems like the coolest, most fun acting. Movie stars, they end up being themselves in every single movie. I'd like to be a whole bunch of different people, y'know. I'd rather be quietly successful than loudly famous.

"And I would like to feel like I was doing a little bit to change the world, change people's perceptions, to make the world a better place. Make people sort of be more liberally minded, y'know, make people less racist, less scared of themselves and not so afraid."

When Andy thinks about the national situation, one issue most concerns him: "Poverty. The urban blight that hasn't really been addressed in thirty years. Ghettos have been allowed to remain ghettos. I think that, especially with the Los Angeles riots just having happened, there is a real chance for this country to undergo an incredible, bloody, nasty revolution if the problems of poverty and the underclass go unchecked.

"We have to think of ways to, rather than disenfranchising people, to make them part of society and part of life. And not just sort of like shoving them into a ghetto and letting them destroy themselves with crack and with drugs and violence.

"We're talking about the American Dream, which is material success, and that is what we are all supposed to aim for. That's sort of like the implicit message of the media, and life. But yet we call crack dealers villains and evil, when that's what they're doing—they are following the path of least resistance to financial success, to creature-comfort success. It just seems terribly unfair to say to someone in the ghetto, 'Work real hard and you might get out of the ghetto,' when 'work real hard' ends you up with a job at the Burger King.

"The United States *is* the best place in the world to live, as far as the amount of freedoms that you have. But people were just burning L.A. There were different news commentators that said that this isn't a political action, this is hooliganism. I don't buy that. For the underclass in our country, rioting is a completely viable, legitimate form of the political process.

"There's sort of an institutionalized poverty, and people every day on TV see the good life being attainable, and the good life is consumer items. And when things go haywire, and they feel cheated and basically just sort of assaulted by the status quo, well, why not go out and attain those things by throwing a brick through a window and carting them back home? Because the powers that be are playing a joke on the underclass by saying, 'Work hard. Work hard and stick to it and you'll end up with all these nice things, just like us.' And that's a lie. That's a lie.

"The underclass doesn't get a proper education. They don't get the proper opportunities to advance themselves. They live in war zones. The riot was just turning a very cruel joke on itself, y'know." In other words, says Andy, the people of South Central Los Angeles had been told that the good life was within arm's reach, and, finally, they took that idea literally.

At the end of our conversation, Andy says, "I think one of the best things for this country would be for it to not be number one for a while. Civilizations have come and gone. Even after Rome fell, there's still an Italy and there's still happy, productive Italians. There's still an Athens, there's still a Greece. We should look at it in terms of, we had our time, and now maybe Japan *is* meant to be the leading economic country. To put it in *Brady* terms, 'It's hard to be the most popular kid in school.' You gotta do a lot of work, and you gotta pay a lot of prices to do that. So maybe not being number one wouldn't be such a bad thing."

■ ■ ■

Note: Since arriving in L.A. in April 1991, Andy has had some close-but-no-cigar auditions. He was also cast in two small roles for television—as a cop in an HBO movie, and as one of John Wayne Gacy's victims in a crime reenactment for a tabloid television news show. ("It wasn't a speaking part," says Andy of the latter. "It was a strangling part.") He is still waiting, optimistically, for his big break.

THE VANISHING
D R E A M

LAURA

"I hated them. I just hated them."

Because she was born in a small town in Guatemala and raised mostly in Honduras, Laura's antipathy for the United States and its people is understandable. In El Salvador, government soldiers kidnapped and tortured Laura's godfather. The Guatamalan government shot and killed one of her mother's friends as the friend was walking with Laura's mother along the street. That government kidnapped and tortured Laura's uncle and three of his children. "We never saw them again," says Laura, matter-of-factly, "so it's for sure they are dead now."

The Guatemalan government also threatened to kill Laura's mother and her family if they did not immediately leave the country. Their crimes? As Laura puts it, they were "against the government."

Laura, twenty, knows the United States is responsible for these atrocities. "They didn't say, 'Go kill the Flores family.' But I know they said, 'Kill everybody that is against the government.' "

Laura's disdain for the United States included more than the federal government. She also despised this nation's people. Laura's father was a Lutheran missionary associated with a politically conservative synod in Missouri. The synod's representatives who were sent to oversee her father's work disapproved of his devotion to the principles of liberation theology, a doctrine that rejects the traditional separation between religion and politics and that commands its adherents to create a better world on earth. Without clearly understanding why the synod's representatives objected to her father's beliefs, she assumed everyone from the United States must be equally closed-minded. She also assumed everyone in the United States agreed with our government's actions in Latin America.

Imagine Laura's dismay, then, when her parents informed her that her father had decided to become a minister for Salvadoran refugees in Houston—and that the family would be moving to the United States.

Laura explains: "I was raised in an environment where they would all tell me that people come to the United States with the dream of paradise. They come here and it's not true. They have to wash dishes. So for me the United States was a bad country and everything.

"But now that I've been here for a year, I think my mind has changed a lot. I still know that the government is not good. I don't believe in the U.S. government. But I have met lots of people here in Houston, like the people where I work. It's not what I imagined. It's not what I thought it would be like when I came here and was afraid. Now I have changed a lot and I think different.

"I thought that I would come here and I would only hear racist remarks because of my origin. I know there's a lot of racism around, but my friends are not racists. So until now I don't feel like I've been mistreated because of my origin. Nothing like that. Also, when I came here I was always reading about Hispanics and black people that were killed for hate crimes, but I don't feel like nothing like that has happened to me right now. I go to a lot of places to visit or to have fun or the place where I go to study. I don't feel like they will look at me with racism. So I feel good right now. Maybe in the future it might change, I don't know. But right now it's okay with me."

Laura lives with her parents and her younger brothers. Klaus, Laura's boyfriend of four years, whom she met in Brazil while her parents were obtaining their advanced degrees from a Brazilian university, also lives with Laura's family. Laura admits that although she used to love Klaus, now she's not so sure. But she'll marry him anyway, she says, once the government changes her residency status from temporary to permanent. That way Klaus, who is in this country illegally, can become a legal resident.

Laura is currently studying at a community college. She has yet to declare a major, but she knows she wants to study psychology. She wants to become a psychologist and work with teenagers from low-income families. "I know I won't solve the problems for all the teenagers in the world," she says. "But if I could at least work with some that I could help and teach them to help others, that would be great for me."

Laura also wants to someday publish some of her poetry. For now, however, her poems are stuffed in a little sugar can, which is wrapped in lots of plastic bags and buried in her backyard. She explains: "Many people think that Central Americans only write poems about war and all that stuff. But I am more romantic about feelings and all those things. If my parents saw my poems, they would faint." She chuckles.

Despite having lived most of her life in Latin America, Laura is quite familiar with one of this nation's fundamental myths, the Horatio Alger version of the American Dream. She describes it: "What we see in movies—a poor man starts getting up in his life and all of sudden becomes a millionaire because he was a very hardworking man. He worked twenty-four hours a day and he managed to build a very large company and now he's a millionaire."

After coming here and seeing America for herself, however, Laura does not believe that that American Dream is real. She tells me, "All of my friends that I have here, who've been here for ten, twelve, thirteen years, their parents came here first and they started working as maids or in maintenance. Thirteen years have gone by and they're working in the same things. Nothing has changed. And all of them live in those small apartment complexes. Families of ten live together in one-bedroom apartments. I don't believe in that American Dream. Not at all."

Although Laura thinks the American Dream is just that, a dream, she still plans to remain in the United States. She says, "When I was coming here I was sure I was just getting my degree and then getting the hell out of there because I thought it would be very difficult for me here. But now I see that I want to stay here. Not because of the American Dream, I-want-to-become-a-millionaire. No. I know that even though it will be difficult, I will be better off here in the United States than in my countries. Because it is very difficult to go back to a country again and start making new friends. All of my friends will have changed when I get my degree. And I'm tired of moving from one place to another. So I think I will just stay here."

For Laura, the United States has been both a pleasant surprise and a profound disappointment. On the one hand, the United States and its people are not nearly as horrible as she imagined when she was on the receiving end of our government's covert and overt efforts in Central America. Yet the United States has not lived up to the promise depicted in the myth of the American Dream.

Laura is also discomfited by the reality that is masked by another great American myth—America the melting pot. She says, "I've seen that Americans are in one group, Chinese in one group, blacks in another and Hispanics in another. It may sound a little bit naive, but I would like for all of us to be together. To work together, to do things together and stop thinking, 'I'm Hispanic,' 'I'm Anglo,' 'I'm black.' I would like people to think, 'I'm a person, and I want to be with other people,' instead of thinking about their origin and their race. I love to get around with all kinds of people. But here it's difficult because if I try to be with Anglos or blacks, many Hispanics feel offended. They say, 'Oh, you are becoming a part of them.' And that's not what I want. I want everybody to be together.

"I just hope that when I do have children, this world I think about does come true. I want my children to grow up with people, not with 'blacks' or 'whites' or 'Hispanics.' I want the world to be different than it is right now."

"How do we make it different?" I ask.

Laura says, "I wish I knew." She chuckles wistfully and repeats, "I wish I knew."

KERRI

Kerri, twenty-five, was born in Houston, Texas. When she was four, her parents moved the family to Woodville, a town of roughly two thousand people about an hour and a half's drive northeast of Houston. Kerri's mother used to teach piano lessons; she was also a schoolteacher now and again as Kerri grew up. Kerri's father, a Presbyterian minister by training, worked for a Presbyterian organization that sponsored medical missions to Africa, the Caribbean, and Asia.

As a teenager, Kerri became an ardent amateur photographer. "It was just kind of a whim," she says. "When I was about fourteen, decided I wanted to try black-and-white photography and developing myself. My mother bought me a darkroom on the spot, very cheap setup. I never was taught how to do it. We got a Kodak 'step-by-step how to process your own pictures' book and turned off all the lights downstairs and just had a lot of fun, shooting film and processing it and printing it.

"And then I really quickly realized that that skill, especially at my age in a small town, was really rare, and everybody wanted me to do things for them immediately. I was working for the high school yearbook while I was still in junior high. Was working for the town paper in junior high just because of the demand, I mean, nobody knew the darkroom skills and I did. And I also realized pretty quick that it's a good way for a fairly shy person to interact with people in a nonthreatening way. People respond to having their picture taken, and I don't have to be in front of the camera."

By her junior year of high school, Kerri was feeling frustrated and artistically limited by the confines of her small town. Kerri's brother, who is one year older than Kerri and had been feeling similarly, had been accepted to study theater at Houston's High School for Performing and Visual Arts. Kerri followed her brother's lead and, halfway through her junior year of high school, earned a slot to study photography and creative writing at HPVA. Kerri's younger sister later joined Kerri and her brother by becoming a music major at the Houston magnet school.

Because all of their children were attending school in Houston,

Kerri's parents decided they should move to the city, too. The family lived in an apartment. Today, Kerri's parents still live in Houston.

After graduating from HPVA, Kerri thought about becoming a professional photographer, but she was not sure that was what she really wanted to do. She was also thinking of going to medical school, so she decided to apply to colleges with strong liberal arts programs. Tulane, a private university in New Orleans, offered Kerri a small scholarship. She visited the campus, fell in love with the city, and decided to enroll. Four years later, she graduated with a bachelor's degree in anthropology.

Sometime during college, Kerri decided against medical school. She explains: "I knew people in medical school and they seemed overworked and unhappy, and motivated by the wrong things— money, prestige. My best friends when I was in high school were med students in Houston. 'N' after knowing them for a few years, they just seemed very stressed out and very unhappy. And they did it so they could play golf when they retired, and that just didn't seem like the right reason. I know that wouldn't have to be my reason, but it just didn't seem like me. I'm not into working that hard *for money.*"

After she finished her degree, Kerri considered leaving New Orleans. "I've applied to some grad schools and haven't gotten in," she says, " 'n' I have a lot of friends here, so it's hard to leave. I love the feel of New Orleans. It's more relaxed than most places. It's more culturally mixed, more tolerant, funkier. The music is much stronger, the art is much more interesting. It's got history. It's not too big, like Houston is so huge, but it's not small like Woodville. Y'know, good size. Close enough to home to visit, far enough away that I don't feel too attached or too close to my parents."

To earn a living, Kerri is relying on her most readily marketable ability—her darkroom skills. She works full-time for a local photographer. "He's in his sixties, I guess. He's been in New Orleans for years and years. He's got all the old-money gigs. He's got the Mardi Gras Balls, which is the thing that turns New Orleans' economy, Mardi Gras. And the reason that is, is because all the old-money people are involved in it. Big money. So he has the biggest gigs, he makes a good living." Kerri spends half her workweek in the darkroom; the rest she spends answering the phone, filing paperwork, running errands, and restoring old photographs.

Although Kerri earns only $8 an hour, having access to a professionally equipped darkroom is extremely valuable to her because she recently decided to devote herself fully to photography. She recently said to herself, "Well, photography is what I'm doing, I'm gonna do it really well.

"And so, over the last year, I've started having exhibits at galleries and really pushing my own work. I'm doing a line of postcards that's selling really well. And when people respond positively to your art, you say, 'Hey, maybe this is what I'm s'posed to be doing,' and keep doing it."

Explaining why she has chosen to become a professional photographer, Kerri tells me, "There's a lotta reasons. I was interested in documenting life the way I saw it. Starting out with an idea of doing it as an anthropologist, tried to take pictures of things that I thought said something about the people that I was photographing or the situation that I was photographing.

"Y'know, you try to say something kind of unique. And New Orleans is such a neat place to photograph. It's visually—stimulating. It's visually—exciting and colorful. That keeps me motivated to work.

"And then I have a lot of feel for art. I wish I could paint. If I could paint, I probably wouldn't be a photographer. I'd rather do oil painting because it's much more of a study, a long-term study of something, whereas photography is very immediate. And I'm not interested in immediate-type photography, like journalism photography doesn't interest me. It's kind of a dime a dozen, I think. But for me, to really work hard and capture something that says something to me is what's important. I'm moving now more into setting up my own situations, so it's more like art. And just to create something beautiful is the only thing I think worthwhile—as an artist—and that's what I'm trying to do."

One thing Kerri is not trying to do is achieve the American Dream. In her mind, the concept of the American Dream "seems like something that's a fiction from the past. Seems that America was the Promised Land. In the prosperous times, when people thought they would have enough forever and that the ecology was totally expendable and there was enough land, they didn't look far enough to see that it would run out, that all the money would run out, that the fresh water would run out. It seems like we're on the end of that now, that we're starting to realize what damage we're doing to the world. And the economy is not going to keep going up like they thought it would. My children are not gonna have it better than I did. That's just logic. So the American Dream seems to me to be a historical myth."

All Kerri wants is to be artistically successful. "I wanna say something about my creative self in my work, and I'm doing that a bit now, more than I ever have. And y'know, the personal satisfaction is the most important thing, but it's great when other people like what you're doing, too. Like, I'm always surprised when somebody likes what I've done, and just lately a lot of people have liked what I'm doing, and that's totally satisfying.

"I'd like to have enough money, not to have material things, but enough money that I didn't have to work for someone else, that I could do what I feel is important to me, instead of what somebody else is doing to make a buck. That's my only real goal."

I ask Kerri where she sees herself in ten years and whether she would ever give up photography. "As a profession, sure, sure," she answers. "I don't think it's the ultimate profession. I don't think it's the ultimate artistic expression. Like I said, I recently decided, 'Well, if this is what I'm doing, I'm gonna do it and stop whining about wanting to do other things.' But there's a million things I'd like to do. I'm not set on photography. I don't think photography is what I was destined to do. I think I'll probably always stay involved in the arts, either in music or art, but I don't know where I'll be in ten years." She laughs.

I say, "I suppose twenty years is out of the question, then."

"No clue," she says with a big smile. "I never thought I'd live this long."

"Why not?" I ask.

Kerri replies, "I don't know. I'm very short-term in my thinking."

Although good relationships, with family, friends, and lovers, are extremely important to Kerri, getting married is not. Kerri, whose parents are still married, says, "I think that people don't find all those things that they hoped would be in marriage, y'know, that marriage holds a lot of false promises. Divorce is so common, marriage just doesn't seem secure.

"And when I'm talking about even the institution, I don't really believe in it. When I think of marriage, I think of living with someone and committing to them. I don't think of the real legally married. I've never even considered getting legally married. I think that

that's kinda useless. It doesn't mean any more than a lease on an apartment—easier to get out of. I don't have much respect for the legal institution.

"I mean, there's things that are desirable about a true commitment and living with someone. But I've been in positions to do that with people that I have cared a lot about, and I've always done everything to get out of any commitment. I think I just need more time to be on my own and do what I wanna do. I'm fairly selfish, I guess, just with my time and—I don't know. Getting too involved in a relationship usually makes me stressed because you have to give so much to it."

Kerri is equally ambivalent about having children. "Overpopulation," she says, "is a big concern to me, maybe because of the travels that I did with my dad in Africa and places where there were just too many people. I always thought if I ever wanted that, I would adopt a child from a third-world country, and I still think that is a possibility—not anytime soon.

"I don't know. My life would have to be a lot different for me to have kids. I s'pose the first thing would be a mate that I was planning to spend the rest of my life with. Financial security and—I don't know. In some ways I'd have to feel better about the future, like, environmentally 'n' financially. I'm not really positive that anybody's doing the right thing in politics, 'n' I'd hate to worry about my children's lives, the quality of their lives, in this kind of insane government."

In Kerri's opinion, the nation is in the midst of an economic decline, and "it's not gonna get any better before it gets a lot worse, as far as the economy and poverty. Those things aren't getting better. Nobody's doing anything to make them any better. I think the economy's gonna continue to get worse, maybe with upturns every now and then. I think poverty's gonna continue to get worse. I think violence is gonna continue to get worse. I think we're moving more and more towards the quality of life that you would expect in, like, a third-world country, in a majority—well, not majority, but in a major part of the society. And that's not a part of society that funds or runs the government or has any say. It's the least educated people, who think that they have no control over—and probably rightly so—no control over their fate."

"How do we change our course?" I ask.

"God—if I knew, I could run for office. I really don't know. It's too far gone maybe, I don't know. There's so many problems with the education system, there's so many problems with—I don't know."

When I ask Kerri to tell me what is most important to her, she mentions something most people in their twenties take for granted—good health.

Last year, Kerri's doctor told her that she had cervical cancer and that it was sufficiently advanced to require surgery. Kerri's doctor also told her that the procedure would cost $3,000. Like nearly 22 million other people under the age of thirty-four, Kerri did not have any health insurance. She had been covered by her parents' medical insurance until she turned twenty-three. After that, she kept meaning to buy insurance but kept putting it off. "I'm young and healthy," she thought, "nothing can happen to me."

After hearing the diagnosis, Kerri told her parents, who offered to pay for the procedure. "It wasn't like I went straight to them and asked for money," she insists. "They immediately said, 'Don't worry. It's your health. We'll pay for the surgery.' I said, 'You shouldn't have to pay for my surgery. There should be a way for people who don't make a lotta money to have surgery.' So they said, 'Okay, find out what you can.'

"The situation was hard because I thought, 'What do people do if they don't have money and they have to have surgery?' I found out." She laughs.

Kerri returned to her doctor. She told him that she did not have any insurance, that she had made less than $10,000 the preceding year, that she did not have any savings or any way of paying for the surgery, and that she just couldn't believe there wasn't a cheaper way for her to have the surgery. "Finally, after all that trauma," Kerri's doctor said he would perform the surgery for free at a local charity hospital—that same surgery that "he was gonna charge me over three thousand dollars for," notes Kerri.

She continues: "So I got admitted to the charity hospital, I got cleared to have it free. And I thought, 'Gosh, what a great country, where people who have no money can get free surgery. Now you're talkin'.' This is what I expected, y'know, everybody deserves medical care. And then I got involved in the charity hospital system and got bumped off the schedule."

"What happened?"

"Just mistake after mistake after mistake. It's an absolute madhouse. It's worse than third-world hospitals I've seen. It's total mayhem. They got my name mixed up with someone else. They did a surgery they should've done on a different day in front of me, so I was prepped and ready for surgery and laid around for eight hours and didn't get the surgery. Took a lot of time off from work, y'know. It was just totally emotionally draining."

Still, Kerri was going to wait for another opening at the charity hospital. "They rescheduled me," she says, "and then I got really scared because they had gotten my name mixed up with someone else, and because there were med students doing surgeries that they had never done before. And because it's like a huge ward and open to all that information, I heard every mistake they were making. They made schedule mistakes. They made a lot of mistakes, and for eight hours I heard every one. The nurses fighting with the doctors, the doctors fighting with other doctors, doctors that couldn't speak English fighting with doctors. Y'know, just too much.

"I just couldn't cope with the added risk of somebody making a mistake. I didn't wanna get the wrong surgery, y'know. And it was just triply traumatic because who knows with anesthesia. I didn't wanna risk taking it, somebody making a mistake, a brand-new med student who's never done anesthesia before. It's my life." Kerri laughs, but it's a nervous little laugh.

Kerri's mother had come from Houston, and she was with Kerri during those eight traumatizing hours at the charity hospital. After that, Kerri's mother told Kerri to have the surgery performed at another hospital and that she and Kerri's father would pay for it.

It was difficult for them, says Kerri. "My dad lost his job, like, about a year ago, and so nobody has any money. And they're gonna have to pay it off on a credit card-type thing a long time. It's gonna be really hard. Everybody's real broke, and we're gonna pay eighteen point nine percent or nineteen point eight percent."

Kerri's parents not only paid for her surgery, they are now paying for her health insurance, too. And Kerri cannot repay them. "I'm in no position to," she says. She lost about $650 on a recent exhibition of her work at a local hotel. She expected this, given the current recession and that an artist's first shows usually are not commercially successful. "Just having my art seen is important," she insists, "and I have to be willing to spend that money." In addition to the loss from the hotel exhibition, Kerri regularly spends more than she earns. She simply puts the balance on her credit cards, on which she now owes about $1,000. As she puts it, her financial life is in constant tension between "getting by" and "going for it."

I ask Kerri whether, as an independent adult, it was emotionally difficult having to depend upon her parents to pay for her surgery. "Well," she tells me, "it was kind of frustrating just because, at twenty-four, I thought I should be able to afford insurance or the surgery. It just kind of made me angry. I work full-time, and because it's a very small business, we don't get any benefits. I don't even get days off paid. And that really made me angry. This happens to me, and it just devastated everybody financially. And that shouldn't happen. That's the American Dream that's lost."

MARINA

"Honestly, sometimes I listen to myself, I'm surprised I have an accent. Why do I have an accent? I feel like I never lived there. And now I'm telling you this and it's very hard for me even to remember it, to remember those feelings. I remember the feelings, that's about it. The constant fear."

Marina, twenty-eight, speaks freely about these inchoate impressions of dread, which are almost all she can recall of her childhood in Leningrad. "School was horrible," she tells me. "The whole idea of Russian society—the way it was, anyway, from childhood, from kindergarten—it's obedience. And the way they achieved it is by scaring people. Since you were a little child, you're always scared of something, constantly. In school you are afraid, constantly afraid. Bad grades, you're afraid. Your parents grew up the same way, so they're conditioned, so they scare you even more. It's like you're afraid to go home, you know, if you don't have the right grade, or if you talk during lessons. There was this thing at school, it was like a diary that you have to bring every day to school. If the teacher doesn't like something about it, she would write in it with red pen. So this is very bad thing, like the worst thing that happened to a child. I remember wanting to kill myself, I was like maybe nine years old, because I didn't get the right grade or something.

"You're constantly lying. You lie from morning to night. You walk into school, if you are three minutes late, they're waiting for you at the door. 'Why are you late?' I know it sounds funny. So big deal, so you were late. So what are they going to do to you? Nothing. But at that time you're constantly scared. You're scared of being late three minutes. And running, you know, your heart is pounding. You are eight years old and your heart is pounding because you're three minutes late."

Yet, according to Marina, this never-ending fear was not the principal reason for her father's decision to take the family out of the Soviet Union. Then an engineer at a Soviet defense plant, her father had learned that, because he is Jewish, he could advance no further in his profession. This convinced him that the family must make a new home elsewhere. Marina's mother, a surgeon, did not want to leave Russia; she would be leaving her family behind. Nevertheless, she agreed to go because her husband so hated life in the former Soviet Union.

Knowing that the Soviet government would never allow him to leave the country—because of national security—if he remained an engineer with a defense manufacturer, Marina's father quit in 1972. In 1973 he applied for an exit visa for himself and his family. The government rejected their application. They became "refuseniks"—people who officially were denied permission to leave the Soviet Union, more often than not for specious reasons.

Marina's family had at least one bit of good luck. Her father was well known to Jewish organizations in the United States. Working through the U.S. government, these organizations pressured the Soviets to grant Marina's family permission to emigrate. In 1978, five years after it had first rejected their application, the Soviet government acquiesced. Although her father had initially considered emigrating to Israel, news of a sluggish Israeli economy convinced Marina's parents to move instead to New York. Marina was fifteen.

Marina and her parents began their life in the United States by sharing an apartment with some Russian friends who lived in a housing project in Astoria, a working-class neighborhood in Queens. Marina notes that they were the only white people in the complex. Within a month her family found an apartment in the area. And some members of a Long Island Jewish community, who had "adopted" Marina's family while they were still in Leningrad, found Marina's father a job as an engineer at a shipyard. Meanwhile, her mother studied to take the examinations that would permit her to practice medicine in New York. She ultimately went to work for the City of New York as a medical examiner.

Marina completed high school in three "miserable" years at a yeshiva, a Jewish day school that provides instruction in secular and religious studies. Says Marina, "The yeshiva I was sent to was in the upper-middle-class Jewish families—very rich, very snotty. We were very poor." After yeshiva came two disastrous years at two schools, first Boston University, then Queens College. The material was not too difficult for Marina; in fact, she found the first years of college easy because she had already studied the same material in the Soviet Union. She just hated what she was being forced to study.

Marina did not want to become a doctor, as her parents wished. She longed to be an artist. Her sole source of joy during those three miserable years at the yeshiva had been the painting and drawing classes she attended on weekends. Without telling her parents, she showed her work to some people at Parsons School of Design, one of the top design schools in the country. They encouraged her to apply. Marina then revealed her plan to her father. After "a lot of screaming and yelling," he told her she could attend design school *if* Parsons accepted her; otherwise, she would have to go to pharmacy school. "At least it's some kind of profession," he told her.

Marina never had to test her aptitude as an apothecary because Parsons accepted her application. Four years later, she graduated, not as an artist, but as a fashion designer. She gave up fine art, she says, because "I don't like to suffer, and you have to pretty much do that" to make it as an artist.

After brief periods at two small apparel companies and a two-year stint with Macy's, Marina became a freelance designer. At first she was so desperate for work that she accepted jobs designing fabrics and worked out of her apartment in Rego Park. Today, she spends most of her time designing sweaters and children's clothes for a company that sells its goods to department stores nationwide, and the companies she works for provide her with office space. When Marina started working three years ago, she made $18,000. This year, she'll earn more than three times that much.

Hearing the circumstances of Marina's life, many people would think that the immigrant edition of the American Dream had come true twice: once for Marina, once for her father. Between 1983 and 1990, Marina's father went from unemployed engineer to cabdriver to vice president at one New York investment firm to vice president at another, larger investment firm. Her parents have moved from Astoria to Rego Park, a more affluent neighborhood in Queens. Marina says, "If you look at my family, the American Dream is you work hard, you achieve. That's probably true. I guess that's the way I see it.

"I have a hard time talking about it now. I'll tell you why. Up until this year, I thought that people who criticize the government here and this country were just spoiled brats. But I am now very disillusioned about what is going on in this country. I thought this was the country of democracy and you are supposed to be spreading about democracy through the world. But it's not really so."

Take, for example, the Persian Gulf War. "When America went to war, I was hundred percent for it. I thought we were doing the right thing. The way they were saying it in the media was that we were going to restore democracy. We were going to the land where women are raped, children are killed and tortured, and we're going to give them their land back. It's not that they didn't do that, but this is not the reason they did it. Because otherwise they would have to go to a lot of other countries besides Kuwait.

"It was disgusting what happened after the war, the fact that they didn't try to kill Saddam Hussein. They just stopped. And the Kurds, they told them basically to rebel and they were going to support them. But they left them to die. This is such hypocrisy."

As a child, Marina was not a Levi's-clad would-be rock-and-roller like so many Russian kids. Yet she still envisioned America as "this amazing place of opportunities." But, she says, "it's changed a lot since I came here."

The condition that seems to distress Marina the most is "the race problem." She explains: "There's a lot more hate—in New York, anyway. I take the subway every day. I know there's more hate now, racial hate. Sometimes you walk into subway and maybe black woman sitting there, or black man, and there's so much hate in their eyes. They just look at you. And it's because you're white they hate you. It's like you can touch them with your shoulder just because you move, you know, and they hate you. They want to kill you on the spot because you touched them. How do I know? They scream. They insult you. They push. I have been pushed many times. This one black man kicked me because I was standing in a way that wasn't comfortable for him to sit. He was sitting. I don't know why it's happening. Maybe economically the country is so bad off, maybe that's why."

Later, Marina adds: "What is upsetting to me is that a lot of black people are anti-Semitic, which makes to me absolutely no sense because in the sixties Jews did more than any other white community for the blacks." And the anti-Semitism in the black community is only one example of the anti-Semitism that Marina believes is growing stronger and more public. She tells me, "We have politicians now who advocate anti-Semitism. Ten years ago, even, it wasn't possible."

Though Marina believes this situation will get worse before it gets better, she sees a glimmer of hope: "I think this generation, the young generation now, is much more mixed. If you look at music or films or art, there's a tremendous fusion of black and white culture which really never happened before. I think it's amazing. The music, there's all this fusion, rap. The white kids are dancing black dances.

"It's neither good or bad. It's inevitable. It's normal. It's better *this* than them fighting each other. It has to happen this way. And no matter how much fighting there will be going on, there will be interracial marriages. It has to happen because otherwise this country cannot survive, because the color of the country is changing rapidly."

Despite having lived here for more than thirteen years and despite having become a U.S. citizen, Marina does not necessarily feel as if she is a genuine member of this nation. A recent trip to Israel vivified her uncertainty. There, she says, "I feel like I belong. I feel my roots." Later she adds, "I felt so much pain for the country, so much more than I felt here. So I don't know if I should consider myself an American."

Yet although she unflinchingly proclaims, "I'm Jewish first, then I'm everything else," and has seriously contemplated making *aliyah*—moving to Israel and becoming a citizen—Marina does not think she will move to the Promised Land. Immigration is difficult, she explains, and she doesn't know whether she could deal with it, "being alone there."

Her voice tinged with wistful resignation, she adds, "Maybe I don't belong anywhere."

I prod her: "You don't feel like you belong here?"

She snaps out of her momentary lapse into pensive silence and responds: "I belong here. Why not. I belong in New York. But when I go outside New York, definitely I don't belong. I mean, I go to Minneapolis on business, and I'm the only person that has an accent for miles around. I'm the only person that has dark hair who doesn't celebrate Christmas."

Almost by default, New York is the only place where Marina feels as if she belongs. Though she once loved the Big Apple, now she does not even like it.

"I read about New York in the fifties," she tells me, "and they say they didn't lock the doors. There was no crime. People used to sleep in the parks because there was no air-conditioning. Neighbors used to get together and, you know, eat and drink together. It doesn't happen anymore. Why? I don't know. Something happened.

"Most of the people here live in their own little world. Family, college friends, whatever. That's it. That's really a life, your own little circle. And basically you don't care about what happens to your neighbor. I can't get used to the indifference."

THE IMPOSSIBLE
D R E A M

JANINE

Janine, twenty-six, has lived almost her entire life in the poor and working-class neighborhoods of Boston's inner city. As a child, she says, her family lived a middle-class life. "I mean, we had a lot of things. We had wonderful Christmases." But Janine also remembers that, growing up, she always wanted more than she had. "Material things," she says. "Y'know, there were times where I would ask for things and my parents weren't able to afford it. I can see that now. But at the time, when they said no, I wouldn't understand why they were saying no."

When Janine was twelve, her parents divorced. This was not only emotionally painful for the family, but financially difficult as well. Janine, her mother, and her younger sister moved in with Janine's maternal grandmother in her apartment in Roxbury, which one writer has described as "Boston's black heartland." But Janine's mother refused to go on welfare. "She's very stubborn," Janine tells me, "she worked two or three jobs at times, when she had to, to take care of me and my sister." Two years later Janine's mother, who had gone back to school and completed her undergraduate education while she was still married to Janine's father, became a teacher in the Boston public schools. Today, Janine's mother has a master's degree, and she still teaches in the city schools. Janine's father, who also has a college degree, works as an administrator for the Massachusetts Bay Transportation Authority.

When Janine was a little girl, several years before her parents' divorce, her mother and father arranged for her to join Project Metco, a voluntary program under which small numbers of inner-city black children were bused to public schools in Boston's white suburbs. "My mother and father wanted me to go. They felt as though I would get a better education, bein' bused," says Janine. Starting in second grade, Janine attended school in Needham, an affluent white suburb.

The first day of class in Needham, Janine was scared. It was not because of the hostility and violence that surrounded busing in Boston during the late sixties and early seventies. Janine was too young then to make the connection between "what was happening" in the city and "us being bused to Needham," and she does not remember any demonstrations in Needham itself. Her fear flowed from feelings of "isolation, and being so far away from home, and not knowin' what to expect, and hopin' that everything would be okay." She also recalls feeling that "something was quite different, and that we were different from the other students that went to the school. And we were definitely the minority.

"It wasn't like we were given proper guidance or information in terms of how to process this thing that was goin' on," Janine says without bitterness. Not that the school's teachers and administrators did not attempt to make the transition smoother for the black children. "They would try to help make things a lot easier for us by having families who would host us for an evening. We would just spend the night to do a couple of things. But I think even though I was able to adjust, I still knew that something was different, and in a lot of ways we were treated differently, and lot of ways we were looked at, we were already stereotyped."

Janine says the teachers assumed that "black kids are a certain way, that they might not be able to be disciplined, or that they might be defiant already and have an attitude and things like that. That might have contributed too—well, it did—because teachers would

respond differently to the black students. If there was a fight between a black student and a white student, the black student would
end up gettin' suspended from school, y'know. The white student
would be sent home and be in school the next day.

"I remember in the cafeteria, there was a fight goin' on. The
teacher came, and when they came to break the fight up, they
grabbed my girlfriend, who was black, and I said to the teacher,
'Why did you grab her, 'cause she [a white girl] was on top of her?'
I had to go to the principal's office for that. I was more frightened
than my friend was."

Janine offers another example of the administrators' treating
black students differently from white students. It's about a black student who was expelled for smoking marijuana. He was not just
thrown out of Needham; he was dropped from the entire Metco program. Meanwhile, says Janine, there was a white student at
Needham who "was basically the guy sellin' the drugs. He had been
suspended on several occasions, numerous occasions. He had problems with drugs since, like, junior high, but they never felt the need
to expel him from the entire school system. They just enabled him
to do what he was doin' and they allowed him to graduate."

Not all of the racism was so obvious. Sometimes black students
simply had the misfortune of being subjected to color-blind rules
that were applied without sufficient thought. "For instance," Janine
explains, "one of the issues that we would get in trouble for was
fallin' asleep in classes. And this is not just myself, but a lot of the
Metco students. We might fall asleep during some classes. A lot of
kids would get in trouble for that." Again and again, Janine and
many of the other Metco students would be sent to the principal's
office; again and again they got into trouble. Yet, as far as Janine
knows, not one of the teachers or administrators ever bothered to
ask why so many of the Metco students were falling asleep in class.

The answer is simple: the kids who were being bused from the
inner city were not getting enough sleep. "We had to get up extremely early in the morning and get home extremely late in the
evening," says Janine. "The ride t'get to Needham is about forty-five
minutes, but that did not include the different households we had to
go in the city to pick up other people. So I could be getting on my
bus at six-thirty in the morning, y'know, six o'clock, to be out to
Needham by eight. School probably would be done by about three,
and it took about a hour and half to get home." Add time to get

ready in the morning and time for homework at night, and you have kids who aren't getting enough rest.

"Looking back at it," says Janine, "I know we fell asleep because we had to get up so early in the morning, ride on the bus the length of time that we did. Our day was very long, but that wasn't considered. That wasn't considered in terms of, 'Well, this could be because the kids had to get up so early in the morning and be bused out here t'go to school.'" But the teachers responded to the Metco students who fell asleep in class as they responded to other students who fell asleep in class three consecutive days—by sending the student to the principal's office and to see the school nurse. "That was something I believe that they coulda handled a lot differently," says Janine.

Janine believes "many people, from teachers to students, were racist. A lot of them were angry that we were there, and we would definitely feel their anger, y'know. And not knowing at that time, when I was young, not really understanding what was going on, and even to call it racism, I wouldn't know. But I knew that somethin' was wrong. Lookin' back at it now, I know that that's what it was."

Race and racism were not the only factors that shaped Janine's experience in Needham. Class was an issue, too. Janine says the suburban schools were very different from the schools in Boston. "They were cleaner. There was more freedom. They had supplies." She laughs. "We would get books, y'know, things like that. And also a lot of the students had cars, but this is like in high school."

I ask, "Were you ever jealous of the kids because they had so much?"

Janine answers, "It was hard to understand *why,* y'know, what was different from them to us. Goin' over some of the houses, the homes, they might have been huge. Different things like that. So it was hard to understand and hard to adjust to, comin' from not havin' that. Feelin' inferior because that might not have been something that we had, and then coming here to the inner city and they had it and not understanding what was the difference.

"Y'know," she says, "we weren't able t'participate in after-school sports because they weren't able to get another bus that would bring us back home after school hours. So that was a bummer. That was another way where we felt excluded, and not understanding why we couldn't have access to the same things."

By the end of tenth grade, says Janine, "I was so fed up and so angry with everything that I had been going through that it really was interfering. An' it got to the point where I just didn't wanna be bothered an' I couldn't concentrate on my work and doin' what I needed to do." For eleventh grade, Janine transferred to Dorchester High School, a predominantly black school in Boston.

Janine immediately noticed the differences between Needham and Dorchester. "There were locks on the doors, y'know. The only time you could go to the bathroom was when classes were changing. We couldn't leave for lunch or anything, whereas in Needham doors were never locked, you can leave at any time if you wanted to go out. The books were terrible."

Janine believes the time spent in the Needham schools was valuable. "It allowed me to see another side that I might not have been exposed to in terms of people and in terms of seein' the difference between the school systems and how they work. But I had more fun when I went to Dorchester High."

After Janine graduated from high school, she "wanted to have fun and travel." For the next three years, she spent time in California, South Carolina, and Barbados, which is where her father grew up. To pay for her travels, Janine's parents gave her some money; she also worked along the way. And she usually stayed with family or friends, so she did not have to pay rent.

Her wanderlust satisfied, Janine returned to Boston. She became a part-time student, working on her bachelor's degree in psychology at a local university. She also took a job as a substance abuse counselor in a women's residential treatment program.

Janine loved working with the women in the treatment program, but it was draining. After three years, she began looking for another job. She accepted a position with Community Servings, a nonprofit organization that delivers hot meals to homebound AIDS patients.

Explaining why she accepted the position at Community Servings, Janine says, "I started becomin' aware of the fact that AIDS was affecting people in the community and just how serious AIDS is. And knowing people personally who have AIDS and who have died from AIDS, y'know, it was a service that I really wanted to do. And really, after being here and seein' what took place and the growth that was happening in this program, I really wanted to be a part of that, because it was a new program and there was room for new ideas."

Janine is the organization's intake and outreach coordinator. She handles all client matters, from ensuring that they are receiving their meals to informing them of social and governmental services of which they might be unaware. "I love the work that I do," she says, "the gratification that I get from when I speak to the clients who get our services. It's really fulfilling."

In addition to her work at Community Servings, Janine conducts workshops on public health issues, especially on AIDS and related issues. She is also a "facilitator" for a support group for women who have been infected by HIV. In addition to all this, Janine is still making progress toward her undergraduate degree, which she hopes to finish within the year.

Indeed, finishing school is her top priority. Once she has completed her undergraduate studies, she wants to begin working on her Ph.D. in clinical psychology. "That's my goal," she tells me, "so I really want to focus on that area of my life." Consequently, although marriage might be a possibility under the right circumstances, having children will have to wait. Says Janine, "I'm not willing to have kids at this moment in my life. It would be inconvenient in terms of what I'm trying to do."

And whatever else Janine may be trying to do, achieving the American Dream is not part of it. "I don't see the American Dream as something that is for me," she says.

"The American Dream is havin' all this freedom, being wealthy, being important, having prestige. Y'know, that's the American Dream, being free t'do whatever you wanna do when you wanna do it. And that's crap. That type of American Dream is limited. It's not for everybody and everybody doesn't have access to even get to that point. Everybody's not wealthy. People can't do what they wanna do when they wanna do it. People don't have prestige. So it's a misconception. It is. It's a misconception, you know, because the majority of people in America are poor. And livin' in poverty, you don't have choices. It's a crock.

"I'm not striving for the American Dream. If I am able to be wealthy, wonderful. If I'm able to have a big house, wonderful. But I'm happy and content right now, and if I don't get that, that's okay. I define success as having myself, in terms of spiritually being content with me, y'know, accepting me for who I am.

"I'm not really looking *for* anything. What I try t'do as an individual is the best that I can do on a daily basis. I never know when my life's gonna end. Nobody owes me anything, so, y'know, I'm not a victim. I have to do what I need to do for myself in order to be happy.

"I have no idea what to expect. But if I continue to do what I'm doin', I expect that my fulfillment an' my happiness will continue to grow—if I'm not caught up in tryin' to strive for the American Dream, tryin', like, t'be somebody and constantly worried about bein' rich. That can be dangerous."

"How so?"

"I think a lot of our youth are trying to strive for that American Dream. I talk about kids in my community, because I'm more familiar with them. And some of the kids who might be sellin' drugs, you know, they're doin' it for that reason, so they can have money and do what they wanna do when they wanna do it, drive around in BMWs or things like that. I mean, they're doing it so they can *have* that American Dream. If they're livin' in poverty and somebody says, 'Well, you can make five hundred dollars a day,' y'know, they're gonna go for it."

Not only is Janine dubious about the notion of the American Dream, she is equally wary of the American government. "Oh, it sucks," she says with a laugh. "It does. I think the entire government's corrupt. I think that they all lie. The government. The CIA, the President, the *entire* government. I think they all work together. It's like an institution that enables people t'continue to lie and be dishonest. They're not for the betterment of the people, in general."

I ask, "Do you vote regularly?"

"No," she replies.

"Why not?"

"Because people who have been on the ballot I haven't been in favor of."

Toward the end of our conversation, I ask Janine why she has turned out differently from the kids who she says are selling drugs as a way to achieve the American Dream. Recalling that both of her parents have college degrees, she tells me: "I think that I am privileged in a way. I had access to a lot of information that others might not have. And I am a minority of my community, you know, because it's not that many people are able to sorta make it. It's hard. Financially, it's difficult. Emotionally, it's difficult. So, I'm definitely a minority. I mean, I think my parents were able to help me sorta see that there were other things out there that I could do. I think that really helped.

"I think I was just fortunate, 'cause I'm not any different than anybody else livin' in the city. I think that I was lucky. I had motivation after a while to sort of not fall into the system. But I'm privileged, y'know. What I try to do is to let other people know that they don't have t'go the route they're goin' and that they can change their lives.

"But it's real difficult if you're living in a subculture that helps breed delinquent youth. The environment, it's dirty. Every minute you hear sirens. Y'know, in some cities, if you're goin' down the street and you hear a siren, that's an alarm that somethin's goin' on. Whereas it doesn't faze me if I hear a police car. It doesn't faze me because it is so much part of our environment. And the environment you live in helps enable you to become who you are.

"Environment has a big impact on people. People who might live or grow up in a very wealthy environment, that will transfer over, I mean, sort of become part of who they are. Their environment, in terms of the thinkin', the attitudes, all of that contributes to who they are, and that's the same thing in this community."

According to Janine, kids in Needham are encouraged by their teachers and administrators to continue their educations, to establish careers, to better themselves and their lives. But kids from the inner city of Boston are not. They are told, directly or indirectly, to settle for what they have; in effect, they are encouraged to do nothing. Janine believes we need to tell these children that they do not have to settle for what they have, that they can have more—they *can* go to college, they *can* have successful careers, they *can* raise families.

Janine says we need to send the people of this nation a message: "You don't need to be makin' two hundred thousand dollars a year to be somebody. It's okay to be who you are with what you have. But just because you're poor doesn't mean you have to give up the fight. You can be anything you wanna be."

VICENTE

Some people call the Rio Grande Valley in far southern Texas "The Valley of Palms," a romantic tribute not only to the palm trees, but also to the rich farmland in the area. Others refer to the Valley as the place "where the sun spends the winter"—a slogan likely invented by a local chamber of commerce to lure frostbitten Northerners, also known as "snowbirds," into migrating south in their campers and spending their winters and their dollars in this sunny clime.

Vicente has another name for the Valley. He calls it "The Valley of Tears."

The fourth of eight children, Vicente, twenty-seven, grew up in Donna, Texas, a town with a population of less than 13,000, a few miles north of the Mexican border. Vicente's father was born in Mexico City but has been in the United States since he came here looking for work when he was eight years old. Except for two summers in the early eighties when Vicente's family headed north to Michigan to pick cucumbers, his father worked as a ranch hand at the same ranch here in the Valley for most of Vicente's life. His father is now retired. Vicente's mother is originally from Donna. She is a house wife and has been married to Vicente's father for thirty-seven years. Vicente lives in Donna with his parents and two of his younger brothers, who are still in school. His other brothers and sisters also live in Donna, in the same neighborhood as his parents.

Raising eight children on nothing but a ranch hand's wages was difficult, says Vicente. "My dad, he worked twenty-four years and he worked real hard to support us. He had to suffer and save a lot of money. He couldn't get what he wanted, just to save a lot of money. And we could make it, but not as fortunate as the middle classes."

Throughout much of junior high and high school, whenever Vicente needed money, he would do what thousands in the Valley do for a living—work in the fields. He picked tomatoes, jalapeños, sugar beets. He tied spinach and mustard. He clipped onions.

"It's shitty work," he says, "but some people say they like it— 'The fresh air, it's better than working in an office.' In a field of one hundred people, maybe ten percent like it. They have always worked in the fields. The rest, they do it because they have to. They didn't finish school. They have no choice."

But thanks in part to his father, Vicente did have a choice. "My dad," says Vicente, "he was strict in one way, on tryin' to finish school." Consequently, unlike so many children in the Valley, Vicente—and all his brothers and sisters—graduated from high school. After that, Vicente wanted to attend an art institute in Houston and learn to design company logos. His parents could not afford to give him any money, and he did not try to get a loan because he did not think he'd be able to repay it. So he abandoned the idea.

Still, Vicente was determined not to go back to work in the fields. Referring to the chemicals sprayed on the crops, he says, "I hear stories about people who work in the fields too long have trouble breathing. They get rashes on their bodies. I know a lot of people who got sick. I'm not gonna risk my health working in the fields, especially when they don't pay that much." Instead of returning to the fields, Vicente moved to California and became a construction worker.

He worked in the Golden State four years. He learned virtually everything there is to know about building a house. By the end of his time there, he was earning good wages—$9.25 an hour, more than twice the then-prevailing minimum wage. But he eventually grew bored with construction work, "the same thing over and over." Construction jobs were drying up, too. He returned to Donna for a few months, then moved to Detroit. After a couple of months spent helping friends sell cassettes and produce at flea markets, Vicente again returned to Donna. He has lived there ever since.

Vicente's girlfriend is Mary. She graduated from high school two years ago; she and Vicente have been dating about a year. Although they are not engaged and have yet to speak with the priest, they are thinking about getting married in December. But before they can settle down, they will have to find jobs that will provide decent pay.

There is precious little work in the Valley, which is only now beginning to recover from a devastating freeze in the winter of 1983–84. The "black ice that destroys everything," as Vicente describes it, so damaged the citrus trees that they had to be cut down to the ground and allowed to grow back again. Eight years later, those trees are only now beginning to produce sufficient fruit to make it economically worthwhile to pick.

That freeze badly damaged the Valley's economy, and it nearly demolished the laborers. Before the freeze, citrus picking provided field workers with jobs for three months of what used to be a seven- or eight-month picking and packing season. Today, there is only four or five months of work, and no more. After that, Vicente explains, "You have to go up north if you want to work. If you want money to survive, it's the only choice." For the laborers who remain in the Valley, he says, "The only way they can support themselves is with food stamps and government assistance."

In the spring of 1991, Vicente went "up north," to a "can shed" near Kalamazoo, Michigan. The work lasted only until November, but he worked lots of hours. A slow week was 60 to 80 hours; a busy week—and there was a full month of those—was 120 hours. If an average work year is approximately 2,000 hours (50 weeks of 40-hour weeks), Vicente did more than a year's work in seven months.

Although there was lots of work, Vicente's sweat did not earn him much money. He received minimum wage, $4.25 an hour, disheartening pay for a man who used to make $9.25 an hour as a construction worker. And there was no time-and-a-half for overtime during those 60-, 80-, and 120-hour weeks. "Just time all the time," says Vicente. No health insurance, either. But Vicente—along with hundreds of other migrant workers from the Valley, Florida, and California—will return to the cannery in a couple of weeks for another season of canning asparagus, raspberries, blueberries, and puddings. While Vicente is in Michigan, Mary will be in Washington state. She will be cutting asparagus as a field worker.

Vicente tells me, "There's no work here in the Valley. And the only solution for us to get money in the years coming is you have to head up north. 'Cause there is nothing here. Everything is dead, how I see it."

Vicente's eyes are not deceiving him. In 1990, when unemployment in Texas peaked at 7 percent, unemployment in Hidalgo County, where Donna is located, soared to 26.6 percent. Although the situation improved slightly in 1991, Hidalgo's peak unemployment rate, 22.2 percent, was still more than three times higher than the highest rate for Texas as a whole, 6.9 percent.* Even more distressing, while the number of people estimated to be living below

---

*Figures from the Texas Employment Commission.

poverty in 1990 was 13.5 percent for the United States and 18.1 percent for Texas, it was 51.7 percent for Hidalgo County.* That means more people in Hidalgo County are living below the poverty line than are living above it—and poverty estimates from the government tend to be conservative.

If anyone thinks that perhaps these numbers might overstate the case, that person need only drive along Business 83, the main commercial avenue in Hidalgo County. The closed packing sheds and abandoned processing plants offer silent proof of a moribund economy.

When Vicente is not working at the cannery in Michigan, he returns to the Valley. There, he spends most of his time as a volunteer at the Mid-Valley Community Center in Weslaco. The center occupies a small store front just seventy-five feet west of the intersection of Business 83 and Farm Road 88, next to Florinda's Barber and New Image (Haircut $3). The only aspect of the center's otherwise unassuming front that might belie the revolution quietly brewing within is a sign posted just above the center's name. It demands in red letters, "PAY ONION WORKERS JUST WAGES."

Inside the center, to the left of the door, is a short bookcase overflowing with issues of *People's Tribune,* a newspaper that exhorts, "Workers of the World, Unite!" and declares, "Is communism dead? *No!"* And from the Central Committee of the Communist Labor Party of the United States of North America, which intends "to end forever the exploitation and oppression in this country we built with our sweat and defended with our blood," there's a stack of the recent issues of *Rally, Comrades!,* a newspaper that prints its articles in both English and Spanish. *(¡Agrupemonos, Camaradas!)*

The wall to the right, covered with a number of Vicente's drawings, posters, and sketches, demonstrates that while Vicente could not afford to attend art school, he did not give up his art. One of the drawings depicts a black man advising the reader, "Take time to learn about Malcolm X." Another warns, "Say No to Drugs," with a circle and slash over the "No." A third commands: "Don't Stop the People." There are also several pictures that plead with the observer to "Support the Strikers."

One of the workers at the community center describes Vicente as if he is the Diego Rivera of Hidalgo County: "Vicente paints the

*From the 1990 Census.

history of this place, what's going on. Someday he may be remembered."

According to its membership form, the center was founded in March 1990 by a group of farmworkers and low-income families in the Valley. They wanted to form an organization that would "speak out and fight in their defense" and would "react to every manifestation of tyranny and oppression."

The center also offers other, more mundane services to its members. For instance, Vicente and other volunteers help people who speak little or no English fill out various government forms and file their taxes. There are pamphlets that tell people "How to Sue in Small Claims Court" and "How to Write Better Résumés," about "Social Security Benefits—1989" and about "Surviving America: What You're Entitled To and How to Get It."

But Vicente believes the center has another mission: "We try to get the people to open their minds to what's goin' on, 'cause lotta people come here and they really don't know."

Vicente offers the workers who pick onions as an example. Crew leaders from the farms will drive before dawn to Hidalgo, a border town on the U.S. side of the Rio Grande. Day laborers from Mexico and the Valley will be waiting for someone to offer them work. The crew leader will offer to pay $.65 a bucket to anyone willing to pick onions. An industrious worker can pick about six buckets of onions in an hour, for a total of $3.90. This is $.35 below the current minimum wage, $4.25 an hour. But the workers either do not bother to figure this out, or they feel as if they don't have a choice but to accept the job on the farmers' terms.

"They're just not using their heads a little bit," says Vicente, his voice charged with frustration and sympathy. "Maybe that's why all the people are living like we are, because they're not using their heads. If they would use their heads, they'd realize they were not making even minimum wage."

To apprise the onion field workers of the situation, Vicente drives to Hidalgo to hand out flyers to the workers milling about in front of the Whataburger. The flyer states: "ATTENTION ONION WORKERS—If you earn less than the Federal Minimum Wage of $4.25 per hour YOUR EMPLOYER IS VIOLATING THE LAW AND ABUSING YOU. . . . for more information call the Mid-Valley Organizing Committee." (The director of the Mid-Valley Community Center later tells me that the MVCC and the MVOC are not officially related to one another.

The MVOC seeks to organize the farmworkers, while the MVCC offers a variety of services to the community. However, the director
also tells me that some of the most devoted volunteers at the community center are also active in the organizing committee. And
throughout our conversation, Vicente makes almost no effort to distinguish the two.)

Vicente emphasizes that the center does not organize strikes.
"We leave it up to the people," he says. "We just tell 'em, 'If you
want to, you can do it. But we'll back you up" by helping to print
flyers and to fill out any paperwork.

One of Vicente's pencil drawings summarizes his thoughts
about the American Dream. The words "Mid-Valley Community
Center" form a circle around an outline of the state of Texas. In the
middle of Texas, a man and woman are crying, and their tears fall
into a river that is lined with palm trees. To the left is a shredded
U.S. flag.

Vicente tells me, "They say the United States or the Valley is full
of vegetables and fruit and everything. It's not really true. It's comin'
apart because the people are struggling. They call it the American
Dream, the Valley of Palms and everything. It sounds pretty and everything. But if you would really see it, people are really struggling
here. That's why I call it the Valley of Tears."

Vicente's current goals are straightforward: "Right now it's really try and settle down and get serious with my girlfriend and try to
get married and raise a family. Just one or two kids. In case I get a
good job.

"The important thing is at least getting a good job, at least that
will pay four twenty-five an hour—that's minimum wage. And try to
get a job where it's gonna be full-time, not just like there's work
and, 'Okay, you can go work full-time,' and after that they'll just
keep you through two months, then they hire somebody else because they don't want to go through that process of insurance policies. A lot of jobs, after you've been six months there, they gotta
give you insurance. 'N' I have been through a lot of work where
they only hire you for three months, and after that they say, 'You're
gone.' You didn't do nothing wrong. Because they will hire a new
guy and they don't have to give insurance. An' I see that.

"I just wanna get a job where I can be really full-time, all the
time working. I want a steady job where I can make enough money

after a month where I can pay at least my rent. And if I get married, my children and my wife can have 'nough money to go out.

"I feel like right now, if you stay here in the Valley and work here, you ain't gonna make it. Anytime, if I go anywhere up there, up north, I know I can make it. Me, because I graduated and my girlfriend graduated. I know we can make it anywhere in the United States that we go. We can get a job in a store anywhere because we know English an' Spanish an' we really know what's going on. But like if we keep on staying here in the Valley, we can't do nothing for ourselves. But I know if we go up north anywhere, we can get a job anywhere we want. That's not hard.

"I see a lot of people ain't gonna make it. Other people are in worse shape than me because I graduated, I finished school. And even that I finished school, I have problems sometimes getting a job and getting paid as good as other people do. I feel that it's gonna be harder for other people that drop out or people that just come from Mexico and they haven't learned any English. It'll be real hard for them."

Vicente is concerned about many problems that face his community and his nation. He worries about abuses by immigration authorities and local law enforcement officers, who often treat Mexican immigrants—and Mexican-Americans—"like you were just trash." He also believes that society gives today's adolescents and teenagers *"les don muchos alles,"* literally "too much wings," too much freedom. "Givin' 'em too much freedom for the kids, that's why they wanna do what they want," such as taking drugs and joining gangs. But Vicente's biggest concern, to which he devotes most of his free time, is the conditions facing the farmworkers.

According to Vicente, "There's work here in the Valley. There's a lotta work. But the ranchers are abusing us. Instead of giving us the work, them that live here, for four twenty-five or five dollars, they go over there to Mexico and hire somebody for a dollar.

"The people won't speak out. They will never do nothin' because the people are really used to bein' scared or somethin'. That's what I feel like before—scared, timid. They just don't want to speak out for themselves. An' because the people don't want to speak up for themselves, the owners of companies, bosses, they take advantage in a way that they say, 'Well, if you don't want to work for me for two-fifty, what the heck. I'll just hire people from Mexico.' That's why I feel they take advantage, because they say, 'We can always go to the border and pick up a load of Mexicans from up there who will have permission for one day or two days of work. We'll just pay 'em whatever we want.' I feel that's wrong. The government or the system here has to do something about that."

He continues, "The system is all wrong. They should put a law—you gonna hire somebody, he has to work for the three months of work there is there, as long as he doesn't break the law. If they never do some kind of contract or that, they're gonna keep on abusing the people here. We're never gonna get anywhere."

Until then, for the migrant laborers and farm workers says Vicente, the American Dream will remain nothing more than a dream.

DALE

Dale, twenty-five, lives in an efficiency in a poor, ethnically mixed neighborhood in East Hollywood. He says he could afford a nicer apartment, but he was in a rush to move out of his old one because he had a falling-out with his roommate earlier this week, and he found this place the next day. Plus, Dale points out, he does not mind paying less rent because that leaves more money for other things, such as repaying money his parents loaned him when he was in college, and helping his younger brother pay for school.

Dale, who is black, was born and raised in New Orleans. He grew up in an area known as Gentilly, a predominantly black neighborhood near downtown. "It was near the housing projects," he says, "but the project in Gentilly, the crime rate wasn't as bad as the others. Pretty safe environment. It was just poor."

Although Dale was raised as a strict Catholic, his parents were divorced when he was six years old. After that, Dale kept in touch with his father, though they did not have much of a relationship. He says, "My father, when he divorced my mom, he divorced us as well. He's around physically, but that's it. I mean, we would go visit him on Sundays until I got tired of it and I was able to see that this was just something to make him look good." Dale says that while he was in college, he learned that his father's second wife "didn't want him to have a whole lot to do with his first marriage. For that reason he had limited association with us. The only reason why I ever maintain contact with him is because I have a brother and sister by his second marriage, and we're all really close. I'm polite to him, but that's it."

Dale's mother never remarried, but when Dale was fifteen, she began seeing an abusive man. Whenever the man came over to the house, Dale would go to his room and study. Dale's mother tried to force Dale to be nicer to her friend, but that only made Dale angry, and he resented this violent man for coming between him and his mother, who had been Dale's best friend.

He says, "It got to the point where when I walked in the house, there was so much tension, like I would immediately get a head ache. I was unhappy. I left home twice. The first time I left and I went back home the same night. But at the end of the week I just couldn't take it anymore. My mother told me, 'As far as I'm concerned, you don't even exist anymore,' and at that point I said, 'Okay, I can't be here.' " Dale was eighteen when he moved out.

"It was a scary time," he says. "I left home making four hundred dollars a month, which is, God, y'know, who can survive off of that? I was basically moving from one friend's home to another's. I didn't like that, but at the same time I couldn't be home. Eventually I said, 'Okay, I'll move on campus when school starts, but in the meantime I would like to be stable someplace.' And my cousin found me. She's like, 'Stay here.' "

The next fall, Dale enrolled at a local university. He put himself through school with a combination of wages, scholarships, and loans from the government and his parents. Five years later he graduated with a communications degree. Later that same month, he left the Crescent City for the City of Angels.

"I'm a writer," Dale explains, "and I felt like I wanted to be out here. I think there's better opportunity."

Dale began writing when he was twelve, short stories and song lyrics. "First of all," he says, "it was always an escape for me. When I had family problems, I used to go into a room, shut the door, turn on some music and write. Second of all, I enjoy doing it and it comes really naturally.

"In the back of my mind, I always knew that I wanted to write. I wanted to do public relations, which entails writing; advertising, which involves writing. But I didn't want to strictly focus on writing because it's hard. It's hard. You have a lot of competition. You have a lot of boundaries to cross.

"You know, one thing my aunt said to me that made sense—but then, it doesn't really matter that much to me—she said that writers starve. She said most artists do starve. And I said, 'Well, I understand that.' So I think initially I put it like in the back of my mind. I said if I can't write and make a living off of it, I'll pursue these other avenues first.

"Writers, as you probably know, sometimes it takes them years to get to where they want to be. I felt like here in Los Angeles I could work on my business skills and my writing career simultaneously, and if the writing career flopped, I still had the business career to focus on."

Dale works full-time as an administrator and supervisor in an office in downtown L.A. He also works eight hours a week as a receptionist at a health club.

For Dale, the American Dream "means that an individual is free to do what he wants to do, free to achieve all his goals and successes as long as he's willing to work at it. And to be happy and accepted as a part of this society. To me, that's the American Dream."

But Dale, who is gay, does not believe the American Dream applies to him. "I think that the American Dream is really for—how can I say this?—the American Dream is structured for the white, American male—*heterosexual* American male. That's my opinion. I could be wrong, but that's what I feel. So I feel like as long as you fit that category, you can probably have just about anything you want, as long as you work for it. But if you're a female or if you're black or any minority, it's like, here's a line and this is as far as you can go. Sometimes you may be fortunate enough to surpass that line, but overall it's like you have a boundary here."

But even though Dale feels excluded from the American Dream, he still has dreams of his own. "I'd like to become an accomplished writer," he says. "I don't have to be a mainstream, like I don't have to have mainstream success. If I could write something as to affect an individual's life, or to make them have changes or to make them see a different point of view, that would be the ultimate satisfaction for me. Of course, I would like to have a little wealth behind it, but I've learned money isn't everything."

When Dale was younger, he believed the secret to a good life was contained in a six-word equation—"money equals power,

power equals happiness." But, he says, "as I went through college, I started to realize, you know, I really wasn't happy. And money didn't matter to me anymore. Just as long as I was happy within, and as long as I was able to share that with someone else, that would be the ultimate satisfaction for me."

Dale has not written much in the past few weeks. "Right now, I'm trying to force myself into doing two hours per week. I'm suffering from writer's block." Dale's muse suddenly became mute about six weeks ago. That's when Dale learned he is HIV-positive.

"I have my good days and bad days, but whenever something traumatic like that happens, I can't write. If it's something that I'm going through or a friend's going through, it's hard for me to write because I get a lot of happiness and enjoyment out of writing. Like right now, it's like I can write for a few minutes, and then it'll pop up in my head. Y'know, you have this thing hanging over your head. So then I'll have a block again.

"But like I said, I think I'm coming out of it. I'm getting used to the idea of being positive and just living my life. So I'm coming out of it. I think I want to get some counseling to completely pull myself out of it and move on."

"How did you find out?" I ask.

"First of all, I think I'm pretty confident of when I contracted the virus. It was at one of my most vulnerable points in my life, in 1985, when I had just moved out of my mom's home. It was my first homosexual experience, and it was unprotected because it just happened. It wasn't anything planned. And when I realized what we were doing, I said we have to protect ourselves, but it had already happened like two or three times unprotected. Eventually I found out that this guy was one of the biggest whores in New Orleans.

"There weren't really any circumstances that made me decide to get tested, like I wasn't sick or anything. I just had been toying with the idea of being tested just to know anyway, and so I just went one day. I said, 'Okay, I'm gonna do this and get it over with.'

"When I found out—God—I felt like I wanted to run for dear life. I felt raped, in a sense, because I felt like life had raped me of doing things I wanted to do. I also felt really raped when I found out because I was an eighteen-year-old kid when I was infected. I heard of the AIDS virus but, being heterosexual up until that point, it wasn't really discussed that much. It was 1985 and the AIDS virus had been around, but first of all, I guess I just blocked it out of my mind because I felt like, 'Well I'm not gay, so this doesn't include me.' And second of all, New Orleans was a pretty small community, and you don't hear about AIDS that much. Well, at that time you didn't hear about it that much *there*. And like I said, I was at a vulnerable point in my life, and I needed someone and I turned to this guy. It just hurt to know that because of my being naive at that point in my life, that this is what happened.

"I was frightened, of course. I was shocked because, like I said, although I'm sure that's when I contracted it, I'm physically healthy. I even at one point felt suicidal. I never felt like I would follow it through, but I just thought for a second, 'So I could just take myself away from all this misery, and from the shame and the pressure and the depression, if I just knock myself off.' I would never do that.

"How else did I feel? Paranoid. Because every little thing that happened, like I have a bad allergy, and whenever I would get congested I'm like, 'Oh my God, this is it.' I felt alone. I felt like a walking time bomb, and sometimes I still feel that way. But I'm adjusting.

"I think I'll tell a couple of friends. My family, no, because my family's like a gossip chain, and if I called and told one person, somebody else is gonna know it, and then my entire family's gonna know about it. And I don't want the sympathy.

"I know that sometimes I should open up, but I don't bring people into my personal situations because I don't want them to feel sorry for me, and I don't want that every time I pick up the phone, every time that I see someone, they'll be preoccupied with what I'm going through. And y'know, I would have relatives, if they knew, they would call me every day.

"It's hard for me to even say it. I have told one relative who's also HIV-positive. I didn't know that beforehand. I suspected it, but I didn't know. And on the day that I found out, I said, 'If I don't share it with somebody, I'm gonna lose my mind.' And I didn't want a stranger. I could have called the one-eight-hundred number helpline, and I decided not to. And also, if something were to happen to me, I want somebody to know so that they can go back and say, 'This is what's wrong.'

"Like I said, I think there's a few friends, a few close friends, that I want to share it with. I don't know how to do that yet. That's one of the things that I'll talk to my counselor about."

Although Dale's mother is no longer his best friend, they still love each other. I tell Dale I'm surprised that he does not want his mother to know about his condition, that I would have expected it to be more difficult *not* to tell her. He replies: "Well, first of all, my mom's going through her own set of problems right now. Second of all, she found out recently that I was gay. That's the first thing that hit her mind, she's like, 'Oh, you're going to get AIDS.' I said, 'Mom'—and at that time I had no idea that I was carrying the virus—and I told her, I said, 'You know, there was only one time in my life that I could have contracted it, and I feel fine right now. So if I haven't got it, I won't get it.' And so that kind of made her settle down.

"Even right now, she's in denial about my sexuality. It's been almost a year since she found out, and, ah, she thinks it's a phase. And I told her, I said, 'Ma, you know what's really weird is that I thought it was too. But phases don't last ten and twenty years.' She said, 'Well, you don't act this way, and you have goals.' I said, 'Ma, gay people have goals, and we don't all walk around in skirts and act real feminine.' That's the ignorance of the heterosexual society, because I think that they see the stereotypical homosexual, and they think that it's all like that. And she said, 'Well, I still think it's a stage,' and I said, 'Well, I think you're wrong.'

Dale, who has had two distant cousins die because of AIDS, says, "My mother's gonna want me to move home, and I don't want to deal with that. I really don't. It's also gonna put her into a type of depression. She's already unhappy, and I'm just a little fearful that she's gonna just lose it. So I don't want to burden her with that. So for that reason I haven't even told her. If it becomes necessary, well then I will."

Dale describes how his condition has affected his life: "Oh, it's put like a rush on it. It's like, you know, 'Okay, I'd better get moving now, because I don't know how much time I have here.' I want to do things and get it out now and work on my future in a more expedited manner."

With his very next breath, he says: "But basically I'm just getting back to doing things on a normal basis. I have a friend who tested positive, and he just went out and bought a home. When I first found out, I'm like, 'Oh, I would never do that,' because you have a home and then what happens if you get sick, you can't make the monthly payments. It's stress right there. But he's just gone on with his life, and that's what I've decided to do."

I ask, "What's important to you?"

Dale replies, "Basically, I just want to be happy, and there's many things that can make me happy. I'm happy seeing other people happy. I'm happy knowing that everybody is doing well and they're getting what they want out of life. What would also make me happy is to know that society is becoming less judgmental. That's been a frustration of mine.

"For my entire life, people look at your race, what you're wearing, who you relate to and associate with, your family, and all of a sudden you have an image that may not be your own, but it's given to you. And I hate that. I feel like we're regressing. I'm starting to feel like the 1960s, with the racial situation that I've read about, is coming back and I'm gonna experience it once again. Well, not once again, but I will experience what my family has.

"I realize that there's no one answer that will solve this problem, but I wish that the government would be there to support its people. 'Cause right now I have very little faith in the government. I'm really—I have no faith in the government right now."

Dale believes that the U.S. government is covering up its malign involvement in any number of activities. For example, he maintains that the CIA assassinated President Kennedy. Oliver Stone's 1991 movie *JFK,* which delineated this and other theories about Kennedy's assassination, only confirmed what Dale had "read about and suspected for years." Dale also asserts that alien spaceships have landed in the United States, that the federal government has seized these spacecrafts and, in at least one instance, probably killed a farmer and his wife who had witnessed one of these landings. "I've always felt like there have been UFO's," he says, "but why is the government keeping it from us? I can appreciate the fact that they don't want a national scare but, at the same time, be honest and open with the people."

He says, "There's also an underground tape that's out right now showing how the government caused the AIDS virus. I'm very resentful of that."

"You believe the government *caused* the AIDS virus?"

"I've always speculated, but I wasn't really sure. But there's a tape right now, an underground videotape in the gay community, that a scientist put out. He shows you everything scientifically." Dale admits he has not seen the tape, and he does not know the scientist's name, though he knows the scientist is in hiding "because the government tried to have him killed off when he started doing his research."

"Why," I ask, "would the government create the AIDS virus?"

"To kill off what they didn't want in the country," says Dale.

"Which was . . . ?"

"The gays. They also injected people in Africa, so as to kill off the black people, and also to trace it out of the country."

He explains: "Basically, it's a combination of a virus from a goat and a cow that creates the HIV virus. This government studied it for years. They injected two hundred gay males in New York and X amount of people in Africa, and that's how it was started."

"You genuinely believe that?"

"I've always felt that. I've always felt that," says Dale. "I could be dead wrong, but this is just how much mistrust I have in the government.

"Everything that comes out now of how the virus started, I read it and I try to look at it objectively. But, like I say, even before I found out my status, even before I knew much about AIDS, you know, even when I was in denial about me being gay, I said, 'Why is this just affecting this small group of people?' Why did it start off in the gay community? I just don't buy it. Like I said, I'm open to the fact that I could be totally wrong, but it's always made sense to me and I've always said that the AIDS virus is man-made. But like I said, the government, I just, I've never had trust in them.

"I know the government's good for some things, but I question a lot of moves they make. And I can't say that I'm always fully objective, because I don't know what's going on *there* that they have to take care of, and they may have to do this for this reason that they're not making public knowledge, and I can appreciate that. But it just seems as though there's a lot going on that I don't feel comfortable with."

He says, "I don't trust the American government. I would like to, but I don't. There's too many secrets."

He realizes that many people will think he is crazy. "Oh, of course I do," he says. Dale assesses his sanity this way: he may be wrong about the government's involvement in the AIDS pandemic, but he isn't nuts.

Note: I spoke with Dale four months after our first conversation. He said his doctor told him that not everyone who is HIV-positive necessarily gets AIDS, and he read somewhere that fewer than 50 percent of those who are HIV-positive will ultimately get the disease. "That has given me hope," he said.*

Like sunshine melting the ice covering a frozen pond, this hope has melted Dale's writer's block. His ideas are flowing once again. He now spends between ten and twenty hours a week writing, a vast improvement over the two hours he was straining to produce just four months earlier.

And now that being HIV-positive seems much less like a death sentence, Dale has a new attitude about his future. "I used to feel like I had five years to do everything that I wanted to do in this lifetime," he said. "But I don't feel like that anymore. Now I treat the virus like diabetes—just take care of yourself and do what you need to do to prolong your life, and everything will be okay."

He said, "I just plan to be around awhile."

---

*I asked a doctor about Dale's claims. He said there is some truth in what Dale told me. Some people who have the HIV virus have not contracted AIDS for longer-than-average periods, and some evidence indicates that there are people who might carry and transmit the virus without ever getting the disease. But this doctor also said that, given what they know today, Dale's second assertion, that fewer than 50 percent of those infected will ultimately contract AIDS, is extremely optimistic.

SAME CITY, DIFFERENT WORLDS III

SOUTH CENTRAL LOS ANGELES

ANTHONY

"This is Vietnam out here," says Anthony, describing his neighborhood in South Central Los Angeles. "AK-forty-sevens an' Uzis an' stuff goin' on. It's a peaceful day today. I'm surprised the police helicopter didn't come around. Usually it comes around every twenty seconds."

The tragic irony of this situation, as Anthony points out, is that this orgy of violence—"gang-bangin' an' drive-by shootin' and crack dealin' an' all that"—has gone on for so long it seems normal.

"Sometime, I be like, 'This don't make no sense,' you know. You gotta just keep your head up high and hope for the best."

Anthony is black. He was born in Watts in 1968, not quite three years after the riot of 1965. (One can no longer refer simply to "the Watts riot" because of the riot—some call it a "rebellion"—that engulfed South Central Los Angeles in April 1992.) A year or so after he was born, Anthony was sent to live with a cousin in Louisiana. Three years later, he moved back to Watts to live with his mother.

When Anthony was ten, his mother "snapped"—the combined effect of trying to raise six boys without a husband (Anthony's parents separated when he was two) and drug abuse ("Those drugs been controllin' her life since long as I can remember," says Anthony). Anthony's maternal grandmother took in Anthony and his brothers. However, "four wild boys," along with Anthony's cousin and uncle, were simply too much for her. After a year, "she just couldn't take it." Finally, after bouncing between his mother's place and a foster home, Anthony moved in with his grandmother's friend Ruby, who lived in an apartment in Nixon Gardens, a housing project in Watts.

As a boy growing up in Watts in the eighties, Anthony had no choice about becoming a member of a gang. "It's like I was born to it," he explains, " 'cause my three older brothers was all gang-bangers and we looked just alike. You can see from the picture." He points to a poster-sized enlargement of a photograph of him and his older brothers. "And people know that I'm they brother, so they just automatically assumed since they were in a gang that I'm in a gang. That's how easy it is. If you stay in a Blood neighborhood, they feel that you a Blood. If you stay in a Crip neighborhood, they feel like you a Crip."

Says Anthony, "Only thing kept me alive was goin' and stayin' in school."

Yet even in school, he was not completely safe. He explains that, at his high school, "there were a lot more Crips up there, and I were a Blood. And so I tried to get me an education, but I wasn't gonna let nobody harm me, so I took me a gun." Carrying this gun to school got Anthony expelled from eleventh grade. He says, as if in a footnote, "I had the clip in one pocket and the gun in the other. That's why I didn't go to jail." Nevertheless, after a semester at a special school for teenagers "who've been in trouble but not really bad," Anthony transferred to a high school in the Valley and became the first of his brothers to graduate.

With high school behind him, Anthony did not plan to go to college. But his father, who by then was the supervisor of custodial services at Langston University, a historically all-black institution in central Oklahoma, asked his son whether he'd like to come to school out there.

Two things convinced Anthony to leave Watts. One was his

feeling that, although he had finished high school, he was still "ta-kin' a wrong path" because he had started selling drugs during his senior year. "Back in '85," he says, "so much money coming through it was ridiculous." Anthony made as much as $500 a day. He "didn't drink, didn't fool with no drugs"; he spent the money on fancy clothes, $75 high-tops, and gifts for his friends and family. But he only dealt for six months before he realized, "Naw, this is not me."

The second factor was his becoming the victim of a drive-by shooting by some Crips earlier in his senior year. Of course, Anthony had been shot at "a lot of times" before, the first time when he was only eleven or twelve. However, this shooting convinced him: "I gotta get outta here." When Anthony's father showed him an opportunity to get out of L.A., Anthony figured, "Sure, why not." And besides, he adds, "I always was smart in school." So he "just up and left" for Oklahoma.

"Oklahoma was all right," he says approvingly. "My first semes-ter I was bored. I was homesick, 'bout to cry an' all that. But after my first semester, I came back home and I was like, 'Man!' As soon as I got off the plane, my heart started beatin' fast. I said, 'I can't wait to get back to Oklahoma.' "

Anthony says wistfully, "It was peaceful out there. It was so peaceful out there." A few moments later he adds, "Peace of mind—that's how you live a long life." Five years later he graduated from Langston University with a bachelor's degree in business administration.

College diploma in hand, Anthony returned to L.A. to find a job. Six months, no luck. Meanwhile, he had heard that a couple of his fraternity brothers from Langston had found good jobs—one as a teacher and coach, the other working with troubled kids—in Columbus, Ohio. So after six fruitless months in L.A., Anthony thought he'd give Columbus a try.

Although the economy there was slow, too, Anthony received more encouraging responses from employers than he had in L.A. Yet the entire time Anthony was in the Midwest, "something" in the back of his mind kept saying, "Go back home. Go back home. Go back home." After three months, he did.

One of the principal reasons Anthony came back is his son, Anthony Jr. Anthony Jr. is almost three. He lives with his mother, her sisters, and one of her sister's four children in a large apartment in South Central L.A. Anthony Jr.'s mother, April, was the only girl Anthony had been "messin' with" for two years when she told Anthony she was pregnant. At first April was reluctant to become a mother. But Anthony—figuring he could help take care of his son once he finished college, and relying on the fact that April could take care of the baby until then—persuaded her to have the baby. He admits, "I had to beg her."

Anthony sees Anthony Jr. nearly every day. He believes his son needs "a good strong father figure, keep his head straight. 'Cause that's all a young man needs growin' up is a father figure. Somebody to keep their head straight, teach 'im right from wrong. 'Cause a woman can't do that. There's some women out there who can, but basically, naw.

"My father left us, abandoned us. An' I know if my father—if a father figure—would've been there, you know, somebody who we respect and listened to, ain't no way in the world we woulda did what we do. We woulda stayed in school, all of us. My mother couldn't keep us in school. At that time, she was tryin' to work and pay bills for us. An' we was drivin' her crazy, runnin' around, gangbangin' an' ditchin' school, all kinda stuff. That's why young boys need they fathers."

"But," I point out, "*you* stayed in school."

Anthony retorts, "I was one outta six boys. That's not good. That's terrible."

He continues: "They always use to tell me to stay in school, my older brothers. 'Man, stay in school. Man, just get that education. Let 'em know that one Crawford can make it.' I'm lettin' people know that Crawfords, they all coulda did this."

Could have, and perhaps some of them will. But right now two of Anthony's older brothers are in jail, and Anthony's other older brother was killed when his fourteen-year-old sister-in-law stabbed him in the leg and severed his femoral artery during an argument with his wife. Anthony's younger half-brother died of cancer when he was a teenager. Anthony's other younger brother is about to graduate from high school. Anthony sadly concludes, "Out of six boys, only me and the youngest one have a chance."

When Anthony convinced April to go ahead and have Anthony Jr., he assumed he'd be able to find a good job once he finished college. "Now, three years later, I still don't have no job," he says, angry and frustrated.

"It's hard for a black man to get a job. And I use to be thinkin' that when people use to tell me that, they just trippin', they don't know what they talkin' about. Now I'm goin' through what they've been tellin' me for years. It's hard. It's like a conspiracy or somethin' that just keep 'em down. They will force you to go sell dope or go rob somebody, try to kill somebody for money."

Anthony thinks that his college education actually may make it more difficult for him to get a job. "It's easy to get a job without a degree," he says. "Get that degree, then that's when things get rough because they have to pay you. They have to pay you then. When you workin' for five, six dollars, they'll pay you that. Five, six dollars an hour, that ain't nothin'. So they have to start payin' you what you worth, then that's when they start gettin' rough."

Back from Ohio for six weeks now, Anthony has so far been unable to find a job—unless you consider just surviving in South Central L.A. a job, which Anthony does. He is living with his aunt and her son in a dilapidated bungalow next door to his grandparents' house in Watts. Anthony does not receive any money from the government; his family and friends will help him until he can get on his feet. "They know it ain't gonna be like this forever," he says. "It can't be."

He fumes, "A woman can have a kid and the government'll give her some assistance. What about the men who can't work, who wanna work and can't get a job? What about them? They just go to waste. I'm liable to go down on skid row. If I didn't have no family, where would I go? Y'know what I'm sayin'. It's like I'm a bum, but only reason why I'm not a bum because I have a family. That's the only reason why. It might be a lotta people down on skid row with B.A. degrees."

From Anthony's perspective the concept of the American Dream is "B.S." He says, "Everybody on the street want the American Dream, but we don't have it. Just a nine-to-five, a nice house, nice car. Basically that's what everyone wants. But we livin' in hard times out here. The American Dream—hmph!—it's a dream all right."

Anthony genuinely believes that the government—"whoever runnin' this country"—is "tryin' to destroy the black man." His

proof? For one, rather than develop constructive ways to help
young black men, the government instead builds more prisons to
confine them. "What are they building these prisons for? What are
they assumin'?" Anthony asks. "It costs more to put a person in jail
than it is to educate 'im. It costs thirty-some thousand dollars a year
just to keep a person in prison a year. Give me thirty thousand dollars. That's a lotta money, you know what I'm sayin'. That's a lot of
money for somebody. If they give everybody in prison thirty thousand dollars a year an' let 'em go free, you think they wouldn't do
no robbin', no killin', or nothin'. Keepin' 'em in there like that, might
as well pay 'em. It don't make no sense."

Anthony offers as further evidence the flow of drugs and weapons into South Central L.A. Visibly agitated, he says: "They can send
a person to the moon, I know the United States can stop this cocaine and stuff coming through here. Automatic weapons? Ain't no
AK's made in Watts. Everybody and Momma got a AK. Everybody
got a gun. AK-forty-sevens, where they coming from? They shouldn't
even sell no AK-forty-sevens. Uzis, nine-millimeters. Man, what happened to the twenty-twos and the thirty-eights, when people get
shot an' still live.

"They could stop all of this," he says. The reason the government doesn't? According to Anthony, it's "racially motivated. They
don't care about black people."

How, I ask, does white society's racism cause black people to
kill each other?

Anthony explains: "The hate that they gave t'us, we couldn't do
nothin' to them, so we take it out on each other. You un'stand what
I'm sayin'? So, we shoot at each other, we kill each other. That's true.
You right about that. But we got that hate from what *they* taught *us*.
So we use it all against each other.

"Some people say I'm paranoid. They think the black man is
paranoid. The black man ain't paranoid. The black man's speaking
the real," he says, talking more rapidly, his voice propelled by emo-
tion. "People say what the government is doing to us and all that ol'
stuff, an' then you come down here and say there ain't no excuse
for me not to have a job. I try to find one. I got résumés written
up, all this old stuff. I dress up, go down there. But when they see
me, they be like, 'Uh-uh.' I look too rough. I look like a hoodlum
to 'em, like I'm gonna do somethin' to 'em. I'm not that type of per-

son. I'm not a hoodlum. I've got more sense than anybody, 'sfar as I'm concerned."

He says other blacks look at him the same way. "They think a young black man is a time bomb. I'm not a time bomb. There's some time bombs out there, though. What can you expect? This is how it is around here."

Ten years ago Anthony believed the United States stood for "freedom, justice, an' all that old stuff." Today, he says, "the United States, it's a slave state to me. They got the police to watch over us, just like in the old days. The police ain't nothin' to me but slave hands. They beat us like the slave hands use to did. So it's the same. The same." And jobs that pay only five dollars an hour, "I still feel that's slavery, it's just a different process. At least with slavery, they was takin' care of us. And now we not in slavery, they just givin' us five dollars."

Anthony tells me about his friend Sean, who works at the parole office. Although Sean's been there three years—and has a daughter to support—he still earns only five dollars an hour.

Anthony says, "He just tryin' to hang in there. He don't wanna sell no dope. He tryin' to do everything the way the United States want him to do it. It's killin' him."

"How?"

"Workin' for five dollars an hour? Three years, goin' on four? That's killin' him. I said, 'Man, I'd rather sell dope.' Don't make no sense. How'm I gonna survive on five dollars an hour? One hundred fifty dollars a week. You know the government gonna get theirs. He's hanging in there, though. I look up to him for that. I respect him for that. I honestly do."

While Anthony considers himself African-American, he does not think of himself as just American. "America don't want me," he says. "They've been showin' me that all my life. They don't want me. Why should I want somebody who don't want me?

"Ain't nobody ask to come over here [from Africa]. I didn't. I wasn't even 'bout to be born, to be honest with you. But I'm here now. I'm here an' I'm in it to win it. An' people out here think like this—'I ain't gonna be out here starvin' an' see the next man with all this.' That's how they feel. I'm just tryin' to do it legit."

Right now, all Anthony wants is "a nice job, a decent job, somethin' a person can be proud of, not no box-lifter or nothin', an' all that ol' stuff. Slavery over with, supposed to be. At least gimme a chance. That's all I ask for. Gimme a chance. That's all a brother need is a chance. That's all anyone ever needs is a chance."

If Anthony ever gets that chance, he'd like to open his own business so he can put others to work. "People need jobs," he says. "People aren't just bad by nature. People are bad because of what they have to go through. People get tired of people sayin', 'Well, wait till you die to get to heaven and get all this stuff.' Why can't we have it now? People need jobs." Anthony adds that his business "wouldn't be nothin' illegal," such as selling drugs, " 'cause it ain't doin' nothin' but committin' genocide."

Observing that "most of these young people around here, they just try to sell drugs for materialistic gain," Anthony tells me, "I'm not a very materialistic person. I just want peace of mind. Just try to take care of my people, my kids, my family, look after them the best way I can." In Anthony Jr.'s case, that means making a good enough living to pay for his college education. "I don't want him goin' on no scholarship in no basketball or no football. We got enough basketball, football players, baseball. We don't need none of that. We need lawyers, doctors, judges, you know, get in the system so you can work things out."

Before I leave, Anthony shows me an album full of color photographs. He points to his family, his brothers, Anthony Jr., April, his friends. Then he pulls out a picture of himself and five of his friends standing on the bed of a red truck, posing like tough guys for the camera. Anthony tells me that four of the five are now in jail—two for attempted murder, one for robbery, and one is serving a life sentence after the authorities reduced it from the death penalty. The fifth guy was killed; someone shot him in the head.

Glancing over the pictures as he slowly turns the pages, he says, "Most everyone in these pictures is either in jail or dead." There is not even a drop of pain in his voice. He is only telling me a fact.

I ask, "Why don't you move? Why don't you go someplace else?"

Anthony explains that although "ain't nothin' but death and destruction" in his neighborhood, he can't abandon his family and friends. "It ain't no use to try to leave the community," he says. "It ain't gonna do no good. I'll be livin' all right. But what about the people who I grew up with? I can't just up and leave. I just gotta try to make things better around here.

"White people don't go through the stuff we go through. I don't think too many white people could survive like this, 'cause it's hard for me to survive. But I just hang on in there. You know, as bad as it sounds, it don't seem like it's that bad, y'know what I'm sayin'. So I just try to make the best out of the worst.

"I wish I could open people's eyes and let 'em see what I see. If you stayed down here, you'd understand everything I'm talkin' about."

DAVID

They came looking "for economic opportunities, just like any other immigrants," says David of his parents, who moved their family from Seoul, South Korea, to Los Angeles. David, twenty-seven, has an older brother and a younger sister. He was ten when his family arrived in L.A.'s Koreatown, a neighborhood where many Korean immigrants live when they first land in the States.

He says, "It was hard at first because I didn't speak the language. I wasn't familiar with the surroundings. But I was so young, it didn't take me too long to get adjusted to the life here."

Although his parents had to work terribly hard—"seven days a week, all day, all night"—within five years they were earning enough money to move from Koreatown to the suburbs. In the early 1980s, however, David's father was laid off from his job. "They wanted to go into business, says David; now they had no other choice because his mother's five dollars an hour wasn't enough to feed everybody. Pooling their savings with lots of money borrowed from a bank, David's parents scraped together enough to open a grocery store in a predominantly Hispanic neighborhood near downtown L.A. The business prospered. Five years later they sold the grocery and bought a liquor store in South Central Los Angeles.

From his junior year of high school until he graduated from college, David worked only limited hours at his parents' stores, Friday after school and Sunday afternoons. He had Saturdays off. After graduating from California State University, Fullerton, David began working for his parents full-time. David's father then devoted his time to the paperwork and the accounting, and under his mother's supervision, David ran the store.

According to David, doing business in South Central L.A. was a "big mistake." When I ask why, he tells me matter-of-factly: "Lotta blacks."

In David's mind, this remark is not an indication of racial bigotry; rather, it reflects his "personal experience." He says that while he worked at his parents' grocery store, he had no trouble getting along with the customers, most of whom were Hispanic, because Koreans and Hispanics "have a lot of things in common." He says, "They had courtesy, common courtesy. I wasn't really intimidated by them. I liked them, as a matter of fact. They were really nice, hardworking people."

But David does not "have good things to say about the blacks" who patronized his parents' liquor store. "I mean, the customers were so—they were scary, to put it bluntly. They were scary. I was intimidated by them," says David, who is short and slight. "At first it was just purely the visual, the physical presence. I mean, they're—I mean, I'm generalizing, but this is what I saw—they were huge, they were rude. I'm not trying to sound like a racist or anything, but this is what I saw. And the way they spoke and everything was just totally different, and the way that their lifestyle is totally different from what I perceive people should be like. Using profanities as an everyday word in front of anybody—my parents, my grandmother, y'know. It doesn't matter who is there, it's 'Hey, you fucking whatever, whatever,' y'know, things like that.

"They have no common sense. At the time there were a lot of frictions between Koreans and blacks, so they generalize us by saying, 'You Koreans are moving into South Central. You guys are gonna take over this and that.' I had to take a lot of that stuff for a few months. After getting to know people, maybe it took about two or three months, and after that it's just like I knew everybody by their names, they knew me, so everything was cool. It was just handful of people that were giving us a hard time.

"After about two years, I was known in the community because I turned the store into sort of like a community center. It wasn't just sell or purchase of liquor, whatever. It was more like they'd ask me, 'Hey Dave, I'm tryin' to fill out this paper, can you help me out?' I said sure, y'know, fill it out for 'em. They need a ride to somewhere, 'Sure, I get off at five. I'll give you ride,' things like that.

"I was, like, well-liked, believe or not. Because there were a few stores around our store and they were—oh, they were hated. They were Koreans, and they were so rude. I don't know if they were rude or just doing everything by the book, which ticked those black people off. But I was like doing everything that I can, within reason, to help 'em out. And you know, we were doing *very,* very good. I mean, we were doing excellent, excellent business. We brought lotta customers in. We had parties for somebody's birthday. All those typical things every businessman should do in their community—give somethin' back, like they say. Which we did."

And to their better customers, David even extended credit, which he says "is unheard of." He explains: "It's a poor neighborhood, y'understand. They didn't have money. 'Hey Dave, let me get this on credit, pay you next week.' Sure, I just write their name down, the amount, and they would come back next week and pay me. Things like that. And I mean, you go anywhere, west side, east side, anywhere, nobody—nobody—does that. But *I* did that because I understood their situation. And it wasn't always liquor that they wanted. It was grocery items, too. So, if a family comes in, needs a few dollars, they don't have money, 'Sure, sign your name, pay me back next week.' " David says these credit accounts regularly totaled $2,000 a month, with individual customers owing as much as $300. He did not charge his customers interest.

David says, "I felt good for myself and the fact that I'm helping them out. And they felt good, too, that they were trusted. I didn't make 'em sign any forms, or, you know, credit applications, whatever. I just said, 'Sure why not?' I've gotta take that chance. It helped. It paid off in the long run because our customers recommended other people come to our store—'This Dave guy, should go see him if you need some help.' "

Another part of David's public relations campaign was to hire a few blacks to work at the store. He had noticed that the previous owner, a white man, was never at the store and had hired blacks to run it. "So before we got there," he explains, "the customers thought it was owned by blacks, but it wasn't. It was just black people working for white guy." Thinking it would not be "good P.R." if his African-American customers did not see any familiar African-American faces at the store, David hired three black men from the neighborhood and "gave 'em decent salary," $7.50 an hour. "I mean, that's pretty good considering that they had no experience in liquor store, or no experience at all. I don't even know if these guys had a job other than picking up cans or whatever. And I hired them not because we needed help, but again, P.R. work. I gave 'em these lame-ass jobs where you don't need no skill. I didn't even do a background check. They were all criminals, after I found out."

None of the men lasted through the month. According to David, two were drunk on the job; the third was a drug addict who did not show up to work for two days after he received his first paycheck. David fired all three.

I ask David why he did not try to hire other blacks from the neighborhood. He says, "I lived there at the store practically. The only thing I didn't do there is sleep. I ate my breakfast, lunch, dinner there. So in a sense I lived in the community. I know 'bout ninety percent of the black people that live around this area, and I know none of 'em are qualified. And if they are, they're gonna turn out just like these guys that I hired." He decided it wasn't worth it to try and hire any more blacks from the area. But, he notes, he "just hired a few Hispanic guys, and, oh man, those guys work really hard, working out really good."

David believes the people in the neighborhood understood his decision—that is, his decision to fire the first three blacks that he had hired. "They know that I tried to hire black people from the neighborhood, but it just didn't work out," he says.

David thinks that, because of his "P.R. work," he and his parents have not faced the hostility that many blacks in South Central Los Angeles have expressed toward Korean shopowners. Indeed, David's customers "were cool" about David and his parents even after the Latasha Harlins incident, in which a Korean store owner was convicted of killing a fifteen-year-old black girl, Harlins, whom the store owner accused of stealing a $1.79 bottle of orange juice. The trial judge sentenced the Korean woman to five years' probation, despite footage from the store's video camera that clearly showed the woman had shot Harlins in the back as Harlins was leaving the store.

Relations between David's family and their store's African-American customers were "pretty calm"—that is, "until the verdict came," the verdict in the Rodney King case, in which a nearly all-white jury found four white members of the Los Angeles Police Department not guilty of using excessive force when they beat a black man, King, as they were arresting him after an eight-mile, high-speed chase. The verdict was announced on the afternoon of April 29, 1992. Says David, "That's the day everything changed."

On April 29, before the verdict had been handed down, an older black man who had lived through the Watts riot of 1965 warned David: "All hell's gonna break loose." Though David knew something would happen that night, he didn't think it would be that bad. But events proved him wrong: hell, or something very close to it, did indeed break loose in South Central Los Angeles. And during this paroxysm of violence—David labels it a "riot," others call it "rebellion," and the L.A. City Council refers to it euphemistically as the "civil disturbances of April 29–30"—the liquor store was destroyed.

First thing the next morning, David, his older brother, and his parents returned to the site where their store once stood, only fifteen or twenty blocks north of the intersection of Florence and Normandie, the epicenter of the preceding night's chaos. "Everything was gone," says David, without any bitterness or anger. Except for two walls that were still standing, everything else was destroyed. "They did a good job," he says. David was glad that his family was alive, and that they had insurance. His parents, however, were speechless.

As David and his family surveyed the still smoldering wreckage, a group of twenty or so people—men and women, blacks and Hispanics, from little kids to senior citizens—gathered in front of the charred husk that had been a profitable liquor store. David says the people asked, " 'Hey Dave, can I have this?' These were neighborhood people. They were asking us if they could have some of the things that weren't burnt. 'Cause we had lotta beer and whatever in the back. So I said, 'Help yourselves, it's yours.' And then, aw man, they just ran inside and took everything that they could. They were going, 'I'm sorry about this, Dave, but you know—' I said, 'Hey, you didn't do it.' And then they were just giving me hugs and they were really sorry. I don't know how, y'know, truthful they were when they were apologizing. But I just said, 'Yeah, help yourself, take it,' and they took. It was gone. They cleaned out."

Watching the people fight over what little had not been destroyed, all David could think about was how poor and desperate these people must be. He says, "It was pitiful sight."

Only six weeks have passed since his parents' store was destroyed, but he shows incredible equanimity about what happened. When I ask how he can accept the situation so calmly, he says, "It's just not in my personality to get overly excited or overly depressed about whatever happens. Of course, I'm bitter. It's like they just took everything that we worked for, and making excuses that it was Koreans that ruined their life or whatever. I mean, the looting and all that stuff that happened, they shouldn't blame it on Koreans, but I see lotta people *are* doing that and that makes me mad, you know.

"For example, if you watch TV, they have like different people for a panel. They're talking about the L.A. riots. It's black people, they're talking shit, you know what I mean. It doesn't make sense. They should have a Korean person to back Koreans' voice, but the Koreans are always missing. It's just always blacks, more blacks, blacks. That's all there is. The things they say, it makes Koreans look really bad, and it's like we're the scapegoat for what the white people have been doing since the Watts riot. I mean, nothing changed after the Watts riot, so, you know, it happened again. But if things don't change, I think it's gonna happen again, and lotta people agree with me that it's gonna happen again if things don't change. But the way it's going, I don't think it's gonna change.

"The Koreans are getting a bad rap from this whole thing. They are just being scapegoated for black people's problems. I hope that's what everybody understands in L.A.—or this whole country—that Koreans didn't bring police brutality and drugs with them when they came to America. It was here. And everybody had the same opportunity to buy the same liquor store while it was on the market. It's just that Koreans got it. But you shouldn't be blamed for that. You should be praised for working hard, paying your taxes, not committing crime, not smoking dope, living a good life. That contributes to this country.

"It's like, if you want to talk about the people that I'm mad at, it's black leaders that I'm mad at. That's the only people. 'Cause people who are actually looting and rioting, these guys were losers to start off with anyway. They have nothing to live for, that's why they did that. If they had any kind of stake in the society or in the community that they live in, they wouldn't do that. But I mean, they don't care if your Korean store burns up. What do they got to lose, you know. Not a whole lot. I blame the black leaders, religious leaders, political leaders. It's all their fault. I blame all this on black leaders—looting, the drug problems, the unwed mothers, the gangsters, the whole problem with the South Central area."

David later remarks: "It seems like this country has become where people can't be controlled. It's like lawlessness. I don't know what it is, but people are just getting crazy. I don't know what it is. It can't be economics, 'cause we've had worse times than we are now and nobody really went out and killed people. I can't explain it to you, to be honest. The only answer that comes close to a solution is that people are uncontrollable, can't be governed."

Immediately after the violence subsided, David began rebuilding and reorganizing his life. He spent most of May standing in lines, making phone calls, filling out insurance forms and applications for financial assistance from the government. He moved out of his apartment in Koreatown and moved back to his parents' house. He also started a job as a bank teller a week ago.

David views the violence that destroyed his parents' store as a setback, nothing more. "I don't expect life to be a cakewalk, you know." Once his parents' store has been rebuilt, which will take anywhere from six months to a year ("red tape," he says), David will return to running his parents' business. Then he will once again be moving toward the goals he set for himself a few years ago: "Save enough money for my own business and a house and two exotic cars."

For David, the concept of the American Dream is just words. "I mean, if you work, and if you're a good person, I think you achieve a human dream." Yet what David believes to be the generally held conception of the American Dream—"a job and a house and a family and that's all"—is not very far from the life he envisions for himself. He, too, wants a job and a house. It's at "that's all" where his views diverge from his hypothetical Everyman's version of the American Dream.

He explains: "The reason I was working so hard was because I want to become a good provider for my family. I want to do everything while I'm still young, have energy to do all this. I'll make money now, have a home, have a dream—American Dream—

house, car. That way I could spend time with my family. So that's why I was working so hard, 'cause I want to save money and have even a brighter future. That's why I'm willing to sacrifice, not dating, not going out every weekend like my friends are. After a while you become used to it. And if you have a goal, I guess, you just gotta strive for it."

And the overriding goal for which David strives—money. "That's what it comes down to, y'know. If you want to do something, you gotta have money. If you want to send your kids to a good school, you gotta have money. If you want to live in a safe neighborhood, you gotta have money. So it's just basically money. I mean, there are people that say, 'Oh, money isn't everything,' but they're maybe about sixty years behind. This is the nineties, you know. Money is important, very important.

"But then you can't lose—how do you say?—the perspective of life. You can't be so wrapped up in money that you lose sight of everything else. Basically, you gotta have money and you gotta be good to others. That's my philosophy."

I ask David whether the violence that followed the King verdict taught him anything about the American Dream. He answers: "Yeah, that you can't obtain the so-called American Dream if you don't work or if you're not applying yourself. If you're just waiting for somebody else to do something for you, or if you're just sticking your hand out for a handout, you ain't gonna get nowhere. You get out of life what you put in, so if you put nothing in, you're not gonna get nothing out. But if you put in a lot, you're gonna get out a lot.

"It could've been very easy for us to be where the black people are now, by not working and just taking government handout. But my parents, they worked two, three jobs combined, two, three, four jobs, in order to get somewhere. And you gotta sacrifice. You gotta get your ass in gear, you gotta do things in order to get somewhere. You can't just sit in front of your house drinking beer and talking about this and that, putting other people down, blaming other people for your misery or whatever. That's what I see when I see blacks."

In David's opinion, the blacks in South Central Los Angeles, the people who were—and will be—his customers, are responsible for their plight. He concedes that discrimination exists to a certain extent, but, he says, "it's not like white people just opened their arms when we came here. There were a lot of adversities also. But you gotta overlook it. I mean, so what if somebody doesn't like you. Who cares? Just go on, you know. But that's how they are. They say, 'Aw, the white people won't do this for us.' That's ridiculous. That doesn't make sense at all.

"If you strip everything down as person to person, whether it be black, white, or whatever, you just gotta work, you just gotta work towards whatever you want to do and do it. I mean, a kid from the Beverly Hills could always go into drugs himself and do whatever. But also the black kid from South Central, he could grow up and go to school and make something out of himself. It's all in their heads, you know.

"I'll give you a good example. There is so much problem with school in the inner cities, or that's what they say. But the kids, once again, they can only get out what they put in. I mean, the teachers are there, the buildings are there, the books are there. The books, everything, all the resources are there. All they gotta do is do everything the teacher says, and if there's a little bit of pressure from the parents to study, they could graduate from an inner-city high school and go to college. And from college, you do the same thing and you could get a job."

David admits that racism may become a factor when an African-American tries to climb the corporate ladder. But, he wonders, "Why don't you work for a black company? There's lotta ways around it. If they won't give you a better-paying job because you're black, you could always just stick it out and go as far as you can get, and then move out of there and get a job somewhere else.

"I'm not qualified to say all this because I'm not black. But I'm a minority, too. I mean, it's not like white people love Koreans or something. There's lotta obstacles for us, too. It's just hard for me to think that blacks blame others for their plight when there's so many options that they could take."

David believes the United States has a mission: "to have a peaceful country where everybody is provided the necessities. And you gotta move on from there. Everybody's given the same chance, per se, and then if you want to get out of that minimal environment, you could work or do whatever to get out of there and make something of yourself."

That, says David, is what the United States did for him and his family, and that is why he believes the United States is a "great" country. "Look what it's done for us," he says. "Although we put in a lot, they gave us a lot, too, in return. What they gave us was just an opportunity and we took advantage of it. That's all we did."

CONCLUDING
OBSERVATIONS

When I started this project, I was content to let other people do all the talking. "What could I have to add?" I thought. As I read all of the transcripts, however, some themes began to emerge. These patterns are not necessarily apparent even after reading this book because it contains only one-fourth of the discussions I had about the American Dream—far fewer, actually, if you include the brief conversations along the way.

Though I believe each individual story is fascinating in its own right, people have continually asked me—and, in the end, I asked myself—what did I learn about my peers after talking with so many of them? At first I resisted answering this question because it invites the same overbroad generalizing that frustrated me when I saw it in previous efforts to define the twentysomething generation. But this question is not just a ploy by trend-spotters and marketing mavens to sell us something. It is another way of asking, "What do the 40

million-plus people in their twenties have in common?" It is a difficult question, but it is a worthwhile question.

These observations are based on my experiences on the road.
They also reflect the reading I've done since I first envisioned this
project, as well as my own opinions.

I. WHAT WE REALLY WANT

So what is the twentysomething American Dream? Even though
people define this concept in different ways, it turns out that most
of them want the same basic things—a family and a "comfortable"
life.

Discussing the American Dream with the people I met, I posed
two questions. I asked them for a general definition of the American
Dream, that is, how they think most people would define this
phrase. I then asked them to define the American Dream for themselves.

In the general definition, although many people mentioned
"freedom" and "opportunity" and a handful discussed concepts of
social justice, these were not the dominant themes. Instead, most of
the people who spoke with me described the textbook American
Dream as a husband, wife, and a decimaled number of kids living
in a nice house with a picket fence and two cars and maybe a couple of dogs. (The American Dream must be for dog-lovers because
no one mentioned cats.) It's interesting that the image they pre-
sented sounds just like the imaginary lives of TV's most famous families. Interesting, but not surprising, given that most people in their
twenties spent as much or more of their childhood with Mike and
Carol Brady as they did with their own parents.

Defining their personal visions of the American Dream, many of
these same people said that being part of a nuclear family, safely en-
sconced in a middle-class suburb, was just the life they were seeking. They see only two clouds looming on their horizons. Some of
them, such as Dave, the would-be firefighter, wonder how reasonable it is to hope for an old-fashioned nuclear family when "I do"
and *adieu* are running neck and neck. Others, like Sergeant Shane

and his wife, Cindy, just hope that someday they will be able to afford what they consider a middle-class existence, that is, owning a house, sending their kids to college, and retiring in economic security.

But many who defined the typical American Dream as neoclassical Cleaver were ambivalent about describing their personal ambitions in those terms. These people reject what they perceive as the crass materialism of this ideal and, instead, often defined their American Dream as "success" or "happiness." Yet when they elaborated on these vague notions, nearly all of them described lives that include what they had dismissed just moments before: they want the husband, wife, or significant other; they want the kids, the house, the cars, and the dog. So what's the difference between the lives they imagine for themselves and the world of the Bradys? Ann, the waitress in Cleveland, summed it up as the absence of state-of-the-art appliances. "I don't necessarily have to have all the luxuries," she told me.

Like Ann, most of the folks I met, including many of those who rejected or were skeptical about the American Dream, said they seek only to be "comfortable." By "comfort," they did not just mean owning nice things. For most of these people, comfort also has a psychological component. Andy, the actor, said a decent life is an "anxiety-free, happy life," and insufficient funds have been the principal source of his anxiety. Many people echoed Andy's sentiments, emphasizing that they want to be financially stable and secure—meaning they want to be able to pay the mortgage and the monthly bills, send their kids to college, and take a family vacation once a year without having to worry constantly about making ends meet.

Who doesn't want such a life? Since the dawn of time, one of humankind's principal goals has been to have a comfortable life. Neanderthals longed for sharper spears, slower mammoths, and caves that were warmer in the winter. Our pioneering ancestors prayed for fertile soil without lots of rocks, sufficient rain, and a cabin that did not leak when it did rain. Contemporary Americans seek affordable houses with central heat and air, jobs that pay a living wage without giving you cancer or repetitive motion disorder, and cars that are safe and reasonably fuel-efficient but that can still go sixty-five miles per hour.

In their pursuit of comfort, people in their twenties are simply upholding a national tradition. Tocqueville observed as long as 150 years ago that in the United States "everyone is preoccupied caring for the slightest needs of the body and the trivial conveniences of life." Many people define the American Dream as parents giving their children a materially better life than they themselves had, even if they must struggle to pay for it.

Not only is it quintessentially American to seek a comfortable life, but several factors reinforced the belief that we should not just hope for, but in fact could expect, a comfortable life. One was this nation's postwar economic boom. Real weekly earnings and median family income bounced merrily upward from 1947 through 1973. The economy expanded at a brisk average annual rate of 2.72 percent, a pace that would double family income in twenty-five to thirty years. It is this experience, economist Wallace Peterson notes, that strengthened the conviction of the baby boomers and their successors that children ought to do better economically than their parents.

As real wages began to stagnate and then fall in the 1970s and 1980s, families compensated by sending Mom to work. As a result, unlike wages, which have dropped 13 percent since 1973, families have managed to keep their median income at the 1973 level. So, although having two parents working created—inadvertently—a generation of latchkey kids and tube junkies, parents could still provide their children with a comfortable material existence.

Television also helped convince many in their twenties that everyone would have a materially comfortable life. Raised as we were, bathed in the phosphorescent glow of our reliable and economical electronic nanny as if we were ferns beneath a grow light, small wonder so many of today's young adults accepted television fantasy as reality when they were children. And in TV's make-believe world, (white) people lived pretty well and only rarely worried about paying the gas bill or affording braces for their children's teeth. (Nonwhite faces were almost nonexistent. And if they were black, more often than not they were cast as maids, crooks, addicts, or pimps.) The commercials also told us again and again, "Yes, you can have it all," as easily as popping open a bottle of beer.

I don't want to give television too much credit. Many kids do not mistake the tube for real life. Furthermore, for children who were poor or who were not white, television may have been too far removed from the circumstances of their lives for them to have confused the two. For Michael, a black man who grew up on Chicago's South Side and who still lives there today, some of the indelible television images from his childhood are scenes of the local rioting that followed the news of Dr. Martin Luther King's assassination in 1968. With tears in his eyes, the little boy asked his daddy, "Are we all gonna die?"

One of the most insidiously powerful influences in the collective consciousness of people in their twenties is the greed-is-good ethos that seemed to dominate much of the eighties. Though virtually everyone I met rejected Ivan Boesky's mantra, "Seek wealth, it's good," the ceaseless parade of opulence on TV shows such as *Lifestyles of the Rich and Famous* and *Dallas* inflated the twentysomething generation's standard for comfort. Again and again I heard remarks like: "I don't want to be rich. I don't need a Rolls-Royce or a Mercedes sittin' outside in my yard. I want a nice house and a decent car, and I just want to be comfortable." Yet when I asked these people to tell me how much money or what kind of material existence it would take to be "comfortable," they almost always described incomes or lifestyles that would place them somewhere in the top 20 percent of the nation's income scale.

I am not an economist, but I suppose it would require a profound redistribution of the nation's income for everyone to earn what only the top 20 percent do today. Either these people are would-be levelers and revolutionaries, or they are going to have a walloping case of sticker shock when VISA sends them the statement for their "comfortable" lives.

What is surprising about this quest for material comfort is how confident most people I met are about achieving it. Unlike Sergeant Shane and Cindy, nearly everyone I talked to said they were certain they someday would be able to afford to live the life they described—despite the pall of economic gloom that has settled on the country in the past couple of years. In January 1992, consumer confidence tumbled to its lowest since they began measuring it in 1969. One of the nonfiction best-sellers of 1992 was Donald L. Bartlett and James B. Steele's *America: What Went Wrong,* a distressing analysis of the dismantling of the nation's middle class by influential Washington rulemakers and wealthy Wall Street dealmakers. A bumper sticker at a convenience store in rural Indiana says it all: "This ain't no RECESSION! It's our new way of LIFE."

Without analyzing whether such dismay is warranted, the question remains, why do these people in their twenties blithely resist the economic paranoia that has become, according to the editorial staff of *The Economist,* "an American habit"? In general, it is not, as sociologist and author Susan Littwin argues, because they refuse to grow up. It is because their parents and their society, through television, inculcated the sunny expectation that the U.S. economy could and would provide everyone with a materially comfortable existence. (This explains in part why a disproportionately high number of people in their twenties—67 percent in 1984 and 62 percent in 1988—voted for the Republicans. Young voters responded to the Republicans' facile optimism and can-do-ism.)

Those people I met who do not believe they will have a better material existence than their parents did not sound hurt or resentful. They did not bemoan the fact that many of them will be older than their parents were when their parents bought their first house, or that they will have fewer things or that those things might not be quite as nice. They seemed to look at it as one of the facts of contemporary life, as something that simply must be accepted.

The people I talked to displayed a similar attitude regarding the families they want or, in a few cases, have. These people are not vainly chasing after the idealized family of television sitcoms, where Mom stays home to raise the kids and Dad's salary alone is plenty to support the family. They realize that without the wages earned by women, many families, perhaps as many as 50 percent, would fall below the poverty line. The men also understand that many women would be unsatisfied if they were restricted to raising children and taking care of the house. At the same time, many of these people, men and women alike, also insisted that, if it is at all possible financially, they would prefer one of the parents to stay home with the children, at least until the children are in school. As with their material lives, when it comes to raising their families, they hope for the best and cope with the rest.

■ ■ ■

There's nothing wrong with wanting a comfortable life. It is disappointing, however, that so few of the people who spoke with me mentioned freedom, opportunity, or social justice when they were talking about the American Dream. Not that the American Dream has ever been without a component of materialism. Horatio Alger taught a generation of Americans that financial wealth was virtue's reward, and the immigrants who came looking for opportunities struggled and suffered so that their children could have a chance for materially decent lives. Nor have noble concepts like equality and liberty disappeared from the twentysomething psyche. Many people talked about these ideas, though usually not in the context of that phrase, "the American Dream."

Perhaps I am wrong, but it certainly seems that the American Dream used to evoke images more stirring than suburban housing and microwave ovens. Poet Archibald MacLeish saw the Dream as nothing less than "the liberation of humanity, the freedom of man and mind." Martin Luther King told the nation of his dream, one deeply rooted in the American Dream, in which people were judged by the content of their character, not the color of their skin. And a forty-nine-year-old former traveling salesman who is now the manager of a submarine sandwich shop in rural Illinois told me that while the American Dream includes a pot of gold and a carefree life, it also means the freedom to do anything you want.

That phrase, "the American Dream," used to epitomize the United States at its best, all of the ideals to which we did, and still do, aspire—freedom, opportunity, and, however imperfectly, social justice. For most of the people I met, "the American Dream" no longer has such magnificent resonance. Perhaps most people in their twenties equate the American Dream with material prosperity because they now take freedom and opportunity for granted, but the noble ideals formerly connoted by that phrase have vanished. Like a sea that has dried up, the water that allowed life to survive has evaporated, and all that is left is the gritty tangibility of things. It is sad that, for most people in their twenties, "the American Dream" conjures up nothing grander.

II. CIVIC INVOLVEMENT: THE
TWENTYSOMETHING PUBLIC SELF

In the introduction I referred to today's young adults as the "dis-" generation. When it comes to politics, this moniker is absolutely correct. We *are* disenchanted, dissatisfied, disenfranchised, disgruntled, disillusioned, disconnected, disgusted—and frighteningly distrustful. What's more, this is not like the distrust of power that ran through much of youth politics in the sixties. Except for the counterculture, the politics of the sixties was designed to break down barriers and include people in decision-making who previously had been excluded—racial minorities, women, people who were openly gay, and young people themselves. The majority of those people did not question the underlying principles of democratic institutions; they objected to their distortion by the wealthy white men who ran them. Today, however, people in their twenties are wondering whether the entire political system is irredeemably corrupt.

Steve, who works for a song publishing company in Nashville, is a good example. Steve has never voted, has never even registered to vote. He blithely told me, "I think the Mafia is running the government. They're going to look after the country, so I don't care. As long as there's some democracy and I do a good job at my work, I'll have a job and things will be okay, I think."

Steve's attitude is not the most extreme. The most dismaying comments came from Dale, the man in Los Angeles who had recently learned he is HIV-positive. Dale genuinely believes that the federal government either isolated or synthesized the HIV virus and infected certain populations that it sought to exterminate, such as this country's homosexuals and blacks. He also thinks the government introduced the virus into Africa just to throw scientists and investigators off the trail.

When Dale expressed his ideas, I told him people will think he is nuts. He was not offended. He smiled and replied that although he may be wrong, he is not crazy. Driving away from his apartment and reflecting on his remarks, I began to realize that his assessment is correct: he may be wrong, but he is not crazy to think that the government could commit such a moral atrocity. After all, the federal government often has treated its citizens as if they were lab rats.

In the Tuskegee syphilis project of the 1930s, the government withheld treatment from 399 black men with syphilis during a forty-year experiment to study the disease. Of course, when the study began, there was no cure for syphilis because penicillin had not yet been developed for therapeutic use. All doctors could do was administer chemicals that delayed the disease's ineluctable progress. Nevertheless, while there is a moral distinction between infecting people with a lethal virus and observing the progress of a deadly illness in people who cannot be cured, the fact remains—the men were studied, not treated.

There is also the government's surreptitious testing of LSD on thousands of unwitting U.S. citizens in the 1950s, in which the CIA and the military intelligence agencies dosed U.S. soldiers—without their knowledge or their consent—because the government wanted to gather information about the effects of the drug. And between 1945 and 1963, as part of a study to determine the effectiveness of combat troops in nuclear battlefield conditions, the government exposed an estimated quarter of a million soldiers to large doses of radiation. These soldiers have been disproportionately afflicted with inoperable cancer and leukemia, as well as other nonmalignant maladies.

Granted, these are extreme examples. Yet one need not head to the morgue to find good reasons to distrust the federal government. Think about the implosion of the savings and loan industry, the bailout of which will cost taxpayers $500 billion—most of which probably will come from the younger taxpayers of today's twentysomething generation because they are just now hitting their peak income-earning, taxpaying years. As early as 1982, Representative Henry Gonzalez of Texas was warning of the impending disaster, but none of his colleagues—or the press—were listening. Many of them were on the back nine with S&L industry lobbyists, musing, no doubt, about the indisputable logic of S&L deregulation. Moreover, those members of Congress who were not gorging at the S&L industry's trough did not want to criticize their colleagues, otherwise someone might seek to clip their access to PAC money.

That's not all. Recall, too, the midnight pay raise the Senate voted for itself in 1990, which vaulted each senator's salary from three to nearly four times that for an average family of four, and which matched a pay raise that the members of the House of Representatives had approved for themselves in 1989. The Senate debate and vote were held in the final hours before the 1991 summer recess and without any advance notice. Meanwhile, those on the Hill were discussing the merits of decreasing funds for student loans and limiting government entitlements. They want to have our cake and eat it too.

The Vietnam War, Watergate, the "covert" war in Nicaragua, the Iran-Contra affair. For most of our lives, democracy has not been the governing philosophy in Washington. Democracy requires at the very least that government officials speak candidly about public issues so that people may think about them. But democracy is cumbersome, anti-intellectual, time-consuming, and just downright passé. So we have instead the government of The Big Lie.

Those inside-the-Beltway types have actually exacerbated voter distrust with their unimaginative reliance on scandals instead of ideas to motivate voters. An occasional exposure of genuine corruption is healthy for a democracy, but scandalmongering—commonly denoted by the suffix "-gate"—has all but displaced ideas and policies as the centerpiece of contemporary politics. Unfortunately, this practice has proved so effective that politicians have undermined themselves. Now most of today's young adults—certainly the vast majority of people who spoke with me—believe government, politics, and politicians are incorrigibly corrupt. Politicians "don't give a darn about us," said one woman from Oklahoma. "They're concerned about their own pocketbooks."

Ironically, despite my peers' thoroughgoing distrust of government—and this includes all levels of government, though they almost always cite examples of federal misconduct—they wonder why the government does nothing about the myriad problems facing the country. Linda, a graduate student in Knoxville, told me she wants a government that can "get things accomplished instead of all this damn talk over and over." But, she said, "I don't know how you distinguish between someone who gives a damn and someone who just wants to be called Senator So-and-so."

The folks I met desperately want government that works, one dedicated to solving problems, not producing a river of grandiose but meaningless gestures. Yet if they are so eager for more effective government, why don't they bother to vote?

Of all the criticisms directed at today's twentysomething generation, one of the most deserved is that we simply do not take the time to make our voices heard through the ballot box. Although the estimates vary, approximately 52 percent of people in their twenties are registered to vote, and only 46 percent of these actually bothered to vote in the 1992 presidential election. This is better than the 38 percent who turned out in 1988, but it is still abysmally low. And even fewer vote in other electoral races.

A 1986 study that measured the political sophistication of U.S. adults is useful in determining how politically active today's young adults really are. That survey found an activist core of 5 percent, which included the regular cadres within the political parties. It described 20 percent as "totally apolitical" and the rest as "marginally attentive to politics." These figures accurately reflect my impressions of the people I met, and they probably describe the feelings of the entire twentysomething generation.

Explaining why he does not vote, Steve, the man who believes the Mafia controls the government, offers a litany that pithily summarizes the views expressed by many of his peers. He said, "I don't have any faith in any of the candidates, for one thing. Secondly, I don't know anything. Even if I were to try to make a decision, I don't think it makes that much difference who gets it. I don't think anybody is that qualified to get it anyway. The people that have always ran, I mean, I can't say that I'm *pro*-anybody. I don't know anything about any of it. I don't believe any of us do."

In addition to those reasons—all of which I've parroted at one time or another—lots of folks said that uninformed voting is worse than not voting at all, and that they have not had the time to learn about the candidates or the issues because they have been too busy or because they have moved so frequently. Many told me that they are not "into" politics because no one in their families ever was.

Perhaps the most distressing reason offered is the fear of being responsible for making a choice. A woman from Philadelphia put it best: "Who's to say that the one I vote for is the right one to run the country or run that particular office? And who's to say he's not? I don't want to be the one to have my hand in the cookie jar when nobody's looking." Democrophobia in its purest form.

Though it would be easy to dismiss these explanations as rationalizations and to blame this political nonparticipation on widespread indifference, that would be a mistake. Not all the reasons offered are specious. For instance, young adults do move around a lot, either for school or for work. Consequently, it *is* difficult to learn or even to care about many local issues.

Nor is the twentysomething generation the only group voting "none of the above." According to statistics from the Census Bureau, between 1976 and 1988, participation in presidential elections dropped for voters for all ages except for those sixty-five and older. (A higher percentage of younger voters has dropped out, but they historically have voted in smaller numbers than their elders.) Like many other habits, people learn to participate in the political process by watching their parents. If more parents voted, more of their children would, too. Children see, children do. Maybe this explains why, when I asked people to define good citizenship, only a few mentioned voting as one of the prerequisites.

Do not mistake this electoral indifference for a more widespread lack of concern or awareness, however. The people I met may be apolitical; they are not apathetic. They are not, as *Time* asserted, "paralyzed" by the magnitude of society's problems. But they do not see any reliable mechanism for channeling their concerns. They do not seem to trust any of the traditional institutions, entities larger than the individual self, that in the past drew people out of their individual shells and integrated them into the community. There does not seem to be any institutional "we" that people in their twenties want to join, no "us" to which they can proudly belong.

Political parties are not a viable option because most people in their twenties have largely dismissed these as inevitably corrupt. And they're probably right. As political journalist William Greider wryly remarked, the parties today operate as little more than mail drops for political money. They are historical artifacts that do nothing more than provide their nominal members with certain legal privileges not available to unaligned candidates. They may try to manipulate voters in some Pavlovian way, but they do not address the everyday concerns of ordinary citizens or enroll them in the process of governing.

Although I met only one person who belongs to a labor union and, consequently, did not have much opportunity to speak about this issue, I suspect that labor unions probably will not serve to unite the generation, either. First, few in their twenties are members of unions. In 1983, depending on which end of the twentysomething age span you look, somewhere between 9 and 20 percent of those people were members of unions. By 1989, that range had diminished to somewhere between 6 and 14 percent of the generation. Moreover, the number of union jobs is shrinking because of the nation's declining manufacturing base. The expansion of the service sector, which is typically not unionized, only hastens this trend. Second, unions currently have an unenviable reputation. They have been blamed—sometimes fairly, often not—for the nation's declining international industrial competitiveness, and they have only recently begun to disentangle themselves from their longtime association with organized crime.

Large corporations won't do the job. Large corporations are increasingly becoming "stateless," owing no loyalty whatsoever to anyone other than their stockholders. Certainly U.S. corporations have demonstrated little commitment to the nation or the nation's workers. Like geese heading south for the winter, the nation's manufacturers have flocked to where labor rates are cheapest, taxes lowest, and environmental regulations most lax—which is usually across the Rio Grande in Mexico, or even Central America.

No rational person today would invest loyalty in a large corporation after General Motors demonstrated its attitude toward its workers. In August 1991, Roger Smith, the chairman who had presided over the company's decline in the 1900s, retired. Four months before he left, the company rewarded him not with a ceremonial saber with which to commit hara kiri, but by increasing his annual pension from $700,000 to $1.2 million. Then in December 1991, GM announced that it would be closing twenty-one plants and laying off 74,000 workers by 1995. The company also canceled the $600 Christmas bonuses for its 100,000 midlevel managers.

RJR Nabisco showed a similar disregard for its employees. F. Ross Johnson, former chairman of the company, left three years after a failed battle for control of the corporation. His "golden" parachute was worth $53 million. (Was it platinum?) Yet because of the company's Brobdingnagian debt from the takeover battle, they had to terminate 2,600 employees.

The chairman of General Electric once said, "Loyalty to a company, it's nonsense." Given this, not many people will volunteer to be the nineties organization person to replace the fifties organization man.

Organized religion probably will not be able to unite people in their twenties, at least not at this point in their lives. Although virtually everyone I met expressed a belief in God or some higher spirit or force, almost none of them attend religious services regularly. More than a few think formal religion is as corrupt as formal politics—like Mike, the police detective from Chicago, who said, "It's a money thing." Most people believe that as long as they know right from wrong and have some sort of personal relationship with God, that is enough. Except for someone extraordinary, like the Reverend Martin Luther King, Jr., religious leaders cannot organize people unless the people are sitting in the pews.

The reluctance of people in their twenties to commit their loyalty to the nation's traditional social institutions would not be so worrisome if there were something else to unite us. But we have not had a New Deal to put us to work, as the WPA did sixty years ago. This generation of young adults has not had a war to focus its energy. (The Persian Gulf "War" could not serve this purpose because the combined air war and ground attack lasted only a month. Moreover, because there was no draft, only those people who had already enlisted in the military were asked to make any sacrifice. People in their twenties, as a whole, were not.) And even if they were inclined to join—which most are not—no widespread social movement currently exists that could rally the twentysomething generation.

Many of the people I met seem to be waiting to get involved in civic life. They long for a genuine political hero, a lightning-rod leader to guide the generation. Dave, the would-be firefighter, said it well: We need a leader " 'cause that's how this country's run."

But the nation has run short of such larger-than-life standard-bearers. In a 1988 poll commissioned by *Rolling Stone,* Americans between the ages of eighteen and forty-four were asked to name the two people they most admired who had been active in public life at some time in the preceding twenty years. The two who led the list: Dr. Martin Luther King, Jr., and Robert Kennedy. What is sad, wrote journalist William Greider, is that both men had been killed twenty years earlier, when many of those surveyed were infants, and before some of them were even born.

Maybe this generation does need its hero. "Without heroes," said one of the characters in Bernard Malamud's *The Natural,* "we're all plain people and don't know how far we can go." The problem is you never know when a hero will show up. If people in their twenties wait for someone to show them The Way, they could be waiting for a very long time.

This generation cannot wait for its leader. Instead, we must find something to inspire us to enlarge our circles of concern to include people beyond ourselves, our families, and our close friends. And in building a sense of the common good, this generation must confront one stubborn, disquieting fact. Assuming the blacks who spoke with me are representative of the nation's black population, the majority of this nation's African-American citizens still feel excluded from participating fully in the American Dream.

III. OUR CONTINUING DILEMMA

Asked what worries them most about the national situation, at least half of the black people I met expressed concern that, in race relations, the nation seems to be regressing. As Lavonda, the black woman in St. Louis who shines shoes and writes screenplays, said, "It just seems like it reverting to worse." Anthony, a docket clerk in one of Chicago's largest law firms, echoed her sentiments: "I think we are going backwards in time to where it was in the fifties and forties." When I asked blacks who did not mention racism to explain why they had not, the answer was always the same: It's a given, they said. Like the air, it's always there, so why think about it.

The story is different for the Hispanic and Asian-Americans I met. No matter how they feel about the American Dream—most in some sense believe in it; a few do not—almost none of them conveyed the same sense of exclusion that so many blacks evinced.

Of course, not every black person who spoke with me feels left out of the American Dream. D'Angelo, a personal fitness trainer in Washington, D.C., said, "This is the only country in the world where you can do anything that you want to do—within reason—and you can be as successful as you want to be. Everything's here for you. That's why the Orientals come over here and it's like a candy shop to them. A lot of Americans just take things for granted. I think this is the land of opportunity. I think this is the best country in the world." In addition, two of the black women I met told me they had never been the victims of racism. There are others, too, such as Dexter, Valerie, and Nathan, who believe that they can achieve their dream as each of them has defined it—though both Dexter and Nathan believe a black person must pay a higher price than a white person to achieve the same level of success. Nevertheless, two-thirds of the blacks who talked with me, even those from solidly middle-class backgrounds who have good jobs and bright futures, said they feel to some degree excluded from participating in the American Dream because of the color of their skin.

Take Dan. A graduate of Duke and Harvard Law School, he is an advocate for the homeless in Manhattan. His girlfriend is white. Her father refuses to meet Dan and has stopped speaking to his daughter. Dan said, "I don't see how a father can stop speaking with a daughter because she dates someone that's of a different race."

Byron, a black man from St. Louis, says he has had to deal with racism his entire life. When Byron was younger, he earned a scholarship to attend one of the most prestigious private schools in the city. One day when he was in eighth grade, he and a couple of his friends were playing, being loud and obnoxious, on the school's lawn. Byron ran by a group of seniors who were sitting on the grass, and he overheard one of the guys say, "Well, look at that little stupid nigger over there."

"My first reaction was to go over and do something about it," said Byron. Then he thought, " 'He's two hundred pounds heavier than you, and you're only five-two. It would be ridiculous for you to go and do something right now.' So I didn't stop. I didn't even look. I just kept on going. I acted like I never heard it. And nobody knows to this day that it happened. I've never told anybody about it, not even my parents. Never told them."

And remember Janine, who grew up in the inner city of Boston. She was bused to Needham, one of the city's affluent white suburbs. Every morning Janine saw what the American Dream could be if you lived in Needham instead of the inner city. While most kids from the inner city realize that there is another way to live, says Janine, they are never told how to get there. They might see the American Dream on television or in magazines, but no one shows them how to make it come true.

Kim, a black woman in Chicago, unintentionally demonstrated to me the racism she lives with, not in the anecdotes she shared, but in her choice of words. I spoke with her over the telephone when I was trying to set up a time for us to talk. She asked if I am white; I said yes. After that, during our brief conversation, she spoke of "us" and "we," never "I" or "me," and she always used the collective noun "blacks"—*we* feel, *blacks* think.

This was not the first time I had heard this. After I hung up the receiver, I wrote a note to myself: "Can blacks in the U.S. ever say 'I' or 'me' and not feel they must speak for *all blacks?*"

Over the course of my travels, I heard this many times—blacks, especially educated blacks, who attempted to speak not just for themselves, but for all black Americans. This never happened with any other group of people I met. None of the Asian-Americans I talked with seemed to feel compelled to speak for all Asian-Americans. The women I met did not say "women think" or "women feel."

Maybe this is what happens when society does not judge you by the content of your character, as Dr. King had hoped, but by the color of your skin. When melanin is a moral yardstick, people are no longer individuals. They are representatives of a group, flesh-and-blood manifestations of statistics and sociological phenomena. Dave is not seen as the decent, caring man who works on behalf of the homeless; he is Dave, the black man who is dating my daughter. Nathan is not the bright, ambitious achiever; he is the black who must have gotten where he is because of affirmative action. It must be wearisome always to be Kim, the living example or counter-example, instead of just Kim.

Those in my generation who are not black do not seem to be aware of how excluded many black Americans feel. While most of the blacks who spoke with me considered racism one of the nation's gravest problems and most of the others thought it was too obvious even to discuss, only a few of the people I met who are not black even mentioned it.

Byron told me, "Racism has always been and it will always be a problem until people realize that we can't make it without the other race—I as a black person can't make it without you, and you as a white person can't make it without me. We just have to realize that we're all in this together."

Are we? In the long run, yes. But the United States is a very large country, and as a practical matter the races in this country seg-regate themselves and are segregated from each other. In some cir-cumstances we might work together, but we go home each night to different neighborhoods. We rarely socialize with one another out-side the bucolic setting of an Ivy League campus; more often, our kids do not attend the same schools. Class divisions play a part in our separation, yet to a very large degree we are not implicated in each other's lives.

I traveled to Los Angeles less than a month after the bloodiest urban violence in this nation's history. Though I was eager to discuss the American Dream with people in the aftermath of this cataclysm, I was concerned that it might overwhelm their thoughts. It didn't. If anything, the opposite was true. Most did not mention the violence in L.A. until I specifically asked them about it.

Even then people interpreted this paroxysm of rage in radically different ways. Anthony, the black man who lives in Watts, sees the riots as a warning to society: *I ain't gonna be out here starvin' an' see the next man with all this.* Rod, the painting contractor who lives in a middle-class suburb not twenty miles from Watts, has a different perspective. The day the violence erupted, he was in South Central L.A. bidding on a job. It forced him to postpone submitting the bid, and he sat in gridlock for several hours because people were fleeing the area. Although the violence frightened him, Rod ultimately sees the riots as just one more reason to get out of Los Angeles. Anthony is warning Rod of the possibility of widespread violence and civil insurrection, but Rod does not hear the message. Instead, Rod, in that noble U.S. tradition, is looking for someplace else to live.

In a sense, the people I spoke with are like Anthony and Rod. Black Americans, many of them anyway, are saying, "We feel excluded from the American Dream. We feel left out." Meanwhile, most of the rest of us either fail to hear them, refuse to listen, question the validity of their feelings, or try to explain away their resentment.

"Americans," political journalist Theodore White wrote, "are not a people like the French, Germans, or Japanese, whose genes have been mixing with kindred genes for thousands of years. Americans are held together only by ideas, the clashing ideas of opportunity and equality—as it were, by a culture of hope." The greatest expression of that hope is embodied in the concept of the American Dream. If some are excluded from participating in this dream, because of race, gender, national origin, or sexual orientation, then this collective act of the imagination that we call the United States inevitably will collapse. Or explode.

This does not mean that there must be only one American Dream on which we all agree. There never has been, and the belief that there ever was a single, clearly defined American Dream is just a sentimental longing for a time of perfect consensus that has never existed in this nation. The dreams of creating a shining city on a hill and of settling the West came at the expense of those who had been here for centuries. The post-War dream of a suburban paradise excluded racial minorities, and it consigned women—and to a lesser degree, men—to specific roles from which it was almost impossible to deviate.

This nation needs the dissenters and doubters. The tension they create forces us to continually redefine the American Dream, and to reconsider the horizon toward which we are traveling. The dialectic they inspire keeps the concept of the American Dream vital. It prevents the Dream from becoming nothing more than a slogan.

Many of the earlier attempts to define today's twentysomething generation seemed to dismiss us, as if the absence of a sequel to Woodstock proves that we are beyond salvation. That is one of the reasons I set out on this journey, to see whether we really are that bad. And after spending thousand of hours with hundreds of people in their twenties, I am quite hopeful about this twentysomething generation.

Admittedly, many of them are cynical, but their cynicism is, at least in part, idealism that has soured because it has never been expressed. Young people often think they can set the world on fire, and though they usually learn that the world is relatively inflammable, they have the satisfaction of having tried to improve it. Perhaps they even learn that small changes are possible and worth the effort. But not the members of this twentysomething generation. They grew up in an age in which the traditional social institutions were seen as corrupt, and in which scandal was the norm. Many of them see the problems facing this nation—a deteriorating educational system, a spiraling budget deficit, decaying cities, rising crime rates, AIDS—and conclude that the social and political actions of the fifties and sixties are a glorified failure.

The people I met seem to be waiting—not only for a hero, but also for a mission. Whether they were founding that shining city on the hill, settling the West, or containing Communism, missions have been central to U.S. politics. They still are. But the guiding paradigm of the last half-century, the Cold War, is over, and nothing has replaced it. This generation is becoming socially mature at a time when our political system offers no philosophical prism that can focus political ideas and transform them into action. The people in this twentysomething generation see the challenges, but they do not have a clear vision of how to overcome them.